A Horn Book Sampler

A
HORN BOOK
SAMPLER

On children's books and reading

Selected from twenty-five years of
THE HORN BOOK MAGAZINE
1924-1948

Edited by Norma R. Fryatt
Introduction by Bertha Mahony Miller

THE HORN BOOK
BOSTON

To my mother

PREFACE

The riches to be found in *The Horn Book* from its very first year, 1924, are so abundant and varied that to choose a few representative jewels from the horde of treasure has been a tantalizing task. Long-time *Horn Book* readers will be sure to miss certain favorite pieces. These may eventually appear in later collections of *Horn Book* papers. In the present selection each paper has its own individuality and quality and has stood the test of many re-readings. We looked especially for vivid, spare writing, for the expression of enduring truths about children and their books with the hope that these pages would speak to today's parents, librarians, authors and illustrators with the same urgency and point as when they were written.

There are in these early *Horn Books* the first stirrings of so many ideas that have since reached fruition — and there is still more to come from them — signs and hints and invitations to future writers, illustrators, editors and critics.

Some of the books mentioned in these articles are now out of print, but can be found usually in any good large-city library. We hope such books will be kept in view and that some day publishers will find it possible to reissue them. Where unfamiliar books are mentioned in an article, we give a detailed footnote and where many such occur, we provide a detailed list at the end of the article.

We have chosen to leave the time references in these papers as originally written since the date of publication at the end of each article gives the necessary perspective.

We are very grateful to the contributors who gave their cordial permission for the reprinting of their early papers in this volume and for their many years of interest in *The Horn Book Magazine*.

Norma R. Fryatt

CONTENTS

INTRODUCTION

This *Sampler,* selected with skill by Norma Fryatt from the first twenty-five years of *The Horn Book Magazine,* is at the same time a sampler of the creative spirit as expressed in books for children published before and during this period. This creative spirit ranges through papers showing how certain books came to be written as in Beatrix Potter's paper " The Lonely Hills " where the origin of *The Fairy Caravan* is described as she watched the dance of the wild ponies.

The *Sampler* shows how the creative spirit works in the research that authors and author-illustrators do in the preparation for the writing of their books, as in Lois Lenski's paper, " The Story of *Phebe Fairchild and Her Book,*" and in Elizabeth Yates's account of her search in Cornwall for Enys Tregarthen. There is creative imagination shown by Esther Averill in her appreciation of Rojankovsky and her presentation of his work in Paris through the Domino Press. There is creative expression in the book reviews presented here, and in the papers about childhood and reading and those about authors and illustrators and their work.

The essays rise to fine heights often as in Frances Sayers' " To Childhood and Beyond "; in Anne Eaton's "Ella Young's Unicorns and Kyelins"; Helen Dean Fish's "The Spring-Green Lady " and John Holmes's two papers, " Medallions to the Thumb " (on Archibald MacLeish) and " Definition of a Poet ".

*   *   *

Late in the 20s Ella Young, the Irish poet and folklorist, came to this country and spoke for The Bookshop for Boys and Girls of her search for the creation myth of Ireland which she set down later in *The Wonder Smith and His Son.* At dinner that evening her face between tall candles became an unforgettable memory, and after dinner she read from her poetry and told of hearing fairy music not only in Ireland but here in America.

The papers of the *Sampler* arouse many memories like this. We had talked, Elinor Whitney and I, during the early years of The Bookshop for Boys and Girls between 1916 and 1924, of starting a magazine, but we did not want to start it until we were sure we could carry it through. Then in the spring of 1924 we went to France and the British Isles, the first time for both of us. Perhaps *The Horn Book* would not have come into existence except for this trip.

In London we had visited Beatrix Potter's publishers in the hope of calling upon her in the Lake Country, but we learned that Mrs. Heelis hated publicity and did not like visits from Americans. So we went sadly to stay at a small inn at Rosthwaite near Derwentwater, walked about the Lake and up into the hills and coached through the region but did not see Beatrix Potter. We would have loved to visit Sawrey and to walk on Troutbeck Fells and the Tongue. Later we came to have some years of correspondence with her.

At Liberty's in London we bought a charming doll with a small wardrobe of lovely clothes for our granddaughter, Nancy Dean. We named this doll " Lucy Brown " after Mr. Ardizzone's Lucy Brown in the book, *Lucy Brown and Mr. Grimes.*

We went down from London to stay for a time at a delightful old inn at Chagford in Devonshire. One day following a bank holiday we engaged a young man to drive us to Cornwall to visit Polperro, the home of Sir Arthur Quiller-Couch whose books—*The Art of Writing* and *The Art of Reading*—were greatly beloved by us. Our driver had driven all the previous day and night and could not keep awake, so we never did find Polperro and we seemed to drive endlessly over the Bodmin Moors, but we did find Foowey.

We had wonderful days in Scotland and Wales and immediately after our return on July 2, full of courage and zest, we knew we were ready to start the Magazine, but what should we call it? We sat on a bench on Commonwealth Avenue near Arlington Street, thinking and talking about the time of John Newbery and the early days of children's books and suddenly the absolutely right name came to us — *The Horn Book.*

One day there came a letter from a young man I did not

know personally but did know to be a poet. John Holmes wrote out of interest in *The Horn Book*. Should we resent two suggestions? First, that we write for each number an editorial which would more or less set the mood of the issue. Second, that we have a front section which would form a kind of portico or entrance. We were grateful indeed for these suggestions and had confidence in their rightness because they came from a poet. The editorials we began at once. As soon as we had the first notes and comments suitable for an opening section, we started it under the title " The Hunt Breakfast," with an appropriate Caldecott drawing — and it still continues.

This first collection of papers chosen from the first twenty-five years of *The Horn Book* and published in the thirty-fifth year of its life embodies the truth which is the heart of *The Horn Book* as it was of The Bookshop for Boys and Girls: " This World is a World of Imagination and Vision." (William Blake's words.) The World of Imagination and Vision is reflected in books. A man — and a child — can be happy in both worlds.

Bertha Mahony Miller

Part I

How the story happened

ABOUT TIM AND LUCY

By Edward Ardizzone

LIKE most parents, I have had and still unfortunately have to undergo that minor torture of making up stories for my children on the spur of the moment, and, what is almost worse, being an artist I have to draw elaborate pictures for them. It is " Daddy, please, please tell us a story. Please, a story with lots of danger in it," or " Please tell us a story about somebody who is very sick and has to have an operation," or " Daddy, please draw us a picture of two elephants having a fight." It was in this way, with much mental labor, that the stories of *Little Tim and the Brave Sea Captain* and *Lucy Brown and Mr. Grimes* were created.

At that time, my daughter Christianna being six, and my son Philip being four, my repertoire was fairly extensive. There was the story of Lizzie who was lost in the snow, and the story of Nurse Matilda, and many others, including the incredible adventures of a small boy and an engine driver. But of them all the story of Lucy Brown was Christianna's favorite, and the story of Little Tim was Philip's favorite, and they both had to be told and re-told night after night without any variation.

One day I bought a large new sketch book, and having, as I thought at the time, nothing better to do, I started to make some drawings for *Lucy Brown*. Before I knew where I was I had got quite excited about it myself, and, putting aside the rest of my work, I spent the next few weeks filling the sketch book with drawings, and writing in the text just as it appears in the finished book. When it was done Philip was indignant, and said he must have a picture book, too. There was nothing for it but to get through hurriedly what other work had to be done and to embark on the story of *Little Tim*.

Knowing how children like to identify themselves with the chief characters in their books, I attempted to make the pictures in both stories as like real places as possible. Some people even say that the drawings of Lucy and Tim are exactly like Christianna and Philip. I think that this is an exaggeration, though I am prepared to admit a faint resemblance.

The likeness to places, however, I can vouch for. For instance, the strange-looking house on the first page of *Little Tim and the Brave Sea Captain* is like the house in which we had just spent our holidays. We had been staying at, or rather near, Deal, a small Kentish seaside town. The beach is the same as the one where the children played, while out at sea there was usually a score or more of small craft: coastal steamers, sailing barges, and schooners riding at anchor, waiting for a fair wind to help them down the Channel.

In *Lucy Brown and Mr. Grimes* the pictures of the gardens in the first part of the book are taken from a small park near our home in London where the children play every day. The park, to give it its full name, is called the Paddington Recreation Ground, but to us locals and the children it is known as the " Rec."

It was not so long ago in the " Rec " that I received a shock, and I have a horrid feeling it is the first of a series of shocks I have yet to receive. I was walking with the children when I noticed them waving to an Old Gentleman who was some distance away. He was waving back to them with great vigor. Somehow his face seemed familiar to me. " Who is your old friend? " I asked them. No sooner had I said the words " Old Friend " than they struck a chord in my memory — Mr. Grimes. Good Heavens! had he come to life? The children answered, " Oh, he is an old gentleman we meet every day. He likes children and he gives us sweets." I hurried the children away, thinking over the embarrassing possibility of meeting a Captain McFee or a Mrs. Smawley. Perhaps all my characters will rise up in a body and confront me. In any case it is disconcerting to find them coming to life, and I shall certainly feel extremely annoyed if Philip runs away to sea the next

2

time we go to the seaside, or if an Old Gentleman offers to adopt Christianna.

You will notice in the last page but one of *Lucy Brown and Mr. Grimes* that there is a double-spread picture of a valley with a white house in it. The white house is fictitious, but the valley is a real Kentish valley with its orchards, village, and small stream where one can still catch crayfish.

I am now at work on a third book which I hope will appear next autumn. In it Lucy and Tim meet for the first time. They go to Portsmouth where Mr. Grimes buys a yacht. The venue of the book had to be Portsmouth because Christianna and Philip had spent some very happy days there on board an old Rye trawler moored near Haslar Bridge, and, of course, they knew the town well. The book is going to be called *Tim and Lucy*, and there is going to be lots of " Danger " in it.

From *The Horn Book* for March, 1938

THE HONEY HEART OF EARTH

In the books of Anne and Dillwyn Parrish

By Bertha E. Mahony (Miller)

> " And the Land of Youth lies gleaming
> Flushed with rainbow light and mirth
> And the old enchantment lingers
> In the honey heart of earth."
>
> Æ in " Carrowmore."*

"THINGS lovely and absurd "— it is with these that the books of Anne and Dillwyn Parrish are concerned. The Parrishes, brother and sister, published their first book, *Knee-High to a Grasshopper*, in 1923. *Knee-High* ends with a poem which forms the *motif* of their second book, *The Dream Coach*, published in 1924. Then in the fall of 1930 came *Floating Island* by Anne Parrish alone.†

Compounded with rare humor, and a microscopic eye for the life of tiny creatures, the three books draw their life from their authors' rich and absorbing joy in the natural world — the same absorption which besets the little French boy, Philippe, in the last story of *The Dream Coach*:—

". . . the whole world, the ox and the ass, the horse and the cow, the tame beasts of the fields and the wild beasts of the spaces beyond, the fox and the rabbit, the mouse and the beetle, the creatures that crawled and the creatures that ran, the cricket and the grasshopper and the inhabitants of air and ocean, the little hills and high hills, the valleys and forests, the voice of water through the land, sky and earth."

*From *Selected Poems* by Æ with permission of Mr. Diarmuid Russell; Macmillan & Co. Ltd., London; and St. Martin's Press, Inc., New York.

†*The Story of Appleby Capple* by Anne Parrish (Harper) appeared in 1950.

Certainly no book is quite so perfect a whole as that in which the author's skill with pencil and brush equals his skill with words. The Parrishes make their own pictures, and pictures and text are so full of delicacy, beauty and genius that one can't possibly say in which lies more. Together they present a rare book-making challenge to the publisher. It is too bad that the publishers of *Floating Island* did not select paper and cloth with the same eye for excellence which they gave to all matters of type.

Knee-High was begun by Dillwyn Parrish. He left Harvard to drive an ambulance at Verdun before America entered the war, and was very ill as the result of exposure and exhaustion. While he was in bed in France he wrote the first part of " Roly-Poly Cottage " to take his mind off some of the things he had been seeing. He put it in a letter to his sister, who finished it and sent it back to him — and so they went on; sometimes a story would be begun by one, sometimes by the other. And there was at no time any idea of making them into a book.

Most people who have had a severe illness know the feeling of one's self having become very tiny, and having retreated far within to a hitherto unsuspected depth. Combined with the feeling of a tiny lost child goes also a strange feeling of world-old age. So it is not surprising that the hero of *Knee-High* is Little Man, who while sick in bed grew smaller and smaller and smaller until he was just the height to give title to the story. But while he becomes so tiny and is so very young, he is at the same time very old.

" He was no bigger than from ' here ' to ' there,' yet he was a fat little old man, for he was very fond of good things to eat and drink. He was rather fond, too, of his little white mustache. He admitted that it made him look something like a walrus. But, as he said, ' I like walruses.' "

In his sick-room he is visited by the Coachman-to-The-World-Beyond, but the invitation of this gentleman Little Man refuses with scornful laughter. From that time on he sets up his home with the tiny people of the fields and woods. The directions for reaching Little Man's enchanting house cover a region familiar and much beloved by the

5

authors. The stories tell of Little Man's adventures among his neighbors — field mice, worms, moles, fish, birds and others, all living lives rich in personality.

The Dream Coach tells four stories of the dreams that came to a Little Princess (everyone knows now that in the midst of riches, pomp and ceremony there is often very little to feed the heart of a Princess who is also a little girl); to the little Norwegian boy, Goran, spending the night alone in a tiny house high above the deep waters of a fjord; to a little Chinese Emperor who put a wild bird in a cage; and last to a little French boy, Philippe. These four stories are charmingly conceived and beautifully written. Each is concerned with subject matter close to the life of a five, six or seven-year-old, as is true of *Knee-High,* but in both books such is the beauty of style, that grown-ups may read with pleasure.

Floating Island was written when Anne Parrish was in the midst of a novel. There came "one of those worrying times that come to everyone, with illness and so on." She could not put her mind on her novel as much as she needed to do and so she wrote *Floating Island* to cheer herself up. No wonder it is so full of fun and good cheer for readers young and old.

There were many fine new books in the summer and fall of 1930, but *Floating Island* was *the* exciting event. The reason is because it is one of those books so whimsically compounded that its like happens rarely. There are many people who can write a fine story of adventure, history or everyday life, but how many can write an *Alice* or a *Story of Dr. Dolittle?*

It is this last kind of book which Anne Parrish has made. The story is of the Doll Family, shipwrecked on a tropical desert island, and in it there is some of the fascination of *Robinson Crusoe* and *Swiss Family Robinson,* combined with a delightful humor. In Mrs. Doll's words and actions, one hears and sees the practical mothers of all times. In Mr. Doll are the characteristics of the imaginative, idealistic and rather wistful dreamer protected and managed by his wife. William, Annabel and Baby are like all children and Dinah the Cook has all the colorful gift for living of her race. The sun shines on the coral island, the waves ripple on the beach, tropical trees and flowers grow and bloom. And with the help of the creatures of the sea and land, the Doll family are gradually united and reinstated in their house.

The author has had set in italic matters of secondary interest. When reading aloud is going on, the foot notes may be skipped, but the reader-to-himself enjoys and chuckles over these interjections. Mr. Doll's drawings are delectable, and the author's pictures are works of genius as before stated.

The author has written about the models for *Floating Island,* and the other two books:—

" I found plenty of models for the *Floating Island* illustrations at the Zoo, the Aquarium, and the Museum of Natural History, but the dolls had to be remembered, doll-house dolls are so modern now. All the doll-houses I looked at while I was working on the book had little radios, and the mothers had bobbed hair and wore labels that said: ' Flirting-Eyed Mama Dolls'."

" The illustrations for *Knee-High* we had done when we were apart, finding what models we could. For instance, for the Dormouse going to bed I pressed into service a stately chambermaid, standing on the stairs in my husband's dressing-gown, with the cord trailing downstairs for a tail. (I never dared show her her completed portrait.) *The Dream Coach* pictures had to be done in a rush, at a time when I happened to be in Delaware, and we worked day and night, running out-of-doors for gulps of snow and air, and then going back to make our poor mother pose as a fat Chinese musician or a thin court lady. I hasten to add that none of the pictures look like her."

Anne and Dillwyn Parrish have done much to enrich the distinguished and permanent literature of childhood, and those grown-ups who love for their children and themselves fine, imaginative prose, rich in humor, with pictures of equal charm, should know the Parrish books and experience the reminder which the driver of the Dream Coach sings,

> " Nothing is real in all the world,
> Nothing is real but dreams."

From *The Horn Book* for February, 1931

THE CLOSED GATES OF THE GUILD OF SILK

By Anne D. Kyle*

A WINTER afternoon with a fine rain falling and night drawing down cold and bleak; — and a little girl who waited shivering on a station platform while her father bargained with the driver of a rickety " carrozza," — a brown surrey with flapping curtains, drawn by an even more rickety horse! Castellammare . . . Sorrento . . . , the musical names fell upon her unheeding ears. For it was Christmas Eve and at home — if she were only there! — there would have been a tree waiting to be trimmed in the big bay window, and a stocking to be hung above the fireplace.

At last the bargain was completed, their luggage piled beside the driver, and presently she too was stowed away on a hard seat beside her father. Children were setting off firecrackers as they rattled through the squalid streets of Castellammare. Firecrackers for Christmas! Didn't they know that such things belonged to the Fourth of July?

They were out of the town now; she knew because the horse's hoofs made a different sound. She peeped through the flapping curtains, — darkness, darkness everywhere pressing close. The wind that blew against her face was wet and salty. From somewhere far below came the strong, deep sound of unseen surf. On and on; now they were passing through a little town, a handful of pink houses shining under the feeble glow of a street lamp. Then darkness again and the smell and sound of the sea. She cuddled closer in the warmth of her

*Author of *The Apprentice of Florence* (Houghton, 1933, o.p.)

father's arm. The wheels of the " carrozza " made a creaking song for her, " Christmas Eve! Christmas Eve. . . ."

Suddenly the song stopped and her father was shaking her gently. She saw a white wall with roses on it and a bright doorway. She stumbled toward it on legs stiff with sleep and cold.

Inside, however, was hardly less cold than the night without, for the pension had once been a convent built centuries before by monkish hands that made no provision for this world's comfort, since they labored for the next. Dinner was in the vast vaulted room that had once served as refectory, and for dessert there was a pudding miraculously and cheerfully afire. . . .

She was awakened next morning by a sunbeam lying warm across her eyelids. The wind that came through the window was soft and heavenly sweet. She slid out of bed and ran to look out. Orange blossoms, a whole garden full below her, creamy white among the glossy leaves! There were oranges, too, like gay Christmas balls. And beyond was a white wall covered with roses and beyond and beyond was the still bay dotted with slant-sailed fishing boats. In the bright distance rose a mountain — Vesuvius! — placid enough in the benevolent sunlight, holding its shallow white cup of cloud against the blue of the sky. She stood quite still, her heart beating fast for wonder and delight. For it was Christmas Day in the morning and, concealed in the dismal wrappings of the night before, there had been after all a present for her, a miraculous undreamed-of present — Italy!

Well, I was that little girl, and that rainy Christmas Eve journey whose details I remember so vividly was but the first of several all too brief visits to Italy, — stopovers on our way to and from the real objective of my archæologist father — Egypt. But even such casual nibbles were sufficient to whet my adolescent and romantic appetite, and I resolved that since my father was not as interested in Cæsars as he was in Pharaohs, I should, when I grew up, return to Italy myself and remain there long enough to satisfy even me. I have since discovered that that was a vain resolution, for Italy like a bad habit once indulged in, plagues one only with greater desire. Of that, however, I was blissfully unaware when, after graduating from college, I set out with a friend on a leisurely trip around the world to be ended by a winter in Rome.

Those were a happy eight months indeed that we spent there; what with picnics on the Campagna and stimulating if footsore mornings in museums and churches dank as the tomb; what with concerts at the Agosteo, some gorgeous rite at Saint Peter's or an afternoon with the marionettes at the Teatro dei Piccoli. Yet for all that I have no desire to spend another winter there,— a week or two, yes; long enough to walk down the Spanish Stairs again, to lunch at Alfredo's or dine at the Ulpia, to walk of a Sunday morning in the Borghese Gardens and sit in the afternoon at some sidewalk café watching all Rome parade up and down the Via Veneto . . . to see a sunset from the Pincio and the fountains playing before Saint Peter's, and I am ready for the high hill road that leads northward to Florence.

For there is a warmer, friendlier atmosphere about that Tuscan city. Even the hills draw close about it, intimately, not stand aloof like the high cold peaks that ride the horizons of Rome. Perhaps it is because, for one thing, Florence is so much smaller than Rome that it has a quality of coziness which the older city cannot acquire; or perhaps it is that the ghosts of the Medici are not as austere as the ghosts of the Cæsars. For Florence has always been a city of common people rather than Emperors, of tradesmen instead of Popes. Her Medici were bankers, her Rucellai and Tornabuoni merchants, her Vespucci enrolled in the Guild of Apothecaries. There was hardly a palace in the city but once had its poles for drying the fresh-dyed wools and silks that bore the stamp of the Florentine Lily to the markets of Bruges and London. Even today you may see them stretching rusted and empty across the front of the Davanzati palace in the Via Porta Rossa, and the iron rings that supported them still protrude from many another sturdy mediæval wall.

In Florence, the past is always at one's elbow. It steps out of some ancient doorway; it loiters in the shadow of a buttressed palace. It kneels in the dim light of some frescoed chapel whose altar steps have known the knees of Cimabue and of Giotto, Botticelli or Leonardo.

10

So it is not surprising that in the course of my ramblings through that maze of mediæval streets that lead off to left and right of the Via Por Santa Maria I began to catch glimpses of a shadowy figure ahead of me. I could tell by the set of his shoulders that he was young and sturdy, used to responsibility beyond his years. I noticed, too, that sometimes he had a book under his arm half concealed by the folds of his worker's smock.

At first he paid no attention to my quickened footsteps behind him; but after a while I think he grew aware of my presence, for he would glance occasionally over his shoulder, or slow his steps as if to give me an opportunity to catch up. But always before I could do so he lost himself in the shadows of an archway, or the turning of a corner took him irrevocably out of sight. Then one day, coming out of what was once the small old church of San Biagio where I had been browsing for an hour or so among the dusty books of Viesseux's library, I met him suddenly face to face; and though the light was not good, — for it was November and a misty rain falling, — I could see the design on his smock quite clearly. It was one I had observed before, carved over the door of a palace in this very neighborhood, — the Closed Gates of the Guild of Silk!

Thus did I come to know the Apprentice of Florence and through him those other friends (and enemies) of his, all of whom, save for the small matter of dress, one might easily find among the crowds that walk today along the Via Por Santa Maria. For the Lucchesis still have their little dye shop and dip the cloth into steaming vats such as Gemma used to bend over; the Clarices who have been born to the freedom of foreign lands still rebel at the old-fashioned strictness with which a proper Florentine maid is reared; the Masos and Vannis still quarrel among the throngs which gather each noon about the broad Piazza that was once the Mercato Vecchio. . . . And still from his stone niche at the Uffizi, the dark, saturnine features of old Cosimo dei Medici brood over that teeming city which he truly loved and for which he and his family wrought so much that was of both good and evil.

From *The Horn Book* for January, 1934

A MODERN PILGRIMAGE

By Virginia M. Collier*

THE very word pilgrimage has a fascination. It means a journey for a purpose dear to the heart. And when that journey leads back into the colorful past, it spells adventure. Such an adventure was mine while working on the *Song of Roland* which I have just finished retelling for boys and girls. To follow the footsteps of the great epic hero of France is to pass abruptly from the present into the obscure shadows of the Middle Ages.

My only guide was the " Song " itself. Yet a study of how it came to be flings a ray of light into the darkness of that vanished period. Who sang it? When? Where? Why? Such are the questions which scholars like M. Joseph Bedier, famous savant of France, have spent their lives in answering.

Doubtless the epic began to take shape soon after the battle of Roncevaux in 778 which it celebrates. So, doubtless, French lips had chanted that song of a glorious death for nearly three centuries before it carried the Normans to victory in England in 1066. Wace in his " Roman de Rou " describes:

> "Taillefer who full well sang
> On a horse that fast went
> Before them went singing
> Of Carlemain and of Roland
> And of Oliver and of the vassals
> Who died at Roncevaux."

The words inspire a picture of the jongleur, Taillefer, galloping at the head of that vast invading army. Twirling his

*Co-author with Jeanette Eaton of *Roland the Warrior* (Harcourt, Brace, 1934, o.p.)

sword, spinning it in the air and deftly catching it again, he sang in a great voice the matchless challenge to courage:

> "As the deer flies before the dog
> So fled the pagans before Roland
> And his mighty sword.
> Strike knights! Do not fly!
> Shame to him who tarries! "

Lustily the army thundered the refrain, " Strike! Strike! Shame to him who tarries! " Thus by the might of a song — the song of their long-dead hero — the French hosts were swept to victory. England became Normanized. And the Anglo-Saxon race of which we Americans are a part was changed forever.

Yet it was probably not until fifty years after that Conquest that the old song was actually set down. Verily, songs were long in the making in those days. Professor Bedier believes they were first fashioned by singers in the monasteries where pilgrims stopped. In France, in Italy and in Spain lay the routes travelled by aspiring feet. When the travellers grew weary at nightfall it was the monasteries which received them kindly and charged them well for entertainment. To hold the guests as long as possible and thus pile up the golden treasury, the abbots engaged the talents of jongleurs to bind a spell about the company with heroic tales and songs.

Thus in the Church were born the great *chansons de geste*. Local miracles and warlike exploits were sung in stirring music to travellers about the fire. The more thrilling the song, the longer lingered the pilgrims. And of all the heroes of these songs Roland was the bravest and the most adorable.

Not unlike those pilgrims of old was I — setting out to pursue the course of the warrior, Roland. My task led me through the magical legends grown thick through the ages toward the true personality of the valiant youth who is known on history's page simply as, " Count of the Breton marches." From the printed script I sought reality in ancient cities and the battlefields of antiquity. It was in Aix-la-Chapelle where I began this part of my quest—" sweet Aix," most beloved of all the homes of Charlemagne.

Just over the border in Germany lies Aix. The soft and

13

smiling town in its circle of green hills is a bright and busy Spa. There, cheerful people throng the health centers where medicinal waters are served for beverage or bath. Few of the visitors stop to remember that these are the very same hot springs which delighted the great Emperor Charlemagne. Yet down in the center of the town one can see the Rathaus built on the site of the ancient palace and part of the old square tower at one end is actually a remnant of the building once famed throughout the world. The octagon of the cathedral is there, too, rebuilt to be sure in 983, but on the plan of Charlemagne's own. Most impressive of all are the bronze cathedral doors, strong, solid and simple, like the man himself and like his age, which open today for lesser folk as once they opened to the mighty Emperor.

In the Rathaus is a wooden model of Charlemagne's palace and cathedral. After studying this with care I climbed to the summit of the wooded hill, looked down upon the pretty town and found the centuries rolling back to show me what Roland saw when he first came there as a boy.

Suddenly the naïve, lusty, aspiring life of those early days seemed to come alive. I saw throngs of tall, blond Franks surround their Kings and move off gravely to the council; or with yelping hounds at their heels, gather tumultuously for the hunt; or I saw them, with lances gleaming and horns sounding, ride forth to battle.

Musing quietly on that hillside I found myself listening in fancy to the lesson so naïvely chronicled in the old documents:

> Pepin (one of Charlmagne's sons) —What is grass?
> Alcuin (the great teacher) —The robe of the earth.
> Pepin—What are vegetables?
> Alcuin—The friend of the physician, the glory of the cook.

Next from my place on the height I gazed into the forecourt of the palace my imagination had reconstructed. I could see ambassadors arriving from far and near, from Saxony, England, Aquitaine and Spain. Perhaps, I thought, I have turned the calendar back to the very day when Isaac the Jew came, leading an enormous elephant, the gift of Haroun-al-Raschid himself.

14

In reviving this life of the Middle Ages, it is hard to distinguish between fact and fancy. For example, the good folk of Aix believed that God intervened when Charlemagne built his chapel too small and, by a miracle, dilated the walls. They were convinced that God suddenly made the waters of the hot springs burst from the ground as a gift to Charlemagne. Yet nothing could be more realistic than the descriptions handed on to us of the daily life of Charlemagne's men. Lusty enjoyment of eating and drinking, hunting and fighting, was matched by eagerness to promote the Kingdom of God. With those tales in mind I found it easy at Aix to visualize the life into which Charlemagne's legendary nephew so eagerly stepped. I saw Roland as the lad he might have been.

And what of the Great Charles himself? At St. Denis, just outside of Paris, I stumbled in the half dark of the crypt on a very early statue of Charlemagne. Like the mutilated figure at Pierrefond, it shows him young and vigorous, with bare knees revealed by a short tunic. This seems far more like the historic Charles than the legendary one of the " barbe fleurie." It is thus we picture him as he conducts with Roland one of those heroic boar hunts in the vast and leafy forest of Compiègne. The sounds, scents and colors of that lively scene bring the King and the young hero vividly before us.

At Laon there is little to remind us that here was born Charlemagne's mother, that touching figure of tender legend. But at Laon, which still stands high above its surrounding levels, one hears again the exultant laughter of Roland and his boy companions as they make their riotous escape down the hill. Over these plains they flew, so says the vivid old tale, to gather horses and weapons as they could and arrive in time to rescue Charlemagne's hard-pressed host at Aspremont.

Likewise, in Rome, one must shut out both the splendor of the old Imperial capitol and the magnificence of the modern city in order to visualize the Frankish King making his way to St. Peter's. Thirty-five steps led up to the portals when Charlemagne mounted them on his knees. Thirteen hundred candles shone down upon him as he knelt to pray.

Of all the places I visited, however, the little city of Vienne was richest in suggestion. On an elbow of the River Rhone, not far south of Lyons, stands Vienne, renowned in legend for the hard siege waged by Charlemagne against his rebellious subject, the stubborn and doughty Girard.

At first, the curator of the museum whom I immediately consulted, shook his head and declared, " Votre problème n'est pas commode, Madame." But the problem became less inconvenient as I wandered up and down the steep-sloped city. I found it sharp, proud, ungiving — the very antithesis of the smiling Aix, but gradually it, too, began to surrender its secrets.

Soon after Cæsar's men invaded Gaul, Vienne became an important Roman city. Throughout the Middle Ages it figures historically as the stronghold of a line of Girards who always appear in the legends as rebels against their lords. Although Vienne may never have boasted a marble palace on its high citadel hill, its contours are in perfect keeping with the setting of the siege sung by the *trouvères*. They must have known the city well. The yellow Rhone flows beneath its steep slopes, and today's line of crumbling city walls follows that of the " crenellated walls that the ancient Romans built "— still impressive at the time our tale was sung.

The cathedral of St. Maurice (the saint upon whom Girard called so often to aid him in combat) casts its reflection in the water of the lazy river. A tower, long since in ruins, still stands guard at the far end of the bridge across the stream. At the foot of a hill where Roman country gentlemen had their villas long before the time of the Girards, there is the level plain where Charlemagne's hosts might have encamped for the duration of the " hard siege." Beyond the plain might have been the meadow where Roland and the young knights held their quintain to while away their boredom.

When I asked people about an island where Roland and Oliver could have fought their epic duel, shrugs and negations greeted my inquiry. " Oh, there is an island just around the bend in the river, a flat, boggy affair," said my informants. " No one goes there, only sometimes cattle are taken there to graze. One can see it close enough from the end of the wall beyond the river bend."

Undiscouraged by the half-hearted advice, I climbed eagerly

16

to the farthest end of the wall which extends around the fan-shaped city. Reward was mine for an incredibly muddy, breathless climb. For there indeed, Aude, Oliver's sister of legendary loveliness, might have watched the island combat between her brother and her lover.

Meantime, while I lingered in Vienne, " the wheat grew greener every day and the sky more blue," just as the old poem says. I could not but believe that the *trouvères* who sang of Vienne not only knew her well, but were enslaved by her proud charm. Even so was I and I carried away in my pocket a fortune — a thin silver coin. On its face is the true inscription, CARLUS REX, that appeared on Charlemagne's deniers. If only one could make the pilgrimage of this coin!

In the legend, it was at Vienne that Charlemagne received the news of invasions from Spain and set out at once on the fatal expedition to Roncevaux. Matter-of-fact historians report that the battle of Roncevaux was a brief and unimportant engagement at the end of a few weeks' or months' campaign in Spain. Charlemagne's rear guard was composed of a mere handful of men and the attacking hosts were a not larger number of Basques, natives of these mountains. Taken at a disadvantage in their heavy armor, Charlemagne's warriors were trapped and quickly vanquished by the agile Basques, who were entirely at home in the mountain defiles. Roland, " Count of the Breton marches," was among those who perished. Such are the bare facts of history. Yet, just as the peculiar ethereal beauty of Assisi produced a veritable St. Francis, so the tragic grandeur of the valley of Roncevaux produced a song which remains today the great epic poem of France.

The old terrain has lost nothing of its compelling impression. On the way to it I stopped at Poitiers where Charlemagne's grandfather, Charles the Hammer, beat back the Saracens. From there on the countryside changes. It becomes more wooded, hilly. This character increases as one moves down toward Spain and the valley of Roncevaux. Once in Spain, despite its green, leafy beauty and the wild foxglove and platycodon which wave from every rocky crevice, the landscape becomes suddenly somber. Mounting steadily, one comes

17

to the tiny hamlet of Roncevaux, which is little more now than the huge collegiate church. Two casual, chatting Spaniards were the only people in sight in the remote and deserted place. One of them directed me in plain English to the entrance of the sprawling church. He had just come home to Roncevaux to live after fifteen years in New York City!

When I slipped into its dark coolness, the church was filled with men's voices in deep-toned song. It was a fitting prelude to the Pass.

We entered the Pass by climbing ever higher and higher. Somewhere outside the sun was shining, but here the mountains interlocked and overlaid one another. Even on the upper road the effect was somber and fearsome. Down in the terrifying gorge where valley dropped below valley, the sinuousness, the darkness, the sheer overwhelmingness of this mountain trap was appalling. Here indeed one felt the compelling truth of the noble and dignified old words: " High are the mountains and dark the valleys, the rocks somber, sinister the defiles."

It took no effort of the imagination to see Saracen hordes approaching from every direction, issuing from clefts and crannies to pour down upon Roland and his desperate band in the valley. Down there one could not look without seeing in poignant clearness the solitary figure of Roland, wounded to death, stumbling through the valley among his slain companions to find the body of his beloved Oliver.

Looking back after one emerges from the Pass he sees the defile like an ominous black crack leading into lost regions. Once more he realizes that there is no poetic exaggeration in the *trouvère's* description, " le vallon d'enfer." Indeed, how true it is that their exact reporting as well as their fidelity to elemental human emotions has given these old epics a power to move and enthrall the listener which remains undimmed today.

From *The Horn Book* for September, 1934

THE STORY OF
"PHEBE FAIRCHILD HER BOOK"*

By Lois Lenski

~~~~~~~~~~~~~~~~~~~~~~~~~~~~~~~

NINE years ago we moved to the country. In the
northwest corner of Connecticut we found a fine
old house built in 1790, near a small village, with
one hundred acres of woodlot, meadow land and pasture.
From the very moment I first entered the house, I began to
wonder about the people who had lived in it and hung their
pots on the pothooks which were still hanging on the crane
in the large fireplace. It had been built at a time when the
surrounding hills were covered with deep woods, when the
roads were mere dirt paths, swimming in mud each year at
the spring thaw — "mud time," they called it. It seemed
an amazing thing that people, plain farmers, should have come
to so remote a spot — it is still five miles from a town and
railroad — and should have built, not a log cabin as the west-
erners did, but a beautiful mansion, a model of architectural
style, with paneled walls, carved moldings and elaborate fire-
places. Instead of using stones from their own fields for the
foundations of the house, they hauled red sandstone with ox-
teams from the Farmington River valley fifteen miles away,
huge blocks of sandstone eight and ten feet long. Common
granite was not good enough. They had great pride, though
they were simple people.

Some time later, while attending a country auction, I
bought an armful of old books. Among them was a little book
in green paper covers, called *Scenes in the Country*. The in-

Phebe Fairchild Her Book by Lois Lenski (Stokes, 1936, o.p.)

19

scription on the fly-leaf was written in a stilted hand, in faded ink: *Kate Daniels Her Book—October 1825—from her Cousins in Litchfield.* And then the quotation:

> " This is a preshious Book, indeed,
> Happy the Child who Loves to Read."

That was the beginning. I began to search not only for early books, but for all the information I could collect about them. I found out that when our ancestors were chopping wood in the primeval forests of New England, fighting battles, building stone walls and driving stagecoaches through muddy, rutty roads, they had the time and also the inclination to prepare and publish special books for children. Children read books in 1776 and in 1800, and on through the nineteenth century. These tiny, frail, paper-covered books tell us more about their inner lives than any other source. They tell us about children's interests and occupations, the morals and religion of the day, parental ideals, opinions and discipline, and they give many details regarding the care and upbringing of children. They open up a brilliant vista of the child's world of the past.

You cannot live in New England without becoming acquainted with your neighbors. Most of mine are descendants of original settlers, fifth or sixth generation. From them I have heard many stories of the early history of the town. Two of my dearest friends are old ladies of ninety-four and ninety-five years respectively; both remember things which happened before 1850. It is a wonderful experience to live in a town with so rich a history.

And so, without realizing it, through the two-hundred-year-old town and the old house and their associations, through the old books which the children read, through the lives of my neighbors and their ancestors, I have been studying New England history for nine years — no, not studying it, but feeling it and living it. The past has come alive for me in a way that it never did in the history books. I hated History in school; to me it was only a meaningless procession of dates and battles to be memorized. But when I decided to tell the story of our house, to fill it with people and describe the life they might have lived one hundred years ago, as soon as I looked at History from the human standpoint, it became fascinating and absorbing and very much alive.

I wanted to describe the ordinary everyday life of a family in a house like ours, home-life as it affected child-life, and village-life as it affected both. For the children did not live lives of their own in those days — they lived in an adult world and were affected by everything that went on in that adult world. The very self-sufficiency of every farm, providing as it did everything necessary for living, in the way of shelter, food and clothing, gave the life of a child an inconspicuous place. Children were taught to be seen but not heard, you will remember — the home was such a busy plant there wasn't time to listen to what the children had to say. Thrown upon their own initiative, they developed inner resources of strength and vigor which enabled them to withstand the rigors of their harsh training and environment.

When Phebe Fairchild came from New Haven to Winton in 1828, the farmhouse was already old and had a past. Benjamin built his house in the new 1830 style because his father's house, built forty years before, was out-of-date. The illustrations in the book show actual views of this house, both interiors and exteriors.

As my story developed, the characters became very real to me and to the members of my family. At one time, after Christopher, the itinerant artist, came to be a member of the Fairchild family, we were afraid the house was overcrowded. So I drew a floor-plan of the house, upstairs and down, put beds in all the rooms and put the family to bed. By putting the two littlest girls on a trundle bed in their parents' room and by sending Timothy up to Uncle Thad's to sleep, it worked out splendidly. To the right of the front entry downstairs is the keeping room, to the left is the north parlor, where Phebe found Great-Aunt Pettifer's bonnet and cape; upstairs, beyond the weaving room, is the little south chamber where Phebe slept, with the window to the east where she crawled out on the roof of the lean-to and dropped to the ground. The road in front of the house leads over Cotton Hill — Phebe followed it when she ran away — then down into the valley

21

to Bakerville, where the old blacksmith shop still stands un-
changed as it has stood since before the Revolution. Not far
away on a side road is an old grist mill, broken and inactive
now; on the back road stands Mis' Abigail's house, plain and
sturdy, where Christopher found Phebe. I might say here
that in all the early records, and on the early tombstones, the
name Phebe is spelled without an *o*.

I spent many months in research. I read old numbers of the
Connecticut Courant; I saw the millinery and hairdressing
advertisements which caught Great-Aunt Pettifer's eye; the
portrait painter's announcement which attracted Christopher.
I studied account books from a local store and found out what
purchases people made in 1830 and the " country pay " they
gave in exchange; I saw invoices listing the actual stock carried; I found records of actual hauling of merchandise from
Bristol Basin on the Farmington Canal. The story of the canal's
opening is based on the actual account of an eye-witness. I held
in my hand a stagecoach time-table, listing the various tavern
stops from New Haven to Litchfield. In my collection of
early American children's books I have a little brown mo-
rocco-covered *Mother Goose,* like Phebe's, which caused so
much trouble; a *Ladies' Pocket Library,* with gloomy black
covers, from which the two blackbirds read about conduct and
behavior to while away the tedium of the stagecoach journey.
I have a pink paper-covered Watts' *Divine Songs for Children,*
with the hymns which Phebe had to learn; a soiled and worn
Memoirs of Miriam Warner, whose forlorn appearance in itself
would give any child the heartache. And I have a tiny little
book, 1½ by 2½ inches, with only eight pages, which is
simply bursting with eloquent objections to *Mother Goose* as
" silly rhymes, unfit for children to read." Another small
eight-page book is called *The Folly of Finery* or, *History of
Mary Lawson;* it tells the sad fate of a little girl who loved
pretty clothes and personal adornments. It was largely through
this handful of little books that Phebe Fairchild came alive.

Phebe lived with me in spirit for many months, as real as
any member of my family. Her ghost will, I haven't a doubt,
continue to haunt my home and my heart forever.

From *The Horn Book* for December, 1937

HOW ENYS TREGARTHEN'S CORNISH LEGENDS CAME TO LIGHT

By Elizabeth Yates

~~~~~~

IN the spring of 1938, Bertha Mahony Miller wrote to me in London of some legends which Enys Tregarthen had collected and retold. Was Enys Tregarthen still gathering legends and why didn't we go to Cornwall to find out? Though we had neither heard of Enys Tregarthen nor the legends, the idea was intriguing; so we started to make some inquiries. Our first query was in a bookshop, but our eager question drew forth no like reply. Only after some searching was the information given: Enys Tregarthen's books had been out of print for twenty years.

We scoured London for copies of the books, but not obtaining any asked Foyle's to advertise for them. While waiting, we read the books in the Library of the British Museum. Little crimson-bound volumes they were with faded gilt letters: *North Cornwall Legends and Fairies* and *The Piskey Purse*. Published in the early 1900's and adorned with old-fashioned drawings, they made only a solemn appeal; but the tales they contained were as fresh as if the winds of Cornwall were blowing through them, and they bore the stamp of the true storyteller. Even our first brief acquaintance with them showed us that they were too good to be forgotten and that they should reach people again — children who would delight in the Piskeys, students who would relish the true vein of folklore.

23

Perhaps Enys Tregarthen was an old lady still thinking about legends. Perhaps — but who knew what might not happen if we found her!

No matter what searches we made or inquiries we launched, we could learn nothing about her. No one knew where she lived, except vaguely in Cornwall. No one had ever heard of her as a person, only as a name on a book. We wrote a letter to her addressed to " Cornwall," but it came back stamped " Not known." We wrote to the Bishop of Truro, as he had written a preface to one of her books, but he replied that it must have been his predecessor as he knew nothing about her, though he thought a writer by that name had once lived in Padstow. However, he could not say.

We wrote to the Vicar in Padstow and waited days for a reply. One came — not from the Vicar, but from Enys Tregarthen's cousin, and in it she said that the Vicar had called on her and shown her our letter. It was quite true that her cousin had written those books, but they had been published so long ago that she thought every one must have forgotten them by now. Enys Tregarthen had died in 1923, a woman of seventy-two, and she had been a bedridden invalid all her life. "A great sufferer but a wonderful person, and I know because I took care of her the last years of her life," the letter came to its close. " I am curious to know why you are interested in my cousin."

It was difficult to explain in a letter so we replied that we were coming to Padstow as soon as we could manage it.

From London to Cornwall is an all-day journey on the train through a storied countryside where natural beauty interwoven with history has made a shining fabric. By late afternoon the wild reaches of Exmoor were stretching out to the horizon and at last — known well because of much reading of it — we saw the graceful curves and changing color of the Camel River, and Padstow where the river makes its last sweep over the sands to flow on toward the Atlantic. We got directions at the Post Office and then walked up the lane from the town and stood for a moment outside the tall, gray stone house which was the end of our search.

Miss R—— greeted us as if we were old friends. " You're

24

just in time for tea and the kettle's boiling," she said brightly. We drew our chairs up by the fire and near a table spread with Cornish dainties — pasties and saffron buns, clotted cream and jam.

" We've got most everything but a pie," Miss R—— said gaily, " and that's a great Cornish dish, too. You know they say the Devil won't come into Cornwall for fear of being baked in a pie! "

Miss R——was eager to know of our interest in her cousin. We told her of how many people in America still delighted in Enys Tregarthen's legends and how they had been brought to our attention. Then she told us of Enys Tregarthen, of how she had been such a gay child loving the open moors and the golden Cornish sands, knowing every flower and bird and cherishing the outdoors as her home; but she was scarcely sixteen when an illness crippled her and confined her to her bed for the rest of her life.

It must have been hard giving up everything she loved, but she had a richly stored memory to draw upon and a lively mind that kept reaching out for ideas to companion with. She started to write from her bed, leaning on one elbow and holding a pencil in her other hand, and she wrote more than a dozen books in the 'eighties and 'nineties, many of them about foreign lands to which only her reading had taken her. They were published and brought her friends and recognition, and no one who read them could believe she was a stay-at-home.

Loving people as she did, many were asked to come to her bedroom; some came from far away, others from the Cornish countryside. These latter she plied with questions and they answered with tales and legends. Then Enys Tregarthen began to realize that the stories told from one generation to another and living only in memory were in danger of being forgotten, that in a world depending more and more upon various forms of machinery the old tales might soon not be told any more. So she asked those who had seen the Piskeys or felt their touch, and those whose knowledge of the Piskeys went back to their parents' and grandparents' experiences, to bring their stories to her, and one by one the old tales were told, written down, and saved.

"There are still many more which she wrote down that have not been made into books yet," Miss R—— ended casually. "Would you like to see them?"

So we followed her up to Enys Tregarthen's old room with its wide view of moorland and winding river. Miss R—— opened a trunk and put the legends before us, musty with forgetfulness, handwriting faded, paper gone yellow, but true Cornish legends saved from oblivion by a loving hand. The splendid thought dawned slowly that here before us was the making of a new Tregarthen book!

We made more trips to Cornwall, visiting the places that figured in the legends, moors and cliffs, villages like busy Mevagissey and deserted Port Quin. We sought out Roche Rocks, Jan Pendogget's farm, Goss Moor and Wheal Glyn, and of them all my husband, William McGreal, took photographs. When the photographs were printed we saw that here were the illustrations for the book. Not Piskeys, for children or students of folklore could best imagine them for themselves, but the wild, beautiful Cornish country where Piskeys frolicked; photographs that would supply a background on which imagination might practice second sight.

A year had gone by and the book was ready for a publisher. Of those who saw the manuscript all sensed the magic of the tales, but opinions varied as to the illustrations; one felt none should be used, another thought an artist should have free rein with Piskeys themselves. To us, the book with legends telling of Cornwall and photographs identifying Cornwall seemed a perfect whole, and Miss R—— stoutly maintained that Enys Tregarthen herself would have wished it so, that children all over the world might know the Cornish country. Then Mr. Richard J. Walsh, Jr., of The John Day Company saw the book as we had seen it — complete.

The happy fortune that has brought the book to light is still tutelar. When the question of end-papers was being tentatively discussed and a map of Cornwall had been decided on, Charles John, a New York artist, chanced to see the manuscript on Mr. Walsh's desk. He felt its charm and, Cornishman that he is, exclaimed, "Why, I even have a Piskey on one of my door knobs at home!" So his knowing hand was chosen

26

to trace the curving coast of Cornwall and find the places where the Piskeys capered. The little chap with the artful eye and pointed shoes and cap that serves as jacket to the book may well have come from Mr. John's door knob if not from a carn on a Cornish moor.

So from faint idea to fulfillment the book has come its way and now is a tangible thing: *Piskey Folk: A Book of Cornish Legends*, collected by Elizabeth Yates with photographs by William McGreal (John Day).

From *The Horn Book* for September, 1940

THE STRENGTH THAT COMES FROM THE HILLS

By Beatrix Potter

~~~~~~

IT seems a long time ago and in another world that *Peter Rabbit* was written. Though after all the world does not change much in the country, where the seasons follow their accustomed course — the green leaf and the sere — and where Nature, though never consciously wicked, has always been ruthless. In towns there is change. People begin to burrow underground like rabbits. The lame boy for whom Peter was invented more than forty years ago is now an air warden in a bombed London parish.

I have never quite understood the secret of Peter's perennial charm. Perhaps it is because he and his little friends keep on their way, busily absorbed with their own doings. They were always independent. Like Topsy — they just grow'd. Their names especially seemed to be inevitable. I never knew a gardener named " McGregor." Several bearded horticulturists have resented the nickname; but I do not know how it came about; nor why " Peter " was called " Peter." There is great difficulty in finding or " inventing " names void of all possible embarrassment. A few of the characters were harmless skits or caricatures; but " Mr. McGregor " was not one of them, and the backgrounds of Peter Rabbit are a mixture of locality.

" Squirrel Nutkin " lived on the shore of Derwentwater Lake near Keswick, and " Mrs. Tiggywinkle " in the nearby valley of Newlands. " Jemima Puddleduck," " Jeremy Fisher " and others lived at Sawrey in the southern part of the English

Lake District. The earlier books, including the later printed *Pig Robinson,* were written for real children in picture letters of scribbled pen and ink. I confess that afterwards I painted most of the little pictures to please myself. The more spontaneous the pleasure, the happier the result.

I do not remember a time when I did not try to invent pictures and make for myself a fairyland amongst the wild-flowers, the animals, fungi, mosses, woods and streams, all the thousand objects of the countryside; that pleasant un-changing world of realism and romance, which in our northern clime is stiffened by hard weather, a tough ancestry, and the strength that comes from the hills.

From *The Horn Book* for March-April, 1944. Reprinted from a letter of Beatrix Potter's to *The Horn Book,* early in 1941 with permission of the Trustees of the Estate of Beatrix Potter.

THE LONELY HILLS

By Beatrix Potter

I HAVE been listening to a Danish girl distilling melody from an old spinet. Her fingers caress the yellow ivory keys. Notes come tinkling forth like the sound of a harp; like a hesitating breeze, away, far away amongst hemlocks. The limpid undertones are the song of a brook that ripples over pebbles. J. Sebastian Bach composed his minuet for such an instrument; an old-fashioned piano propped against the wainscot on seven fluted legs. The maker's name, " Clementi," is painted above the keyboard in a wreath of tiny flowers.

Music strikes chords of memory. Big golden-haired Ulla spoke of Copenhagen; of Hans Christian Andersen; of the little bronze mermaid sitting on her stone upon the strand where Danish children bathe and play beside the summer sea. She spoke of long frosts in Denmark; of skating on lakes and canals. No letter — another month and still no letters from Denmark; poor Denmark; poor Europe; silent behind a black curtain of fear.

For me the pretty jingling tunes bring memories of Merry Nights and of our English Folk-Dance Revival twenty years ago. The stone-floored farm kitchen where first we danced " The Boatman " and heard the swinging lilt of " Black Nag." The loft with two fiddles where country dancers paced " The Triumph," three in arm under arched hands. The long drive home in frosty starlight with a load of rosy sleepy village girls wrapped up in rugs. Coniston, and the mad barbaric music of the Kirkby-Mazzard Sword Dance, when a beheaded corpse springs up and holds a wheel of wooden swords aloft. Chapel Stile in Langdale where we came out into deep snow from a dance over the store. The " Running Set "— the twinkling feet! " Nancy's Fancy," " Haste to the Wedding," " Pop Goes the Weasel " and "We Won't Go Home Until Morning! " The Morris bells and baldricks! The plum cake and the laughter. Fat and thin, and high and low, the nimble and the laggard, the toddler and the gray-haired gran — all dancing with a will.

There were summer festivals, also, most lovely to remember. Quivering heat and smell of trodden grass, the lawns of Underley Hall, a stately setting. Deep below the woods and hanging gardens the River Lune meandered in wide sweeps through Kirkby Lonsdale meadows. The " County " perched precariously upon a grandstand made of planks. A fine wind and string band with big drum and bassoon, very hot and thirsty, fiddled furiously under a tree, a lime in scented bloom. At Underley the dancers were marshalled behind lilac bushes and azaleas. They danced on in converging strands of colour to weave a tapestry that glistened like shot silk.

I remember another unforgettable pageant, held on the Sportsfield at Grasmere. The fells towered around like a wall, and white clouds were piled over Helvellyn and Stone Arthur, with distant rumblings of thunder. And the dancers! The merry dancers! They had come in their hundreds from all over the north, a rainbow-hued kaleidoscope. In spite of roughish turf I have never seen better Morris, or prouder beauty than the Durham reels danced by girls in corn-coloured smocks. The reels pleased me especially. Folk dancing, if it is to take real hold, ought to be an indigenous revival. " Three Reels," " Petronella," and " The Triumph " were traditional in this Border country. My farm servants danced them at our Christmas suppers long before Morris dancing was introduced from the south. Well-trained Morris dancing is a miracle of graceful agility; a display for international meetings. But give me the swinging, roaring reels — the sparkling pretty long sets — the maze of intricate dances surprisingly remembered — follow the fiddle, forget your feet! Or dance with style and bend and sway; a bow and a curtsy for man and maid; and an inextricable tangle of laughter for beginners! Give me reels and spontaneous unsophisticated country dancing all the time for dancing in a north country village.

Another time all by myself alone I watched a weird dance, to the music of Piper Wind. It was far away in that lonely wilderness behind the table-land on Troutbeck Tongue. In the midst of this waste of yellow bent-grass and stones there is a patch of green grass and stunted thorn. Round the tree — round and round in measured canter went four of the wild fell ponies. Round and round, then checked and turned; round and round reversed; arched necks, tossing manes, tails streaming. I watched a while, crouching behind a boulder. Who had taught them? Who had learned them to " dance the heys " in that wilderness? Oftentimes I have seen managed horses cantering round the sawdust ring under a circus tent; but these half wild youngsters had never been handled by man.

I stood up. They stopped, stared, and snorted; then galloped out of sight. While I was watching them I remembered how I had been puzzled once before. In a soft muddy place on the old drove road I had seen a multitude of little unshod foot-prints, much too small for horses' footmarks, much too round for deer or sheep. I did not know at that time that there would be ponies on the Troutbeck fell; though I knew they were at Haweswater and Mattisdale. I wondered were they footmarks of a troop of fairy riders, riding down old King Gait into Hird Wood and Hallilands, away into Fairyland and the blue distance of the hills. Over the ferry where mountains are blue, the finding of those little fairy footmarks on the old drove road first made me aware of the Fairy Caravan.

In the calm spacious days that seem so long ago, I loved to wander on the Troutbeck fell. Sometimes I had with me an old sheep dog, " Nip " or " Fly "; more often I went alone. But never lonely. There was company of gentle sheep, and wild flowers and singing waters. I listened to the voices of the Little Folk.

Troutbeck Tongue is uncanny; a place of silences and whispering echoes. It is a mighty table-land between two streams. They rise together, north of the Tongue, in one maze of bogs and pools. They flow on either hand; the Hagg Beck in the eastern valley; the Troutbeck River on the west. They meet and re-unite below the southern crags, making the table-land almost an island, an island haunted by the sounds that creep on running waters which encompass it. The Tongue is shaped like a great horseshoe, edged by silver streams, and guarded by an outer rampart of high fells. From the highest point of the Tongue I could look over the whole expanse: Woundale and the Standing Stones; Sadghyll and the hut circles; the cairns built by the stone men; the Roman road; Hallilands and Swainsdale, named by the Norsemen; and the walls of the Norman deer park stretching for miles —" Trout-beck Park."

Far away in Dalehead the black Galloway cattle were dark specks moving slowly as they grazed. Sometimes I came upon the herd on the lower slopes of the Tongue; which was a reason for not taking Nip. The little shaggy cows were quiet with me, but fierce in defence of their calves against dogs. Sometimes I timed my ramble to cross the track of the shep-herds when they drove down a thousand sheep from the high fell for dipping. Rarely, I saw a hiker who had lost himself. Once there were two ravenous boys who had been out in a mist all night on Caudale moor. Usually I saw nobody, the long day round.

Mist is beautiful I think, though troublesome for sheep gathering. It takes strange shapes when it rises at sunset. During storms it rushes down the valleys like a black curtain billowing before the wind, while the Troutbeck River thun-ders over the Cauldron. Memories of " old unhappy far-off things and battles long ago "; sorrows of yesterday and today and tomorrow — the vastness of the fells covers all with a mantle of peace.

From *The Horn Book* for May, 1942. Reprinted with permission of the Trustees of the Estate of Beatrix Potter.

WANDA GÁG AS WRITER

By Ernestine Evans

~~~~~~

ALL I knew about Wanda Gág were her pictures. I had seen them at exhibitions and reproduced in magazines. They were beautiful, and very simple, and full of the wonder of common things. They excited more senses than one. I always wanted to reach out and touch them. It was this that made me sure that if the new publishing house of Coward-McCann was going to enlist America's artists in the service of children, Wanda should head the list. An appointment was made to see her, and I set out for the Weyhe Gallery.

I meant to ask her if she cared for Ouida's *The Nuremberg Stove*. What I found was an artist, and a storyteller as well. Stories with pictures, stories without pictures. She was an old hand with them, as entertainer and comforter and exhorter of a whole family of little Gágs. And more than that, as was plain when, years afterward, she dedicated *Gone Is Gone* " To My Peasant Ancestors," she had inherited a wonder-bin of tales to begin with. She had the hang of setting a scene and putting her characters in motion, of sharing what she remembered, and inventing surprises. I forgot about the Porcelain Stove. The girl before me in a quiet businesslike manner was showing me her portfolio. The story strips she had done for a Minneapolis newspaper to earn her living had been tried out on the little Gágs. We talked about New Ulm. Yes, she had thought of trying to make a book. She had one under way, a book about cats. And when, a month later, we had in the office the marvelous manuscript of *Millions of Cats*, I hugged myself, as children all over the country have been

34

doing ever since for nearly twenty years. But the bits she told me that first day — shyly, but directly, in answer to questions, never piling it on, but making you see New Ulm by words, and the table with the children eating supper and governing each other with " Eat fair! "— were proof that she was a writer.

> Tell me where is fancy bred
> Or in the heart or in the head?

I suppose " fancy " there means love. But with Art it is as mystifying. Too many children's books are fancies from the tops of not very good heads, and more are too full of heart with hardly any head concerned. Not so any of Wanda's tales, the ones she invented herself, or the ones she carefully chose to translate and rewrite from those gathered, in cottage and forest by the Brothers Grimm, which represented the experience and wishes and dreams of generations of hard-working peasants, so few of whom could read or write, so many of whom were dependent on oral relation for what there was to remember of the past.

Wanda's style in telling stories, a very conscious and conscientious style, gained immensely from the old patterns which were often half song and half story, handed on to be retold and remembered. She used devices like repetition and cunning simple rhyme well. " They followed it over this and that, and over things both round and flat, and over things both small and tall." See, even I can remember that from *Snippy and Snappy*. "We rolled it up, we rolled it down, we rolled it up and up and down, we rolled it up and down and down, we rolled it up and down." This is a minor touch of art and very pleasurable, and sometimes only noticeable when you discover from some young Patsy or Jossie that it tickles them, or when you vaguely miss the easy sway in the sentences of some other little book the children have brought you on a rainy day.

I always liked the moral note in Wanda's stories. Oh, no moral sticking out like a sore thumb, or even one wrapped in a cracker, but there, all the same, to cheer a body into being good rather than " bad." There is a universal moral in telling your child or your neighbor or yourself to go on and on and try harder, and I always enjoyed the part in *Nothing at All*

35

where it says: " But do you think he sat down and cried? Oh no, he had a plan."

Her care about format was part of her writing and drawing. She wanted to squeeze the last possibility of communication out of each story. I wanted the shape of *Millions of Cats* to be the same as Nicolson's *Clever Bill,* which was both small book and large one, a wide page and yet not " big merchandise." She agreed to that, for it suited her notion of the old man journeying home. The hand-lettering seemed to make the book something special and closer to the children. They drew letters before they wrote script. Nice round expressive letters were not as formidable as type. Everything was done to make the story as simple as possible and as clear. She was painstaking in her choice of words, and there was a sort of sureness about the stories, however surprising they were, as if they had already stood the test of time and were by way of being classics. This is most true of *Millions of Cats.* It was, from the beginning, as sure-fire as *The Three Bears,* another story written by a known author, that has a sort of patina — as if it had been handed down by your Grandmother, who got it from hers or dear knows where:

Once upon a time there was a very old man and a very old woman. They lived in a nice clean house which had flowers all round it, except where the door was. But they couldn't be happy because they were so lonely.

" If we only had a cat," sighed the very old woman.

Have you ever told a child to sleep on *Millions of Cats* without the book in hand? Without the pictures? " Cats here, cats there, cats and kittens everywhere, hundreds of cats, thousands of cats, millions and billions and trillions of cats," letting those double-l's slide slower and slower and softer and softer, like a lullaby?

The Funny Thing I liked much less than *Millions of Cats,* but I learned from it that neither I nor the public had a storyteller who meant to pander to us or repeat herself; and after *Snippy and Snappy* and the *ABC Bunny,* it was a pleasure to see the same skill used on different characters and in new forms.

Perhaps I am wrong, but in herself, and in her stories, or so it seemed to me, there was never any pattern of humor in the conventional sense. When she decided to be, in part, an editor herself and select certain of the old folk stories for re-telling, there was an impish humor in her selections. She was always aware of the political and social issues in the world around her. I do not think I am imagining that she often found in some of the oldest stories much that was slyly apropos to high policy in Washington and grim struggles in farm and factory. Read " Clever Elsie " again, one of the stories in *Tales from Grimm*. " There was a man. He had a daughter who always tried to use her brains as much as possible and so she was called Clever Elsie." I still think the story appealed to her because she thought that less brains, maybe, and more common sense, and a little less exploitation of crises and imagined crises might be wiser politics. As an editor, she had a sense of spoof; and it amused her that old sense, like old wine, was so good in the flasks.

When she simplified stories, she was an ideal barber. She cared for the shape of an old tale's head. She never fussed up curls. She brushed out the natural wave. Styles might change and local historical customs confuse. Some such bits she snipped out. The old story itself she never changed. She respected the past in the sense that she recognized lasting values. Stories were for use. And by use she meant the sharing of experience, and her art lay in making the sharing so very entertaining and so simply put that there was meaning and rhythm for the widest possible audience. Her ear was as concerned as her eye in relating a story. And if you as reader could bring your own experience, you were welcome to write " between the lines " as you read. Which is, isn't it, what all the enduring classics do for an audience?

Her need for growth and her performance were like a tree's. She did not need to travel widely, " to get away from it all," even to see strange and foreign places. Her penetrating eye gave her a constant sense of search, of discovery of form and color, and her reading was always a search for expansion, a basis for discussion with others, not an avoidance of realities about her.

That there is another collection from the Brothers Grimm coming this autumn, is a certain joy to look forward to. There will be the same quiet retelling in well-carved words. Her selection will be as aware of what the stories meant to the peasants of the past as of what is still valid in our own society. The book will be presented as " a children's book " and yet all of us, however old, will have a sense that once again Wanda is writing for *us*. In pictures and in words, the fountain she made of her life continues to play for all.

From *The Horn Book* for May, 1947

Part II

Let us now praise artists!

FLOWERS FOR A BIRTHDAY

KATE GREENAWAY

MARCH 17, 1846

By Anne Parrish

CHILDREN are safe to play in the sand on English shores again. A century is nothing to the sea. It might have been this morning instead of ninety-five years ago that two children played, flooded with sunlight and serious with contentment. Everything was wonderful, and " life would go on forever just as it was. What a beautiful long time a day was! Filled with time —"

A wisp of fog hides the child named Dollie, but Mrs. Greenaway's Kate, in pink frock and white sunbonnet, still gathers the dove-colored pebbles to fill the white-and-purple basket.

She remembered the colors fifty years later. Waking or dreaming, she remembered what she saw. When her illustrations for *Marigold Garden, The Language of Flowers* and *Little Ann* were exhibited in Paris, these " runaways from the nursery " " *vêtus à la mode bizarre et charmante qu'on appelle maintenant ' la* Greenaway ' " enchanted the French with their freshness and innocence. They said her water-colors awakened memory.

"You can go into a beautiful new country if you stand under a large apple-tree and look up to the blue sky through the white flowers," she wrote when she was fifty. " I suppose I went to it very young before I could really remember and that is why I have such a wild delight in cowslips and apple-blos-

41

soms — they always give me the same strange feeling of trying *to remember*, as if I had known them in a former world."

She remembered going to her own country when she was two. She was sent to a farm in Nottinghamshire, where Ann the farmgirl was kind to the little London girl. The things Kate saw because of Ann glow through her work. A cabbage-leaf of strawberries, a spray of harebell, are gifts to us from Ann as well as from Kate. When Ann took tea to the haymakers, she carried the child on one arm, and all her life Kate remembered the warm sun, the smell of steaming tea and new-mown hay, the meadow flowers, and her complete happiness.

She needed flowers. They made her happy, but the church-bells made her sad. She swung between gaiety and woe. Coming treats must be kept secret; her anticipation was too intense.

Lizzie, five years older, took care of Kate; the little sisters roamed the London streets, connoisseurs of shop-windows and Punch and Judy shows. Once a man dressed in skins, blowing a trumpet, cried that the end of the world was near. For months Kate was frantic with terror. She could read now, and she tried to find relief in stories. But her favorites were frightening or sad, and she was what she read.

She dreamed too much. When she woke from nightmares, shivering and weeping, One-Eye, beloved rag-doll, was always in bed with her to wipe her tears on and be companion and consolation. There were china dolls for whom she made exquisite, tiny clothes, coaxing feathers from pillows to trim their bonnets. There were wooden dolls; Queen Victoria and Prince Albert, a halfpenny each, the Royal Children, a farthing apiece. They were sewn into ballet costumes of gauze bonnet-lining, alike except for three rows of cerise satin on Prince Albert's white skirt. The Greenaway children were fascinated by the Family in Buckingham Palace. Thirty years later Kate sat in the Palace, " with the nice little princes and princesses hopping about," losing their hearts to her, while she remembered that other Royal Family, so small that a child could hold it in one hand.

There was tea with Aunt Mary, with sugar on the bread and butter. It was with Aunt Mary that Kate and Fanny, four years younger, were walking home, so absorbed in looking at the stars that they both fell off the curb, and the two red pelerines, the two plush bonnets, the two grey muffs, were covered with mud.

Kate remembered those costumes, and the costumes of her brother, born when she was six, and always her companion. Years later she painted his scarlet pelisse and his white felt hat, his blue frock and Leghorn hat with ostrich tips.

The baby was named for his father. John Greenaway was a wood engraver. Often he worked at home all night. Through love and determination Kate would wake in the dark of early morning and creep down to him. Shadows filled the room except where gas-light fell on the tired man and the child, still languorous with sleep, leaning against him while he buttoned her frock. Then the coals glowed, the kettle boiled, the toast on Kate's toasting-fork smelled good. After the chill, warmth was a peculiar pleasure, and there was the warmth, too, of love and the fun of a shared secret.

When she was eleven, Kate's art schooling began, and continued for about eleven years. Overwork, and effort to follow the ideas of others, wrapped her in the quiet dullness of a cocoon.

But wings were growing, strong for flight in her own air.

Edmund Evans, master-craftsman of color-printing, long-time friend of Mr. Greenaway's, so believed in her that he printed a first edition of 20,000 copies of a book of pictures and verses. The edition sold before he could print another. With French and German editions, 100,000 copies were sold. The book was *Under the Window*, and Kate Greenaway was famous.

Another man helped in bringing about her almost overwhelming popularity. John Ruskin showed the young gentlemen of Oxford " a baby thrown into a basket of roses " and " exhausted the splendor of his vocabulary in his praise " of Kate Greenaway. He continued to lecture and write about her, and although Whistler made fun of the prophet of the Pre-Raphaelites, and Rosa Bonheur said that he saw nature with " little eyes, like a bird," Ruskin was the most influential art critic in England.

There were floods of praise from Europe. At home Mr.

Punch crowned her with glory. In the Christmas number of 1880 he is shown among writers, illustrators and publishers of children's books, and she has the place of honor. A friend wrote of Linley Sambourne's caricature: "What a horror! It is actionable really! " But Kate, who could laugh at herself, was elated.

Children were dressed like hers, in what *La Vie de Paris* called " the graceful mode of Greenawisme." The high blue sashes, the mitts, the coral beads became a carking care to many a child.

She was copied. Her tulips are painted against other hedges, her clothes are on other children. But the children are changelings, leaden-heavy, while hers seem to move to delicate music.

Her children were never born; they have grown like primroses. A mother in a pale pink tulip of a gown, holding a baby among other tulips, is really a taller flower. The father and godfather in *The Royal Progress of King Pepito* are elder sisters, dressed for home theatricals. Their pretty faces, their delicate hands, betray them.

There is a family resemblance to some of the paintings of Burne-Jones and Watts. One can imagine her children going carefully down " The Golden Stair " with their gentle aunts, or having a quiet ride on Uncle Sir Galahad's horse, their faces wistful, for, dancing or rolling hoops or running among the lambs, they do not smile. When Frederick Locker-Lampson begged her to allow them sometimes to look happy, she answered: " Of course, it is absurd for children to be having a game and for their faces to be plunged in the deepest despair and sadness . . . I hope to do better." But she could not change.

Their prototypes drift across the spangled grass of Botticelli's paintings. Look at his " Madonna with the Pomegranate," or, in the " Madonna of the Magnificat," at the angel in yellow. Compare Venus, from " The Birth of Venus," with the children on the cover of *Marigold Garden*. There are the pointed chins, the wide-apart, dreaming eyes, the sweet, serious lips; they are all as remote as the moon from the laughter and tears of the world.

Ruskin, who for two years had written about her, wrote to

her. In his first letter, when she was thirty-four and he was sixty-one, he wrote of "your gifts — and your graces — and your fancies — and your — yes — perhaps one or two little tiny faults." She answered at once, and the long correspondence, with its praise and its scolding, its playfulness and petulance and kindness, and its deep importance to her, had begun.

Two years later they met. She looked forward so much to the meeting that she was again the child sick with anticipation. " But then the first moment I saw you I was glad — so glad."

Loving her work, he at once began urging her to change it. She was to do glass-painting for " sacred places." She was to " do nothing but patches of colour with a brush big enough to tar a boat. . . ." " I want your exquisite feeling given to teach — not merely to amuse." " Now be a good girl and draw some flowers that won't look as if their leaves had been in curlpapers . . . and then I'll tell you what you must do next."

She felt there was " a holiness " about him. But the innocent incense she burned did not get into her eyes when she worked.

He was not well when she sent him *The Language of Flowers,* with some of her most exquisite paintings. He wrote: " You are working . . . wholly in vain. There is no *joy* and very, very little interest in any of these Flower book subjects, and they look as if you had nothing to paint them with but starch and camomile tea." *A Apple Pie* vexed him. "All your faults are gaining on you. . . ."

Sometimes praise and blame mingle. " The ivy is very beautiful . . . but the colour is vapid and the leaves too shiny. Shine is always vulgar except on hair and water. . . . " But a Christmas card of hers is "a greater thing than Raphael's St. Cecilia." Another drawing " is lovely, beyond all thanks or believableness or conceivableness . . ." " . . . ineffable . . . a marvellous piece of beauty . . . a caught dream." He tells her she will have the joy " of doing more good than any English artist ever yet did."

H. Stacy Marks, R.A., urged her not to " let *any* success or praise make you puffed up or conceited, but keep humble and try to perfect yourself more in your art each day." Never was advice less needed. She overworked, she was overtired. " I long to be out . . . I even envy the cats as they run along the wall."

45

Sometimes she went on visits. She went to Coniston. Out-of-doors were mountains and lake and the moor where bees droned in the heather; indoors the parlor-maid came to the study door each fine evening to announce " The sunset, Mr. Ruskin." She visited Lady Jeune, but the house was full of young beauties, and she cried, " Oh, let me come away . . . from these sirens." She sat in the best dress that did not fit very well, and made little jokes with the young men who were yearning to be with the sirens; she reminded herself that she loved the gorse and the new lambs, and went for another walk alone.

She was happiest when she stayed by the sea with Mr. and Mrs. Locker-Lampson. Here was no anxious trying to please, no feeling of inferiority. Others spoke of her as a gentle mouse; the Locker-Lampson children loved her " roystering spirits." Randolph Caldecott was often there, kindest friend and most admiring rival, and although Mr. Ruskin could not be induced to like his work, Kate delighted in it and in him. They all played hockey, the children dressed " *à la* Greenaway," the gentlemen in their blazers and straw boaters, the ladies in long, tight dresses that burst into pleated frills and little trains. Miss Greenaway's shining hair came down, as usual, of its own softness, about her delicately strong, vulnerable face, pink from laughter and running. Tiny and clear in the past as figures seen through a diminishing-glass, they run on the velvet lawn, their laughter comes from far away, through sea-sound and the water-sound of leaves.

Better not to risk discouragement among the sirens, nor too much happiness with other people's children, in other people's gardens. Better not to disturb the routine of work. She had a garden of her own, now, at the new house that horrified Mr. Ruskin. "You *shan't* live in London . . ." 39, Frognal, was too ugly; he would not write it. Kate kept him supplied with addressed envelopes.

Mr. Locker-Lampson did not like it, either. He said of the new studio, "What a frightful falling off. . . ." But Kate liked it. It was big and uncluttered. There were prints of Michelangelo's figures, a Velásquez baby in hooped brocade, and a lay-figure that frightened her after dark. There was a glimpse

46

of the shine and coziness of her tea-room beyond, with cushion-heaped basket-chairs and a fireplace. Her mother, her father and her brother Johnny protected her. She worked almost all day, then gardened or walked with Johnny's dog Rover. From tea until supper she wrote her endless loving letters, illustrating them with watercolors, or made dresses for her models, as she once made them for her dolls. After supper she read. She wanted more happy endings than she found; she always wanted happy endings. At ten o'clock she went to bed.

Tea-time was her time for friends. Often she went to see Lady Dorothy Nevill, very old, and gay as a girl, who would make her laugh, would plan to take her to the latest play. " Miss Greenaway thoroughly appreciated these efforts to enliven her," Lady Dorothy's son writes.

Certainly Miss Greenaway was appreciative. In gratitude, she gave her paintings " as if they were leaves off the trees," Ruskin said, to the friends who tried to buy them.

Slow at making friends, they became essential to her, and she went into constant, causeless panics for fear of losing them. " *Don't* begin to find me very dull — don't begin not to want me."

She was painting portraits; getting likenesses of living, lively children was a strain. Painting with oils bewildered her, and the big brushes, after " the fine point I've passed my life with." " But . . . I'm going to emerge . . . triumphant????"

She began to feel " the *go* of things " in oils, and to find the colors. Her white became particularly beautiful in its subtle variations. She began to see subjects large. A study of a baby walking is masterly in its strength, freedom and simplicity. " I can draw a little, but I can't paint," she said.

She was told that it was the east wind that kept people away from her third exhibition, but did not believe it. ". . . whatever I do falls flat. It is rather unhappy to feel that you have had your day." But she must go on earning. She felt driven and lost. " I *do* take a time — far too much —." But " it . . . is fatal to me to have to do anything in a hurry . . . nervousness comes in."

She was still happy while she worked: " the morning rushes by." But when she stopped, depression poured back.

She felt as though she were under the earth. Then Lady Mayo sent her striped tulips, and she was a child, so small that she was bending them down to look "at their wonderful centres." There were narcissus, too, lilac anemones, and "a new beauty, the lovely greeny white ranunculus." "I always rejoice over a new flower."

The Peruvian lily she had planted four years ago, that had never flowered, burst into a glory of orange trumpets. She said "Perseverance does it!" She saw a bee "as large as the Coniston ones that kick so furiously." It gave her the visits to Ruskin, the bees and the lake and the mountains. She would see them again, some day.

But Ruskin died, and the comfort of his scolding and praise was over. Once she had written to him: "After such wonderful life, it seems such a miserable ending — to go out of life with pain. Why need it be?" She pondered it, through sleepless nights. In the three worlds of her friends, the fashionable, the æsthetic and the pious, she remained herself, as precisely and as purely as a crystal. She said, "I am very religious . . . but it is in my own way."

She took a walk by the sea; two shining green acorns in the sand lifted her heart. "I go on liking things more and more, seeing them more and more beautiful." She tried to write a play; she tried to write her life. She planned a dressmaking business. She made other plans when the pain of acute muscular rheumatism let her think, in the restless resting between the nine takings of medicine, the eight beef teas. But her heart was in her painting. "Nothing I do pleases anyone else now . . . so I will please myself." She wanted to paint "a life-sized hedge" with all the hedgerow flowers and berries. She was sick of the words "little" and "dainty." She wanted to paint Night, with an angel rushing through a sky full of stars. "One day I shall."

She went on writing the verses that fill four thick manuscript volumes. Her verses for children are right with her pictures as the leaves are right with the rose. Her "love poems," written by a school-girl, would be silly and sweet. Written by a woman, they are wholly sad. Dreams without hope are cold shelter when night is near.

She was never the first, the belonging one. Welcomed, she came from outside for a little while to touch completenesses that loved her and were kind and did not need her.

But, like Hans Christian Andersen, Lewis Carroll, Edward Lear, like a blessed and valiant army of others, she found release from loneliness in her work for children.

Autumn came. The cold bees clung to the cold flowers. " If it would get warmer I could go out; then I should get stronger."

But it grew colder. Dead leaves flew on the November wind, and winged seeds from her garden, to take root in other gardens.

Pain ebbed; she rested, half-dreaming. Fifty years floated away, she was five years old, gathering shells by the sea, and " life would go on forever...."

Her storms were her secret; their waves left only loveliness on the shore, drawings as precise and prettily colored as seashells. She gives them to us, shining and fresh as though she had gathered them, wet with the sea, this morning.

From *The Horn Book* for March, 1946

ARTHUR RACKHAM AND
"THE WIND IN THE WILLOWS"

By George Macy

I MUST have called at least a dozen times upon Arthur Rackham in his studio in London, yet I never once approached that studio without feeling a fresh delight. It was as if the Artist who drew us all set out to provide Mr. Rackham with the kind of studio Mr. Rackham would have drawn for his own favorite artist to occupy. It was only two minutes from the Zoo in Regents Park. The moment you walked away from the park you went through streets lined with drab identical workmen's houses. In Fitzroy Road, between two of these drab houses, you found an arched sign reading " Primrose Hill Studios." You walked under the arch, along an alley between the two houses. Behind them you found a short cross-street, a sort of Pomander Walk cross-street, lined with a dozen small cottages directly out of *Hansel and Gretel:* ivy-covered cottages with red roofs. Mr. Rackham occupied cottage number six; he told me he had occupied it ever since he was a struggling young artist, ever since the strange and philanthropic landlord had built these studios for struggling young artists. I now wonder whether Mr. Rackham was from the beginning the kind of artist who would naturally occupy this gnome-like kind of studio, or whether he became the kind of artist he was at his death *because* he occupied this gnome-like kind of studio.

Not only did it seem to me that he occupied a studio looking like a cottage in one of his own drawings, it also seemed to me that Mr. Rackham himself looked like a character out of one of his own drawings. In the last years of his life, when I knew him, his head seemed always cocked to one side, bright and eager and smiling and cheerful; his cheeks were pink and bright; his eyes bright blue and clear; his emotions used his face as a field to play on. You must not think this romantic nonsense, you must not think that I imagine the artists I know to look like their own work. Nearly all of the artists I know look like somebody else's work! Indeed, of all the artists I have met, I can think only of Jacob Epstein as an artist out of his own work, for Mr. Epstein looks in his studio like a giant hewn out of one of his own blocks of stone with his own somewhat frightening chisel.

It was in the summer of 1936 that I became painfully aware of Mr. Rackham's emotions. I had called upon him, to persuade him to illustrate *The Crock of Gold;* I thought that he would make some effective drawings of the pixies and the leprechauns and the gnarled old Philosopher of James Stephens' book. Mr. Rackham agreed with me, and said he would make these illustrations.

Then he told me that he was at a loose end. He had just finished a series of illustrations for Poe (what an unhappy idea I thought this!) for an English publisher. All his life he had been accustomed to having in hand commissions for books which would occupy him for three to five years to come. Now he felt at a loose end because he had no commissions in hand at all. He wondered whether I had other ideas, in addition to *The Crock of Gold;* he would, he said, work upon *The Crock of Gold* with greater happiness and a greater sense of security, if he knew what book he would take up after *The Crock of Gold* was finished. We sat in his studio for hours, in a desultory discussion of other books he might do. I am sure now that it was in a desultory fashion that I said: "What about *The Wind in the Willows?*"

Immediately a wave of emotion crossed his face; he gulped, started to say something, turned his back on me and went to the door for a few minutes. Then he came back and said that he had for many years been trying to persuade an English publisher to let him illustrate *The Wind in the Willows.* He had been asked by Kenneth Grahame, nearly thirty years ago, to

51

illustrate that book; and had for all those years deeply regretted his refusal.

It may not be generally known now that *The Wind in the Willows* was not a successful book when it first appeared. Kenneth Grahame was in 1908 the Secretary of the Bank of England. Despite his occupation of this unlovely position, he was already famous as the author of those lovely little books, *The Golden Age* and *Dream Days*. The editor of *Everybody's Magazine*, the American magazine, sent his European representative to call upon Mr. Grahame to persuade the author to contribute some new material to *Everybody's*. Grahame proceeded to assemble a series of letters he had written to his small son at school, letters in which the adventures of a mole and a toad and a badger were narrated in serial fashion. He called the manuscript *The Wind in the Reeds*.

The editor of *Everybody's* turned it down; and it is nice to know that, years later, the editor of *Everybody's* built a house in the Adirondacks which he proceeded to call " Toad Hall." When the book appeared, this time under its permanent title, *The Wind in the Willows,* it had a slow beginning.

It was then that Kenneth Grahame called upon Arthur Rackham, and asked him to make illustrations for a new edition. Mr. Rackham told me that he recognized the delight of *The Wind in the Willows* even then; but that he had many commissions for book illustrations in his studio at the time, and he said No to Kenneth Grahame.

The Wind in the Willows became world-renowned. A playwright in England and the President of the United States joined in creating this renown. As Mr. A. A. Milne himself put it: " *The Wind in the Willows* was not immediately the success which it should have been. Two people, however, became almost offensively its champions. One of them was no less important a person than the President of the United States, Theodore Roosevelt; the other was no more important than the writer of this essay." Mr. Milne wrote, around *The Wind in the Willows,* a play called " Mr. Toad of Toad Hall," which enjoyed a huge success in London and delighted Kenneth Grahame in addition.

The English publishers of *The Wind in the Willows* have

always been Methuen and Company, and they have issued *The Wind in the Willows* in editions illustrated by several artists. When Mr. Rackham decided that he wanted to illustrate the book, Methuen's had stocks of the other illustrated editions. So Mr. Rackham lived in disappointment, until that summer afternoon four years ago, when I suggested the title to him.

He immediately insisted that he would illustrate *The Wind in the Willows* first, *The Crock of Gold* after that. He said that he wanted plenty of time for making the illustrations, so we arranged a contract by which he agreed to deliver the water-colors for *The Wind in the Willows* to me in the spring of 1938. He also insisted that we should not proceed at all until I had obtained the approval, not only of Methuen, but also of Mr. Grahame's widow. It was through Curtis Brown, the literary agent, that I got in touch with Mrs. Grahame. Mr. Brown told me that she expressed immediate delight. In several later meetings, Mr. Rackham told me that he had been in correspondence with Mrs. Grahame, and that the aged lady had several times gone with him on walks along the reaches of the Thames, to show the artist exactly in what delightful elbows of that river the author had found the mole and the toad and the badger. Of the sixteen water-colors which Mr. Rackham finally delivered to me, two contain clear panoramas of the Thames at just those points which Kenneth Grahame had in his mind. It is possibly too romantic a hope that the artist met in his wanderings the direct descendants of the little animals who were the author's friends.

When the spring of 1938 came around, Mr. Rackham could only report progress. His own health was not good, and Mrs. Rackham's health had been so bad that he had been prevented from doing effective work. In the fall of 1938, and in the spring of 1939, he wrote me to say that he was now himself confined to his country house in Surrey, he was permitted to work only a short time each day, but he was giving every minute of his time to the completion of this job which he now considered his final labor of love. He sent the water-colors to me in London only a short time before England declared war on Germany on the first of September, 1939;

and he sent them with a letter saying that he had been permitted to work only a half-hour each day, so he regretted the fact that he could not clean the pictures as well as he would have liked, or mount them as beautifully.

Once these water-colors are given to the world, it will be seen with what affection Mr. Rackham made these pictures. I think them the finest pictures ever made for *The Wind in the Willows* because I think Mr. Rackham has affectionately personalized the little animals, more affectionately and therefore more effectively than did Mr. Shepard. You will find in these water-colors all the soft and glowing tints which are in the best of the Rackham drawings, all the scrupulous attention to detail, all the superb draftsmanship evidenced in each firm strong stroke of the pen.

It was Mr. Bruce Rogers who brought me the news that Arthur Rackham had died on September 7. I had just come back to New York, and had written to Mr. Rogers to ask whether he would like to design the book in which these Rackham pictures would be printed. When he came to my office he said that he had read, in that morning's newspapers, which I had not yet seen, the news of Rackham's death.

It is, I think, the first time that Bruce Rogers has designed a children's book. Not that *The Wind in the Willows* is a children's book! Although Kenneth Grahame's two previous books had been about children, this one is about animals, the kind of animals to be loved by child and adult. *The Wind in the Willows* is no more a children's book than *Alice in Wonderland* is a children's book; which means that it *is*, in the phrase used by so many publishers, " a book for children from six to sixty."

From *The Horn Book* for May, 1940

THE GENIUS
OF ARTHUR RACKHAM

By Robert Lawson

ARTHUR RACKHAM had died and I never knew it. I had seen no newspaper and even if I had his name would not have figured largely. He had never robbed a bank or deceived a people or sent young men to death.

It must have happened that evening when the rabbits acted so strangely. That evening when the sunset bathed our valley in a golden glow so all-enveloping that separate colors were swallowed up and the whole landscape took on a mellow tone seldom seen — except in a Rackham drawing.

And then in the twilight the rabbits came, more rabbits than we had ever known at one time before. Through the shrubbery and over the lawns they played, soundlessly as always, but driven by some queer excitement. Later we heard a fox bark in the pine woods and saw the vague shadows of deer. A fringe of dead trees along the hilltop lifted their gnarled arms against the western sky and seemed to wave them, although no breeze was stirring. There were tiny rustlings among the grass and we felt that somewhere, Something had happened.

It was not until weeks later that we heard, and then we knew it must have been that evening that Arthur Rackham had rejoined the earth he loved.

Small wonder that little creatures rejoiced, that his beloved trees held out their arms and that the Wee Folk raced through

55

the grass. For they were his and he was one of them come home, from a strange, unreasonable world.

And in the halls of whatever place good illustrators go there must have been rejoicings that night, too, when the Great Ones welcomed him as their peer. Gloomy old Doré was there, I am sure, Leech and Tenniel and Caldecott, Abbey and Beardsley and poor crippled Vierge, Remington and Frost, young Clark and great, bluff, honest Howard Pyle. There his chair was placed among the Great Ones and there he will sit through the generations to come.

The appreciation of Rackham's genius has suffered, I think, by its complete perfection. All his drawings appear so polished, so finished, so graceful, that many fail to realize the great strength and firm knowledge that underlie this seeming ease. This would be especially explainable by the period which we are now enduring and, let us hope, passing through.

I often hear people say, " Oh yes, Rackham. But his work is too *sweet*. His color is not real. His drawings lack strength, they lack guts! "

Poor blind people, brought up in a time when the symbol of strength is the bludgeon and the trenchant skill of the rapier is unknown. Poor dazzled eyes that have never seen a Chinese painting, Nantucket moors in November, a Persian rug, or a world swept into complete harmony by a sunset glow or the cool blue wash of moonlight.

It is understandable, but very sad, that in a time when Strength is indicated by bulging muscles (in the wrong places), distorted figures and a sign-painter's technique, the incisive power of Rackham's pen should be completely missed. That in a time when the ill-matched juxtaposition of all the rawest pigments is hailed as Color, the lovely harmonies of Rackham's tones should go unnoticed.

In an age when the roaring, lumbering efforts of artists to compose strikingly are so blatantly obvious, it is not surprising that Rackham's flowing skill in arrangement is laughed off as Weakness.

More important than any technical attributes were his point of view, his understanding, and his unfailing sense of fitness and beauty. It is a dangerous thing to say in these times, and one most easily misinterpreted, but Rackham was in his work a Gentleman.

This may be, in many eyes, a complete condemnation of him and his works. But in the quiet corners of our noisy and complex modern existence there are thousands of minds that cherish the glimpses of quiet beauty and of a clean and color-suffused world which his sensitive genius gave us. As the temporary fads and madnesses wane and blow away, his high repute will remain clear and unsullied in the hearts of our generation and of many to come.

I think that a thorough appreciation of Rackham's technical skill can come only to those of us, and there are many, who have, consciously or unconsciously, attempted to adopt his distinctive style.

It is then that one begins to realize his almost unbelievable sense of restraint and taste, his sureness of drawing, his sensitivity of line and his daring of arrangement and handling. One realizes it and steps back in awe, seldom again venturing into that particular field.

One question bothered me for a long time and that was why his pen and ink work, purely as black and white, fell so far below the level of his color work. It was only after some years of study that I came to realize how he had developed his pen line for one particular purpose, which was as a foundation for his color, and to what an extent he had so developed it.

Where in his black and whites the excessive variation in line seemed disturbing and the harsh contrasts between heavy blacks and a flowing hair line caused a lack of richness and tone, these very qualities were what made his pen work so perfect in combination with his color.

One who has not struggled with this problem can hardly begin to appreciate what a supreme master he was in this field. Black and white line is comparatively simple, it is all there and visible as one goes along. But to know the exact weight and quality of line, the exact amount to do or to leave out in a pen drawing that is only a foundation and definition for color to be applied later, is a very different matter.

In this aspect I have never known Rackham to drop below the level of complete mastery by so much as a single line.

To study his work and see how his delicate sensitive line will suddenly sweep into a great clean-cut black is a revelation in skill and courage. And to see how these lines always take their correct and foreordained place beneath the soft, enveloping glow of his color is a chastening lesson in knowledge and sureness of craft.

The beauty of his color is clear to any one, or should be, but it is, I think, even more interesting to all illustrators, whose task it is to evoke by every possible technical means the *mood* of any particular incident. Here, again, he never fails, but accomplishes this objective with such an ease that it passes almost unnoticed. Only a faint stain of color, a flowing skillful wash, and each drawing takes on, through its color alone, the exact mood that the author hoped to convey to his reader.

For make no mistake, Arthur Rackham was an *illustrator*.

In spite of the great individuality of his work it was always in its proper place, which is to carry out and make visible the ideas and moods of the author.

Washington Irving's *Rip Van Winkle*, for example. Here, perhaps, the gnomes and gnarled trees might be labelled "Rackham," but simply because no one has ever done gnomes and gnarled trees as Rackham did. But Rip *is* Rip. The little houses of the Hudson Valley towns *are* Hudson Valley houses of the period, the Kaatskills *are* the Kaatskills and the moods and color and details are Washington Irving's vision enlarged and enriched by the sure touch of a true Master Illustrator.

For many years *The Wind in the Willows* has been a subject of controversy among illustrators I have known. Who could do it? It has never been done as it should be done, with all due respect to Ernest Shepard (and all disrespect to the publishers who gave the United States a cheap and horribly mangled version of his delightful drawings).

In these discussions the name of Rackham seldom entered, I don't know why, except that the perfect solution of any problem is always the last one thought of.

Arthur Rackham has done *The Wind in the Willows* and there is no longer any question. It was, I understand, his last work, and what a fine way that was to wind up things! I have seen only one small reproduction of one of the drawings,

58

but a single glance has assured me that here was the man. The Gilbert of Kenneth Grahame has found his Sullivan, another perfect collaboration has been achieved.

The other day I was re-enjoying Rackham's drawings for Milton's *Comus* which have always puzzled me somewhat. For in this book there are what seem to me to be some of his very finest drawings and some of his worst. Mind you, when I say his worst, I mean *his* worst, which still leaves them very high up.

This day the signature on one of these drawings suddenly caught my eye, "Arthur Rackham, 1914." Perhaps that ominous date explained this strange unevenness. 1914 — the year the world that Rackham knew and that knew and loved him burst into flame. The year that the youth of his world was plunged into mud and filth and hate that would always cloud their eyes to the gentle beauty of work like his.

Perhaps an era was dying then and perhaps Arthur Rackham knew it and for once his sure hand faltered.

From *The Horn Book* for May, 1940

59

LESLIE BROOKE:
Pied Piper of English Picture Books

By *Anne Carroll Moore*

W HO is Leslie Brooke? " we asked, as we delightedly turned the pages of Andrew Lang's *Nursery Rhyme Book* at Christmas time, 1897. "Who dares make new pictures for Edward Lear? " we said in 1900, with a scornful look at " The Jumblies " and " The Pelican Chorus " in gay new picture book covers. " Why, it's Leslie Brooke again," we exclaimed. " Now, can that be the real name of an artist — be it man or woman — or is it a name out of a nursery rhyme? ' The most beneficent and innocent of all books,' this artist, with his own sense of nonsense, calls the Nonsense Books of Edward Lear, and wants the children of a new generation to know and love them. That's why the books were given a new form, and I do believe more children are going to like them. This artist ought to make a picture book of his own. He is no mere illustrator. He's a picture book artist."

And that is precisely what Leslie Brooke did do. He made a picture book of his very own and called it *Johnny Crow's Garden*. This jolly, timeless book, with its priceless gifts of true humor and original interpretation, went straight to the hearts of children of all ages, and for twenty years and more has held first place in the affection of American children.

With the coming of *Johnny Crow's Garden* we began to feel personally acquainted with Leslie Brooke, for the words of its dedication are revealing words:—

> " To the memory of my Father, who first told me of ' Johnny Crow's Garden,' and to my Boys, for whom I have set on record these facts concerning it."

60

And as the Christmas holidays brought one after another of his inimitable picture books — *The Three Bears, The Three Little Pigs, The Golden Goose, Tom Thumb, The Man in the Moon, Oranges and Lemons,* and all the rest — we said: " These are picture books out of England itself. There have been none to compare with them in their simplicity of drawing and clearness of color since the golden days of Randolph Caldecott, Kate Greenaway, and Walter Crane. Why doesn't some one tell us who Leslie Brooke is? "

The dedication of *Johnny Crow's Party* —" To my nephew Somerset, happy in a name that assures his welcome to Johnny Crow's, or any other party "— deepened our impression that behind the pictures was a personality in full touch with childhood, past and present, but still we knew not the artist.

Our Fairy Godmother, Marie L. Shedlock, brought the first actual tidings of Leslie Brooke. " He is a man and he's alive and living in London," she said. " He lives in a charming house in St. John's Wood." She had visited his studio with a friend, a friend who probably knows him and his wife — a daughter of Stopford Brooke — better than any one else in England. Leslie Brooke had never before been told how much the children of the American public libraries cared for his picture books and he was deeply touched, the Fairy Godmother said, and then she added: " You must go and tell him yourself, some day, just what it has meant to have had such books appear at a time when the vulgarities of the comic sheet were being repeated in picture books for American children."

It was close upon Midsummer Eve in 1921 that, by invitation of the same dear friend of Leslie Brooke, I visited his studio on behalf of thousands of American children who love his picture books. Unfinished drawings for *Ring o' Roses,* published in 1922, were there, but I was taken back and back, as I had hoped to be, by earlier work and delightful talk, to the days when Leslie Brooke began to paint portraits.

As a young artist, he had painted Barrie, then a young writer, and from memory he had painted his friend, Arnold Glover. Over and over again he had painted the beautiful face of his wife, with the golden hair, and I saw at once that she lives for children in *The Golden Goose Book.* One of the two sons for whom *Johnny Crow's Garden* was made did not come back from the War, and Leslie Brooke had published no new picture book since 1916.

" I'd like to do another *Johnny Crow* if you think the children would still get fun out of it," he said wistfully.

" There's no shadow of doubt about it," was my reply. " They love *Johnny Crow* and it's the best book on gardening I've ever seen."

For many years, Leslie Brooke's studio was in his garden at Hampstead, and there an immense amount of work was done with the modesty and degree of technical skill which have given him his unique place among living artists of children's books of the first rank.

Leslie Brooke has since gone to live in a little village near Oxford, close to the meadows and slopes associated with Scott's Amy Robsart and with Matthew Arnold's dearly loved haunts.

" His extraordinary powers of observation and delicate sympathy with every phase of life have linked his own creative faculties as an artist to a rare understanding of ' the inner side of things.' Even his thumb-nail sketches bring a smile of happy amusement to any one who understands ' children,' whatever the age may be.

" He is a lover of the countryside and a first rate walker. As a companion on the open road, or by the running stream, his charm is a part of the surroundings, and leaves the same memory of ' far-off days,' never to be forgotten. A keen sense of humor is his by inheritance, and speech is hardly needed to illustrate his intuitive appreciation of wit or wholesome fun."

Such is Leslie Brooke, lover of Caldecott and Edward Lear, himself no less beloved by the fortunate children of his own time.

From *The Horn Book* for March, 1925

L. LESLIE BROOKE

By *Anne Carroll Moore*

EONARD LESLIE BROOKE was born at Birkenhead on September 24, 1862. He was of Irish ancestry, a descendant of Henry Brooke of County Cavan who wrote *The Fool of Quality,* a novel in five volumes published in 1766.

Childhood was then an unexplored continent. "Children were still the immature young of man; they had not been discovered as personalities, temperaments, individuals," says E. V. Lucas. "But the way toward a nicer appreciation of the child's own peculiar characteristics was being sought by at least two writers of the eighteenth century, each of whom was before his time: Henry Brooke, who in *The Fool of Quality* first drew a small boy with a sense of fun, and William Blake, who was the first to see how exquisitely worth study a child's mind may be."

Blake's *Songs of Innocence,* published in 1789, gave children a new place in the world, and I like to speculate on what Henry Brooke might have said had he written a letter to William Blake. No letter was written so far as I know. There is no record that novelist and poet were ever in communication. But there is a letter from William Blake which bridges the century that lies between the birth of Leslie Brooke with his clear recognition of a child's right to fun, beauty and truth on his own terms and the small boy depicted by an Irish ancestor with a daring sense of fun. And so, since I propose to rely on Mr. Brooke's own letters in this personal sketch of a singularly beautiful life which came to a close at Hampstead on May Day 1940, I will take from the pages of

Behold This Dreamer! this letter from William Blake. Walter de la Mare does not comment on The Reverend Dr. Trusler to whom the letter was written. He merely places the Blake letter under the heading Reason and Imagination and leaves the reader to use his own imagination as to what Dr. Trusler may have said. Blake's use of capital letters indicates the need he felt for making a rousing reply.

Fun I love, but too much Fun is of all things the most loathsom. Mirth is better than Fun, & Happiness is better than Mirth. I feel that a Man may be happy in This World. And I know that This World Is a World of Imagination & Vision. I see Every thing I paint In This World, but Every body does not see alike. To the Eyes of a Miser a Guinea is far more beautiful than the Sun, & a bag worn with the use of Money has more beautiful proportions than a Vine filled with Grapes. The Tree which moves some to tears of joy is in the Eyes of others only a Green thing which stands in the way. Some see Nature all Ridicule and Deformity, . . . and some scarce see Nature at all. . . . As a man is, so he sees. You certainly Mistake, when you say that the Visions of Fancy are not to be found in This World. To Me This World is all One continued Vision of Fancy or Imagination, & I feel Flattered when I am told so. What is it sets Homer, Virgil & Milton in so high a rank of Art? Why is the Bible more Entertaining & Instructive than any other book? Is it not because they are addressed to the Imagination, which is Spiritual Sensation, & but mediately to the Understanding or Reason? . . .

I am happy to find a Great Majority of Fellow Mortals who can Elucidate My Visions, & Particularly they have been Elucidated by Children, who have taken a greater delight in contemplating my Pictures than I even hoped. Neither Youth nor Childhood is Folly or Incapacity. Some Children are Fools & so are some Old Men. But There is a vast Majority on the side of Imagination or Spiritual Sensation. . . .

In this dark hour for childhood over the world and with Blake's water colors commanding fabulous prices in American auction rooms, we probably find his words more significant than did Dr. Trusler in the age of reason. *Songs of Innocence* have become poignant everyday experience. The Little Boy Lost and The Little Boy Found are no longer lovely poems in a book. They are ways of life in a strange world from which for millions of children the sense of security and the right to happiness have disappeared. Yet out of darkness and terror comes Johnny Crow with his perennial welcome into a sunlit garden.

64

"Like Johnny Crow, the abbot of Reichenau did dig and sow till he made a little garden," wrote Helen Waddell in her *Wandering Scholars* in the midst of an enchanting picture of a medieval garden and the poet who planted it. On learning of Leslie Brooke's pleasure in his discovery that Johnny Crow had made his way into her book, Miss Waddell sent him this message: "Tell Mr. Brooke I consider *Johnny Crow* a great book. I give a copy to every child I know."

As Johnny Crow is at home in any garden whether of the ninth century or the twentieth, so Leslie Brooke was at home in any age and in any country he traveled in or read about. "He was a man of wide interests, ranging from fine printed books to gardening, as well as a water colourist, a portrait draughtsman and above all an illustrator of children's books who had imagination and charm," *The London Times* said of him.

Concerning the facts of his personal history, Mr. Brooke wrote in 1928, "There is really so little to tell. I was born at Birkenhead and received most of my art training at the Schools of the Royal Academy in London. My brother and I were always drawing — like any other children — and I went on drawing; there is my whole story.

"My pleasure in pen drawing began early in copying Tenniel as a small boy — so that when the time came that small commissions began to arrive from publishers that seemed the natural medium to use for them. I began drawing for Blackie and Cassells. Also, I succeeded Walter Crane as illustrator of Mrs. Molesworth's annual story for Macmillan's and held the job through a number of years.

"My connection with Frederick Warne and Company began in the winter of 1895-96 when I suggested to them the idea of a new volume of the Nursery Rhymes. As a result *The Nursery Rhyme Book*, edited by Andrew Lang, was published in 1897 and since then all my books have been published by Warne. Next came Lear's *Nonsense Songs* which appeared in two parts — *The Pelican Chorus* drawn in London in 1899 and *The Jumblies* done at Harwell in 1900."

At this village near the Berkshire downs the Brookes lived for a number of years. In 1894 Leslie Brooke had married Sybil Diana, a daughter of the Reverend Stopford Brooke, who was his cousin. To the two sons born of their marriage their father dedicated *Johnny Crow's Garden,* published in 1903, but it is to Mrs. Brooke he gives credit for suggesting that he put Johnny Crow into a book. " There never was a time when the name of Johnny Crow was not familiar to me," he says, " yet I had never thought of making a picture book of his garden until Mrs. Brooke suggested it."

It was while living at Harwell that Leslie Brooke illustrated *Travels Round Our Village,* an adult book by Eleanor G. Hayden.

He says of it, " There are chapters in it that I think you might like. As to the drawings which were mostly done at the turn of the century,— so long ago that I may speak of them, — I think that they have caught something of the hard roughness of surface of the Berkshire village life that is unconscious of its own underlying humanity. ' The Village ' was West Hundred, but the book, both in text and illustrations, is an amalgam of three neighbouring villages — West and East Hundred and Harwell (where we ourselves lived) and there are few figures in my share that were not drawn directly from, or from memory of, individual inhabitants, if not always from the same person that the author had in mind. Possibly had the illustrations been done with less respect for fact they might have been more amusing! "

It is interesting to note the effect of this close study of village life upon the characters who figure in *The Golden Goose Book* whether animal or human kind. This picture book, worth its weight in gold, was done in four parts during the Harwell period, as was *Johnny Crow's Party.*

In London again, between 1909 and the War years, drawings were made for *The House in the Wood,* a selection from Grimm's *Fairy Tales, The Tailor and the Crow, The Truth About Old King Cole,* whose author, G. F. Hill, a distinguished authority on coins and medals, was years later made head of the British Museum. The first part of *Ring o' Roses* was also published before the War.

It was in 1921 that I met Leslie Brooke for the first time in his studio in St. John's Wood. He was finding it hard to go on with his unfinished drawings for the second part of *Ring* o' *Roses,* for he was not in touch with any children. The War was over, but his eldest son, Leonard, had not come home. He was killed in action in 1918 while serving in the Royal Air Force. I had just come from a stimulating visit of several weeks to the children of the Devastated Regions of Northern France. There I had sensed with fresh insight the potential power of the picture book in freeing the spirit of childhood. *Ring o' Roses* must be finished. The children need it, I urged. Mr. Brooke was eager to know everything I could tell him of picture books in action in American libraries and homes, in French libraries and schools. Out of that first exhilarating meeting grew a strong friendship fed by frequent interchange of letters and books.

We met again at his home in the village of Cumnor in 1927. Ten years later, in 1937, there was time for a more leisurely stay with the Brookes in Hampstead, close by Hampstead Heath. They had moved from Cumnor a few years before to be near their son who was living with his family at Hampstead. It is to Peter, Henry Brooke's eldest son, that *Johnny Crow's New Garden,* done at Cumnor and published in 1933, is dedicated. Peter, nearing his fourth year, darted in and out of his own house and his grandfather's like a swallow. He was already beginning to draw pictures as well as to enjoy them. There was time to look over old drawings in the studio, time for a long morning at Keats' house culminating with a toast in mulberry wine made by the Curator from the fruit of the tree under which Keats wrote The Nightingale. This was highly amusing to Mr. Brooke. There was time also for tea with Robert Charles, the lucky author of *A Roundabout Turn,* time for walks and drives about the countryside in April, time for delightful talk, for Leslie Brooke had the happy faculty of fully identifying himself with the interests of a friend. Whether by letter or in conversation he entered in, with ready wit or with silent understanding of a mood for silence. Small wonder that Johnny Crow became " the perfect host."

It had been my intention to present Leslie Brooke as a perceptive critic of the work of younger contemporary artists and in so doing to take from his letters such comments on the books I had sent him as personal gifts from year to year as seemed representative, but I have been unable at this time to achieve a design in harmony with his taste and my own and I quote only from one letter, dated December 29, 1938.

"I am having such a feast that I only wonder whether I can convey any digested impressions of the books before the year is out. They are so individual this year and their personalities are so varied.

"I have least knowledge so far of *Nino** which seems one of the most beautiful. I can only say at present that it seems to have had one individual influence over it all the time in the making, and that a delicate refinement of mind. (There is always something to be anticipated more eagerly when there is ' Written and Illustrated by ' on the title page.)

"With *The Three Policemen* I had a wholly new experience with its ' Written and Illustrated.' For I never recall a book exactly to compare with it. Its assurance is so delightful and with it all so simple. And what remains most for me after an hour of surprised enjoyment — even astonished enjoyment — is the portrait of William Pène du Bois on the dust wrapper. He knows such a lot of things — and such a lot about drawing them — yes, and shading them, too. And every minute of the time he realises that he is solemnly pulling my leg. And at the end he turns out to be that very healthy, wholesome boy, with a face of real quality. The drawings from pp. 47 to 57 seem to include many of his characteristics, one of them being a remarkable sense of volume.

"Then I come to *Mei Li* (which I am learning to call May Lee). This book is a most thorough and conscientious piece of work, on a par with the painting of an elaborate picture. What strikes me first is the amount of skill shown in the blending of groups of figures with a background of buildings — or of another smaller group of figures across the pages, attending always to the blocks of text which have always an integral effect in the design. The blending of the figures with the landscape across the pages in the Bridge outside the City (with

*By Valenti Angelo (Viking, 1938)

the beggar girl)—and specially in the scene when they arrived at the Great Square — which seems to me wonderfully good pattern — gives me a lot of pleasure. But besides all this Mr. Handforth is carrying on a lot of activities — there is the sense of a family party of the Wangs out for the excursion — and the anxiety about their getting back too late — fended off by Lidza the beggar, and in between one gets a sort of impression of the family relationships — Uncle Wang and San Yu, and the circus folk. The modelling of many of the heads is a pleasure in itself. It is a book for artists and author and publisher and printer all to be proud of, for it remains throughout a children's picture book.

" *The Cautious Carp** (perfect title) comes as a very happy relaxation in these strenuous days. It recalls the German animal picture books of more than fifty years ago — with Wilhelm Busch at their head, but it is on the whole more kindly, less callous, than they. I am looking forward to trying it on Peter who will, I think, appreciate the simplicity of it — for the drawings are so straightforward that they hardly require the explanatory rhyme, while the mechanism of the various ' plots ' is as it were rather more casual — less inevitable — less ineluctable than the German — who had a less kindly sense of Fate than Mr. Radlov's. These, I take it, are all drawn direct on the stone, and in this the colour is very well managed. It's very cleverly done, for the effect of the atmosphere in the different stories is varied. ' The Porcupine's strange experience ' and (opposite) ' Where is the Ball? ' are excellent specimens of this variation in atmosphere by colour, as they are of the quality of the humour, while ' How the Little Bird Escaped ' shows in 'And put it in a cage ' very understanding drawing of two types of children."

*By Nikolay Ernestovich Radlov

From *The Horn Book* for May, 1941

A PUBLISHER'S ODYSSEY

By Esther Averill

THE year 1925 was a good one to go to Paris, and those of my generation who went then will always feel that the period which followed, except for the very end, was the best of all periods. I realize that each generation of Americans in Paris thinks its own days were the best. Perhaps, in other times, there was more tranquillity in the world. But ours was a restless generation, enjoying life as it was.

And 1925, technically speaking, was a memorable year for those of us who loved the pleasures of the eye. In the spring came the Exposition Internationale des Arts Décoratifs, which gave the official signal for the unleashing of many artistic forces that had been pent up by the War. For three or four years I drifted about as a reporter of the decorative art movement in France — a job that brought me in contact with all the new forms, colors and materials used in fashions and in the furnishing and construction of modern buildings.

Then, towards 1929, I became associated with Lila Stanley, another American living in Paris, on the specific job of buying French designs for an American stationery manufacturer anxious to inject a little of the modern spirit into his merchandise. It was a privilege to watch the various artists who collaborated with us develop their decorative patterns for watermarks, monograms, borders and boxes. But our employer in America was of the opinion that the majority of the designs we sent him were too novel for the general public. The few designs he did print in America were rather badly mutilated in the process of color reproduction.

70

Among the artists who free-lanced on our stationery project there was a Russian, Feodor Rojankovsky, whose decorative talent expressed itself in a distinguished arrangement of gay, infectious colors and with a fantasy of theme which we felt had great popular appeal. It seemed an especial pity that his work, too, should fare so badly in America. Rojankovsky, luckily for his own peace of mind, was in a transition stage which permitted him to look in a semi-detached way at the outcome of his writing-paper efforts. Perhaps at heart he thought, "After all, a piece of writing paper is an empty thing until it has words or pictures scrawled across it."

One day Rojankovsky came to his appointment with an animal *A B C* tucked under his arm. He told us that he had made this *A B C* in Warsaw, and that he hoped some day to become an illustrator for children. He wondered if we could find an American publisher willing to print an edition of the book. As a matter of fact, we had no connections with the publishing world. We had never given much thought to children's books and were ignorant, even, of how a book is made. Then, too, it seemed to us that, since his Warsaw days, Rojankovsky had progressed considerably as an artist. Like many Russians of the period, he had had a broken career. He had been just old enough to serve in the Russian army during the War. Afterwards, he had left Russia at the time of the Revolution and worked his way across Poland and Germany, stopping here and there to do commercial art work, a bit of book illustrating and an occasional stage set. He had reached Paris in 1926, and in the writing-paper days was employed as a designer by a Paris publicity firm specializing in *de luxe* catalogues. In that capacity he was increasing his knowledge of modern layout. Also, his imagination was beginning to ferment.

Rojankovsky came to us not once but several times with the little Polish *A B C* under his arm. And in the end we told him that if he would illustrate a new book for children, we would finance its printing in Paris, where color processes seemed superior to those in America, and that afterwards we would try to place the book with an American publisher. I do not know what else we could have said, longing, as we did, to see for once a series of Rojankovsky's designs adequately reproduced.

We chose Daniel Boone as hero simply because we wanted an American theme for a book intended for American children, and a theme associated with Indians, animals and trees would be preferable for Rojankovsky. Indians would give him a point of departure, for many generations of European children have played " Indian " and read Cooper — and Rojankovsky, as a boy in Mitava, had been no exception to the rule. Then, at the time when we first knew him, animals and trees were the subjects that absorbed him as an artist. *Daniel Boone* would be his book entirely — a sequence of his brightly-colored pictures which would tell the story of Boone's life and adventures through the wilderness. It was planned originally as an album of pictures without words, although we afterwards decided to add brief captions.

One evening in 1929 — or possibly it was early 1930 — the three of us, Lila Stanley, Feodor Rojankovsky and myself, with Boone for hero, met in my studio to find out how a book is made. On the bright red stool by the glowing candle we placed the guest of honor, Monsieur B——, a technical director in the publicity firm where Rojankovsky was employed. Monsieur B—— was no common mortal, like you or me, but a glamorous individual who had been with the circus in former years, in just what capacity, however, we were never sure. We had hoped that he would talk to us about circus people, especially those we had seen perform night after night at the Cirque Medrano and the Cirque d'Hiver. Unfortunately, he preferred to assume the attitude of a professor in a boarding school for young girls, and to confine himself to the subject of books.

"*Mesdemoiselles,*" he began, taking a sheet of typewriter paper, and from the deftness of his fingers and a slight quirking of the wrist we wondered if he were not perhaps the magician who pulls rabbits from his sleeve — "*Mesdemoiselles,*" he began again, calling us to attention, " imagine that this piece of typewriter paper represents one very large sheet of paper. The inside pages of a book are made from similar large flat sheets of paper printed first on one side and then on the other, and afterwards folded down the middle and again down the middle and again and again until the pages fall into their proper sequence.

" For Rojankovsky's book I should advise using the simplest method of printing — just one large sheet which, after being folded, would give you thirty-two pages in the format *à l'italienne*, that is to say, about the size of a Boutet de Monvel song album. To be sensible, you must keep down your costs of printing by avoiding too many colors; three colors on one side of the sheet and two colors on the other ought to be sufficient. Offset should be a satisfactory and not too expensive means of reproduction. For the binding, use a buff-tinted paper, or something not too soilable. If you wish, I will send you a dummy in the format I have suggested, and if I can be of any further service. . . ."

Then our technical advisor departed; perhaps he had had enough of being sensible. He sent us a dummy, as he had promised, and shortly afterwards word came to us that he had joined a traveling circus.

I cannot remember much about the period that followed. It must have been the moment when we ransacked unsuccessfully French bookshops and libraries for pictorial documentation on the life and times of Daniel Boone. Often we wondered if we had not been a trifle rash in choosing an American hero for a Russian artist who had never been further west in the world than Paris. Eventually, however, we located enough material in the American Library of Paris to give him a start.

If work had not progressed satisfactorily, if we had not studied production costs sufficiently to be able to offer what seemed to us a reasonable proposition to American publishers, why should my next clear memory be of another night, late in the spring of 1930? Miss Stanley and I were waiting in my studio for Rojankovsky. On the floor lay printing estimates, suitcases and all the other paraphernalia of departure. She and I were to leave early in the morning for America, to see publishers in New York. Nine o'clock struck; ten o'clock struck; and still there was no sign of Rojankovsky. Three or four weeks previously he had dropped from sight with the little dummy on which he was to put a few last touches. Since then he had failed to keep his appointments, he who was habitually so punctual.

He came, finally, not in an apologetic but in a radiant mood. He had been off into the heart of the American wilderness with Daniel Boone, fought with Indians, seen nature as a living thing, talked with birds and squirrels and white-tailed deer. He untied the string of a large package he was carrying and to our astonishment took out a tall dummy of a book in folio size, saying, "*Voilà*, the new *Daniel Boone*."

Rojankovsky had arranged this folio size by reducing the number of pages of the little oblong dummy from thirty-two to sixteen, so that they could be twice as tall. Then, in a freer, surer style he had drawn a few sample illustrations for his new format and each of them had five glowing colors, while the cover was of fragile white to match the generous spaces of the inside pages. It was a rather different, a more expensive conception of a book, Rojankovsky admitted. Yet he hoped, he did really believe that he had found his style, his method of approach. And then he added, " One cannot put the American wilderness into a little book."

For a moment we wavered between the old and the new format. We had counted on producing a fairly inexpensive, sturdy book for children. But it was impossible for us, having seen the new *Daniel Boone,* to revert to the earlier format and style.

After all, it apparently did not make much difference that we reached America with only a few of the pictures worked out into folio size and without any definite ideas as to production costs of such a format. Experienced publishers could tell at a glance that a five-color book of the size in question would demand a large edition in order to bring the cost per copy into the popular price range, and they felt that *Daniel Boone* was too risky a project for large quantities, that it was too big and fragile for small children and too pictorial and thin for older ones. During our visits to the publishers, we heard very little about the needs of the special child who will love pictures all his life, even to the extent of becoming an artist.

As for Rojankovsky's illustrations, we learned how true

it is that when a new artist with an original touch appears, his work is apt to shock people who have their own notions about the aspects of the life he is trying to depict. Rojankovsky was judged to be too gay a fellow, too Russian an artist to tamper with the early American scene, and beneath the brilliance of his colors and the fantasy of his imagination it was hard for most Americans to detect the seriousness of his artistic purpose. The few publishers who were kindly disposed towards *Daniel Boone* told us that it was a stunt book that might possibly succeed in prosperous times. But America in those days lay in the depths of the financial depression. Perhaps just around the corner we might have found an interested publisher, but we had already turned so many corners to no avail that we sailed back to Paris in a mood one-third sad and two-thirds stubborn. We decided to continue with the book and have it printed to the best of our ability, for we hoped that once the printing had been completed in a manner worthy of the originals, we could find somewhere a publisher willing to give *Daniel Boone* a home.

Rojankovsky set himself to the task of finishing his illustrations. His capacity for work and his tenacity amazed us. Some of his full-page pictures were drawn five or six times, with all their colorings and details, and to the end they kept their quality of prodigious freshness. He wanted the book to be as beautiful as he had the power to make it. And when the time came for printing, he urged us to use not offset but lithography, so that the pages could be printed directly from stones on which he, himself, would redraw his illustrations.

We found a firm of lithographers, Mourlot Frères, whose director, Fernand Mourlot, was sympathetic towards our project. I remember that he arrived late at one of our first appointments in his office, for he had been detained along the way by the purchase of an old print that enchanted him. It was a large lithograph of a fox, and Mourlot said that in the brush strokes of the fur on the tail of the fox there was a lithographic technique that could not be surpassed. When we glanced at the signature on the print and read the name of J. J. Audubon, we laughed and said, "After all, this is by a Frenchman."

" *Tiens*," said Mourlot, " I have never heard of Audubon. Perhaps he is not very well known in France."

"Audubon was an artist and an ornithologist who tramped through the American wilderness in the early days. He traveled across the Boone country many times. In fact, he paid a visit to Daniel Boone when Boone was a very old man."

And Mourlot said again, " *Tiens*,"— for this Russian artist, this Daniel Boone, this Audubon, the Frenchman of whom Frenchmen had not heard, were bewildering in their range of nationality and space and time. And who were we? Were we publishers? Did we have an imprint? Of course, Mourlot could not ask too many questions or express too much surprise, for he is a courteous man.

He led us down a winding staircase into an *atelier* with presses, darkened beams and a chiaroscuro worthy of the crayon of Daumier. There, in a maximum of pale light, a place was cleared for the great slabs of stone on which Rojankovsky was to render his designs with lithographic crayon — a separate stone being necessary for each color in the book. In Poland, Rojankovsky had had previous experience with lithography, and he now set about to increase his skill, to force the stone to yield those soft shadowy effects which are peculiar to lithography and which gave relief to the bright patches of flat color used in *Daniel Boone*. From time to time as the months passed, Mourlot tiptoed down the perilous staircase to take inventory of developments. " This Russian artist is a good lithographer," he said to us. " Will there be a French edition of *Daniel Boone?* "

For Rojankovsky, too, it would be advantageous to make the book available in the country where he was starting a new career. But when we went the rounds of the publishers in Paris, we had, in our small way, a taste of what the Ballet Russe had experienced twenty years before, when its bright colors outraged the retina of eyes overused to pallid tones. Chronologically, we were a year or two ahead of our time, and the upshot was that we decided to become publishers in France by running off a small quantity of our edition with text in French, under an imprint of our own: Domino Press, Paris.

76

II

WHEN the lithographs of *Daniel Boone* were finished in the summer of 1931 we were anxious to submit our sample pages to American publishers as soon as possible. Therefore we went to that well-known landmark for Americans abroad, Brentano's Bookshop on the Avenue de l'Opéra, to inquire whether any publishers happened to be in Paris on scouting trips for new material. We had the good fortune to meet Mr. Brentano himself, for he was making one of his annual visits to Europe. He looked carefully at the lithographs, reminisced when he saw the illustration of Boone drifting down the Ohio River in a flatboat — the landscape showed the country of Mr. Brentano's own boyhood — and then, reverting to the purpose of our visit, told us that there were no American publishers in Paris at the moment and none were likely to arrive until their Christmas books had been launched. At all events it was far too late in the season for us to hope that *Daniel Boone* could be published in America in 1931. But Mr. Brentano did propose that we go immediately to London and make an effort to place part of our edition with an English publisher.

His remark astonished us, and we replied that we doubted if England would be interested in a picture album dealing with the hero of a colony she had since lost. Furthermore, the text of *Daniel Boone* was simply in the form of captions, and we felt that in England words mean more than pictures. But Mr. Brentano offered to give us a list of London publishers and said that we might tell them we came at his suggestion.

We went from London publisher to London publisher. Gentlemen of the old school, friends of Mr. Brentano, received us courteously, and showed us pictures of the kind they themselves prized: pencil drawings of the lovely head of Keats, pale watercolors of the Scottish moors. From publisher to publisher we went. How tiring it is to tramp the streets of foreign cities. Yet publishers continued to give us " leads " until at last, one torrid afternoon in Russell Square, when literally we could go no further, we rang the door-bell of a quite

77

young firm, Faber and Faber, who agreed to import a small edition of *Daniel Boone* for publication in England.

Afterwards, how good it was to cross to Paris, to see the quais along the Seine, and Notre Dame, and then to lose ourselves in that cosmopolitan world, which was a kind of isolated world within the world. For foreigners who liked to experiment quietly with schemes, Paris was the most favorable of cities.

That is why, among the Americans who lived there in the post-war period from the early 1920's through the early 1930's, perhaps a dozen of them spasmodically, when the mood was on them, took to publishing. The names of the first of those expatriate publishers escape me, but I remember that about our own time were Sylvia Beach, who had brought out the monumental *Ulysses* of James Joyce under the imprint of her bookshop, The Shakespeare Head; Gertrude Stein, who issued several of her own works under her own imprint, Plain Editions; and Harrison of Paris, a small firm specializing in illustrated editions for bibliophiles. We ourselves were simply the most inconspicuous and the most naïve of those expatriate publishers. We were the last to enter the field and the last to leave it at a time when the devaluation of the dollar and the political unrest in Europe rounded out a cycle of American activity abroad. I believe also that none of the others were concerned with children's books.

Yes, all things seemed possible to us in that lovely isolation, *couleur de rose*. But we had merely to pass beyond the gates of Paris to realize that we were also living in France, a foreign land. After we returned from London, we began going almost daily to Argenteuil, a small suburb on the Seine, to supervise the printing of the text of *Boone*. We could never make the train trip to Argenteuil without thinking of Monet, who had painted so many of his atmospheric scenes there. The town had changed much since his times, but actually, we saw in our mind's eye only the delicate, divided tones of Monet.

We could not help wondering what the good folk of Argenteuil would think of Rojankovsky's bright, flat and decorative patterns. As a matter of fact, the foreman in the press room, with whom we worked, regarded us as barbarians. He looked

78

with horror at the *Boone* pictures yet held his tongue, for pictures, after all, were not his concern. But type and its composition were the core of his existence. Bred as he was to the tradition of the noble page of type, he could not endure the plan that Rojankovsky had devised for blocking the captions above, adjacent to or beneath the illustrations. And now, because we had had no experience with the translation of manuscript into type, we found that our poor captions sometimes overflowed and sometimes fell far short of the patterns intended for them. We cut or added to our sentences as best we could, and pleaded with the foreman to use those little trade tricks by which printers who set type by hand were able, so we had heard, to achieve optical illusions. He did his work well, but with a grudge. " How can I help you? " he once said. " This is not a book."

" It is an album of pictures," we suggested meekly.

" Call it what you will," he said, " it is not a book."

His comment pricked our conscience, made us sensitive to the fact that, absorbed as we had been by the pictures, we had overlooked what he would have called the fundamental element of a book, that is to say, fine typography. I realize, now, that a few beautifully designed type pages would have rounded out *Boone* from a picture album into a book, yet we could not have attempted that without some finely written words, and I am glad we did not try to be more pretentious than our literary means allowed. We have also learned since then how ticklish is the problem of designing a child's book, even under favorable conditions, for the designer, like the author and the illustrator, must see with the eyes of a child. And the best picture books that I have seen, both of today and of times gone by, have an air, often intangible, of spontaneity and warmth, even at the cost of classical perfection in typography.

At Christmas time in 1931, *Daniel Boone,* with English text, appeared in England under the imprint of Faber and Faber, London; and with French text, in France, under our own imprint, Domino Press, Paris. In spite of our weakness in text and typography, the *London Observer,* recognizing the vitality of Rojankovsky's work, called *Daniel Boone* its "choice among all the children's books of the season." We began to think that the destiny of a book is a strange thing which no one can foretell.

The sales of the book abroad are a story in themselves. It is enough to say here that they came less from the ordinary channels on which we had counted than from unexpected sources. As I look back upon the period of the early sales, I have the sensation of listening to tiny firecrackers popping here and there — sometimes close at hand, more often far away, in other European countries. In Paris we succeeded in placing *Boone* in the better shops, but the financial returns, although they increased as the years passed, were not very brilliant that first season. No expensive book for children sells widely in France unless it has a sumptuous or pseudo-sumptuous binding, and furthermore, even skilled publishers there found it difficult to struggle against the inertia that blocked most attempts to market new juveniles. Once when I called upon a book dealer, who bought an embarrassingly small number of our books, he said to me as I was about to leave, "And yet, *Mademoiselle*, this may be an item for collectors, after you are dead."

He had meant to cheer me, but instead, he plunged us into an abyss of gloom. In a vision we could see ourselves saddled, for the remainder of our lives, to a stock of slow-selling books. We were still holding in reserve the whole American edition, and no American publisher had given us the slightest cause to hope that we could dispose of it. We must think twice before involving ourselves further in this cumbersome business known as publishing.

Perhaps we did think twice, I don't recall. I do remember that Rojankovsky was champing at the bit to continue illustrating, and not long after *Daniel Boone* was finished, we began work with him on our second book, *Powder*, the story of a pony and the circus. The real reason for our going on must have been that, after having known the fun of being associated with the creation of a book, we would have found it very dull to quit. Useless, however, to think of another picture book of American history, for America had become, for us, a distant and mysterious land, while the little one-ring circuses of Paris stood just around the corner. This time, too, we wanted to produce a less expensive book. We chose a smaller and more economical format and planned to have the pictures printed in two- and three-color lithography, with a slight story to accompany them. Late in the spring of 1932 we went to London with the rough dummy of *Powder,* arranged for Faber and Faber to import an edition for English publication, and then sailed to America, where eventually Harrison Smith and Robert Haas won our gratitude by accepting the book for publication in America.

On that trip, *Daniel Boone* also found a home, not with a regular publishing firm, but with the Bookshop for Boys and Girls in Boston. No arrangement could have pleased us more, for Miss Mahony, then director of the Bookshop, had always been a guide for us as we groped our way along. Without her steadying influence, it is doubtful whether the Domino Press could have lasted; she encouraged us whenever encouragement was possible, and, even better, tried never to discourage us. We first met Miss Mahony on that earlier visit to America, when we came to show Rojankovsky's *Boone* pictures to the publishers. We were then so absorbed in Rojankovsky's work that one would have thought no other illustrator existed. But in the course of time she tempered us, in such a kindly manner, and opened our minds to the fact that there were many other gifted artists in the world, and other publishers who knew the joys of collaborating with them on picture books. She also helped us to see that publishing for children is a complex thing and that some day, if we were to survive and find our place in the field, we must catch a spark from the children's editors in America, those experienced editors who, through years of intelligent work, have given a new vitality to children's books. And her influence continued to reach out to us in Paris — how, I do not really know.

There was still another American, Miss Anne Carroll Moore, who meant much to us, for every one of her critical writings that drifted to us overseas threw light upon problems that confronted us while we were developing our picture books. Even in her short reviews of books, new American books that we would probably never see, she found the means of linking a specific, sometimes local incident to the " general stream " in a style that engraved many of her phrases upon our memory. All in all, she left us haunted, as we still are, by the thought that in our own work for children the beauty and the imaginative power of the written word have eluded us.

III

At the risk of being over-personal I have tried to describe the obscure origin of a fly-by-night publisher in Paris in days that now seem strangely far removed. If I have taken the liberty of mentioning freely the names of artists, printers and various authorities in the field of children's books, it is because we were the product of circumstances rather than of a preconceived plan to become publishers. The early part of our story is really the story of the people who influenced us and interested us in the publishing of books for children.

At first we turned to contemporary French juveniles — they were the ones nearest at hand — for the stimulus which most people need when they begin to specialize in a given line of work. Yet we went as far back as Boutet de Monvel and Job without finding a vast amount of material that satisfied us. Then, about the time when we were beginning *Powder,* a streak of fortune led us one day to the ancient Cour de Rohan, which is older than the time of Perrault. There, in a tiny, vine-clad bookshop we met a youthful dealer, J.-G. Deschamps, and his aunt, *Tante Emma,* who spoke the magic words: *dans le temps:* in times gone by. His shop brimmed with Old French children's books and pictures ranging from penny prints to the finest illustrated editions. The Deschamps were the people who for the remainder of our stay in Paris helped to educate our eye and improve our taste.

How our eyes loved to caress the details of those old French children's books: the flower-colored paper bindings of the Romantic period, the morocco bindings of the *ancien régime,* the Gothic woodcuts of the sixteenth century and the

82

soft copper engravings of the early nineteenth century. How thoroughly publishers long ago had worked out the basic types of juveniles: A B C's and fairy tales, picture books and chapbooks, fables and fiction, books of knowledge, books of fantasy and books of song. I doubt if one could plan a modern juvenile whose counterpart did not exist in times gone by. It is true that each period must weave its own material on the framework of those basic types, yet it was an unforgettable experience for us to turn the pages of rare volumes in which publishers had achieved such a delicate harmony of imaginative content and visual effect.

Meanwhile the Domino Press dragged itself slowly on its way. It took us an interminable time to make a book, partly because we had so much to learn as we went along and partly because we were hampered — no, almost beaten — by commercial problems involved in the fall and fluctuations of the pound and the dollar. The printing of our second book, *Powder,* was not completed until the summer of 1933. We kept the edition with French text for ourselves and published it under our own imprint. The English and American editions were imported and published respectively by Faber and Faber, London, and by Harrison Smith and Robert Haas, New York (now Random House). To our knowledge this was the first time that a child's book had been printed in France for simultaneous publication in France, England and America. *Flash,* a sequel to *Powder,* was issued in 1934 under the same imprints.

The formula of international publishing for children was an appealing one, although the brief period during which people had had a tendency to think in international terms was drawing to a close. But this method of publishing meant that every time we wished to change a format or an artist we must make those long selling trips by land and sea. The circuit was too large for us to cover by ourselves and we did not wish to become an organized publishing firm with an overhead expense that might force us out of the experimental field. We had no ambition other than to remain a fly-by-night publisher, free to issue occasional books that fall outside the regular channels of publishing. Therefore it seemed advisable for us to try in the future to experiment with fairly small editions for a single country. Besides, our only chance to improve the quality of our texts lay in working in the country whose children spoke an idiom that was our own.

So, towards the end of 1934, we packed our trunks with books and journeyed homewards. Before we left we brought out our fourth and last picture book in France: *The Fable of a Proud Poppy*, illustrated by the Hungarian painter, Emile Lahner, a collaborator in the old writing-paper days. His little book, the most European-looking of our series, is filled with his own woodcuts which he hand-colored delicately.

Viewed from turbulent Europe, America still seemed to be the promised land, the land of youth and energy and golden opportunity. All these things we knew and I wish that I could say that we set sail in a lively spirit adequate to the event. But actually we came with that sinking feeling peculiar to many Americans who leave their beloved Paris.

We brought with us the rough projects for two books which we have recently published under our new imprint: The Domino Press, New York. The first of these, *The Voyages of Jacques Cartier*, appearing in 1937, marks our first attempt to work with a relatively long text for older children. However, in design the book is in the picture book tradition. Very little is known about Cartier, the Breton sea-captain who sailed beyond the misty, much-feared region of Newfoundland and discovered Canada. Therefore, instead of writing an imaginary story of his life, we have simply linked the brief and often broken records of his explorations to the background of his time and leaned heavily upon Rojankovsky's illustrations for dramatic interest.

But in the *Tales of Poindi* (1938) we have had the more delicate task of making an illustrated book in which the written word plays the leading rôle. The original French text (which we have published in a separate edition entitled *Contes de Poindi*) is by a French poet and novelist, Jean Mariotti, who was born in the bush of New Caledonia, an island in the South Pacific. In the blue half-light of the Caledonian forest live exotic birds and other curious creatures that have become legendary themes for the tales told by native

84

women to their children. In writing these tales in French, Mariotti has developed a style both primitive and elaborate, simple and at times slightly precious, as if the complexity and intensity of tropical nature defied straight-forward description. His sentences are sometimes formally constructed and again they are elliptical. His sensitiveness to individual words induces him occasionally to coin one, and he weaves the threads of his story through a pattern of recurrent themes and repeated words that suggest the monotony and the eternity of the immense forests. Unfortunately the peculiar poetical quality of his style is one that for technical reasons cannot be rendered literally into English.

Rojankovsky has illustrated the *Tales of Poindi* in a quiet vein and we have placed his illustrations on the pages so that they accompany the text rather than dominate it. The make-up of an illustrated book is not an easy matter in these days when the graphic arts tend toward bold pictorial effects. To catch this modern spirit and at the same time to use illustrative material so that it may enrich but not intrude upon the images evoked by the written word is a problem to which we must give more serious thought if we are to continue experimenting with books for children.

From *The Horn Book* for September, 1938, December, 1938, and February, 1939

ILLUSTRATIONS TODAY IN CHILDREN'S BOOKS

By Warren Chappell

CREATION is adventure. Regardless of how often the trials are made, it is not humanly possible to material- ize imagination. Artists then can never hope to sense the full satisfaction that can come to an able craftsman. To be sure, there is a good deal of craft in illustration; one must work for a printed result, and the job is done only when the presses stop rolling. But it is the elusive creative ad- mixture which keeps the greatest technique from being empty. One of the gravest dangers facing any illustrator is the pigeonhole, for though it may aid his ability to produce in quantity, it stifles both the creative capacity and the very natural enthusiasm of adventure.

It should be obvious that there is no such thing as an expert, that experience carries with it such a broadening of vision that it vitiates any tendency toward becoming almighty. Whether the pigeonhole or the individual artist is responsible for today's plethora of tired illustrations, it is difficult to say. One thing, however, is certain — the superior attitude, the attitude of talking down to the audience, can never produce good work.

An illustration is a pictorial statement. It should never be a technical manipulation, and only in the rarest of descriptive instances should it be a costume exercise. Hollywood has shown us that it is possible to serve up costumes which, though correct in every detail, fail completely to be clothes and to be worn as such.

Every illustrator must of necessity have a method, and he should be aware of the vast background of pictorial art with all its devices of composition and means for describing shapes. This knowledge, however, cannot lessen the anxiety with which he must approach each piece of work, large or small. How often, as praise, one hears a comment on an illustrator's technique, and yet the very fact that it has called attention to itself suggests a mannerism. The artist's method should only be apparent to another artist.

There are few illustrators who enjoy a more enviable reputation than Sir John Tenniel, and this reputation has been built on a single collaboration with Lewis Carroll. Let us look back of that association and see what had prepared Sir John for his assignment. For years he had been a regular contributor to *Punch,* and he was in the habit of observing, and of crystallizing his observations for publication. Our own A. B. Frost was trained in a similiar way. It is to be noted that both these men had a high average for gag-free humor, the only kind which can outlast its own generation.

In any discussion of illustration, it is impossible to escape consideration of the author's responsibility in the final result. God certainly never intended that every one should be an author, else he would have spread the talent more evenly. It is no more surprising that *Treasure Island* is a piece of literature than that *Alice in Wonderland* is a major illustrated book. Author and illustrator, in these instances, were prepared to make a real contribution. One may assume that neither had any preconceptions about his undertaking, yet both seem to have been aware of the necessity for simple, straightforward treatment of their themes. The quality of the manuscript is of prime importance to the illustrator. The greatest illustrations are those which Rembrandt made for the Bible, Daumier for *Don Quixote,* and perhaps those of Delacroix for *Faust* should be included.

The position of the publisher is not an enviable one. To produce an illustrated book is expensive, and parents, not children, are the purchasers. This unfortunate combination of factors produces the dreaded pigeonhole, and sooner or later each illustrator is liable to be tucked into one which is reserved for him. Many of our best artists seldom make an appearance in books because they defy classification and refuse to imitate drawings which they have done before. To them each manuscript is a new problem.

Today we are faced with a new influence on bookmaking for children, in the big offset factories which have usurped the editorial initiative of many publishing houses and now will provide finished books for them. In this way the publisher is turned into a mere selling agency. Naturally by keeping the presses constantly rolling, the factories can produce illustrated books in color at a very low cost. Such a stereotyped solution of the problem of the high cost of books seems most unfortunate. If illustration is to be governed by so-called " art directors," and on the factory principle, both the child and the illustrator will be the losers. Nothing but admiration can be held for those houses which insist on doing their own work, even if it is less profitable for a time, for they are the publishers who are most certain to carry on a standard and a tradition.

Technique has always been a will-o'-the-wisp, but now there is added the quicksand of the " original lithographic drawing, done directly on the plate." It is impossible to gain the experience necessary to draw on stone or zinc by spending a few hours in an offset shop. This method of reproduction does not lend itself to bravura drawing on the one hand, or to piddling on the other. It is a stern, slow craft. Transparent tones must be built up slowly so that the grain will be kept open. It should be remembered, also, that the old lithographic illustrations, in color, were made with many more than three colors and black. This was true for letterpress as well, as can be seen in the wood engravings which Edmund Evans did for Caldecott.

In most instances, the best method for hand-separated color plates today is through the use of drawings on paper, where a proper saturation of color can be achieved. Among the fall books there are two outstanding examples done by this method: Kurt Wiese's *Captain Kidd's Cow,* which is handled in washes, and William Pène du Bois' *The Flying Locomotive,* produced in line. In the latter, the artist has competently employed cross-hatching to produce middle tones, and he has used solids expertly, to heighten the sense of silhouette in his illustrations.

Among the fall books illustrated with lithographic drawings two seem to stand out: *The Matchlock Gun,* illustrated by Paul Lantz, and Robert McCloskey's *Make Way for Ducklings.* Lantz has achieved a fine mood in his drawings. The color plates, though successful, suffer from the graininess which has been alluded to above. McCloskey's drawings have a great deal of variety and interest, achieved through a change of scale and pace. He has wisely chosen a warm color to overcome the usually unhealthy pallor of offset. The cleverness of his manipulation of the crayon has some tendency to cheapen the whole very capable effect.

The successful way in which McCloskey has changed the pace of his pages brings up one of the most important factors involved in a picture book, and that is variety. The audience should not get the feeling that it has seen this one before. It is particularly important that there be constant changes in the silhouette. Those who recall William Nicholson's *Clever Bill* will remember how the heroine packed her bag for several pages, and each page was fresh and interesting.

The part played by typography in the making of children's books can be overestimated, but it has a definite rôle. Just as the individual picture must be organized within itself, so is the relationship of these individual pictures in the whole scheme a part of the problem. And just as the individual illustration should not be design-ridden, so the whole is not improved by self-conscious typographic treatment. The finished book must not elicit the comment that it is a good-looking package — that's merchandising language, not critical.

Illustrators should be interested in the past, and should learn from it. The idea of originality is an invention of progressive education. Shakespeare and Molière drew on their forerunners, Rubens spent much of his time in Spain copying paintings in the Prado, and Rembrandt made dozens of copies of Persian miniatures. In each case the result was something new. It cannot be said too often that art thrives on continuity, and that the work of any individual becomes a part of the general heritage.

For those who do not want to go back to Michelangelo to be inspired by pen drawing, there are always the files of *Century* and *Harper's,* embracing the 'eighties and 'nineties, which will show how rich a medium pen and ink can be. Photoengravers should spend some time studying that period, too, in order to find out why they are not able to make line cuts as well as did their ancestors.

Both editors and illustrators should remember that a child cannot be drawn showing his teeth and smirking, and that all children do not look alike. It might be well for every artist to think back on his own childhood and recall that he didn't want to be beautiful himself, and rather looked down on children who were afflicted that way.

An artist should be encouraged to illustrate around most of the main passages of a manuscript, rather than laboriously to reconstruct those scenes which often are already adjective-laden and overdescribed. After all, the artist is a collaborator, and his task is a complementary one.

Illustrations fall roughly into three groups: narrative, descriptive, and decorative. In the first category is to be found the greatest work, the illustrations with true literary content. Here the illustrator is making a contribution from his own experience and creates a story held in suspense among the various characters and objects of his composition. Descriptive illustrations range from a diagram of a monkey wrench to a battle scene by Meissonier. The decorative classification runs from Burne-Jones to wallpaper. There are not more than a half-dozen designers today who can do really fine decoration, so it is safe to conclude that book illustration in this last category has everything against it at the outset.

In so short a treatment it is impossible to do more than touch on some of the problems which loom large in the book field in general, and among books for children in particular. When one considers the comics, the movie cartoons, and the textbooks, it is safe to say that the average child's pictorial experience is all but bankrupt, and that a good ninety-five per cent of the illustration he sees is little more than competent art student work. This is not to underestimate the art student's work; it is simply to say that time and maturity add something completely beyond the realm of technique, and that through living himself, an artist is able to bring life and reality to his characters and his statements about them. Realism is a very different thing. It is reality which can be created by experienced minds and hands.

From *The Horn Book* for November, 1941

Part III

Reviews and Criticism

CRITICISM OF CHILDREN'S BOOKS

By Bertha E. Mahony (Miller)

A RT flourishes where there is sound critical judgment to examine and appraise. The critic must, first of all, have a real point of view about his subject. The essential point of view grows out of acquaintance with the best children's books past and present, and also with the world's best literature for everyone. This point of view — this measuring stick — must also bear some relation to children themselves and their reactions to books today. The critic should have experience of sharing books with children or of seeing them choosing and reading books for themselves. It is a truism — and yet it does not seem to be generally understood — that criticism is just as importantly concerned with pointing out excellence as weakness.

From its first issue in October, 1924, *The Horn Book* has owed much to the writing of Alice M. Jordan on children's books old and new. As editor of the magazine's Booklist, Miss Jordan has since October, 1939, written for each issue notes on books which are miniatures of positive criticism and fine prose.

Comment on children's books is valuable in exact proportion to the judgment, honesty, fairness, and skill expressed by their critics.

From *The Horn Book* for May, 1946

AN AUTHOR'S VIEW OF CRITICISM

By Howard Pease

TOO often today we hear adults deploring the lack of criticism to be found in our spoken and written reviews of children's fiction. Not that there isn't plenty of justification. Familiar to all of us is the reviewer who narrates everything we don't care to know about the story. Familiar, too, at the other extreme, is the egocentric reviewer who gives only his own reaction to the story. When we find the problem of criticism evaded like this, it is no wonder we become baffled or annoyed. Yet few of us realize, I suspect, how difficult criticism is.

Criticism will always be personal and always inexact. Even the words we use reveal how inexact it is. We say vaguely that a certain book is delightful. But are we sure it will also delight the young reader for whom it is intended, especially since experience has taught us that adult praise has no assurance of a youthful echo? Then when we try to be more definite in our criticism, we find that we must use terms taken from other fields of work. We speak of the *form* of a novel, its *structure,* its *design;* and these are architectural terms. We speak of *viewpoint,* and here our term comes from the artist who paints a scene or a portrait. We speak of *dramatic method,* and this phrase stems directly from the theater. We mention *craftsmanship* and remark that a novel is in need of polishing, as though the author were a cabinetmaker; and here we often fail to differentiate between the craft of fiction and the craft of prose writing. Moreover, in criticizing a book we find it difficult not to reveal our prejudices as well as our enthusiasms, and people who know us well may rightly be skeptical of us on both of these counts. Not many of us are so commendably candid as the librarian who faced her colleagues to review a new book. " I didn't like this story at all," she announced. " But then, it's all about horses, and I never did like horses."

Our minds, fortunately, are not like chain drug stores stocked with identical goods. Each one of us has his own accumulation of ideas and experiences; hence one person's reaction to a novel, a play, a movie, a painting, will be different from another's. Unlike a picture which hangs on a wall to be viewed and studied and pondered, a work of fiction exists in time, like music. It is only when we have finished reading a book that we can judge it, and then we can only think back; and what we remember most vividly may not be what other readers remember. The narrative has faded away like a strain of music; it no longer exists, though the book itself may stand on a shelf for another reading, just as a symphony score may lie on a shelf for another concert.

For anyone to become even a fair critic is not easy. The attempt, however, should do much to make us more humble. We shall find that we must be more realistic, more definite. In the first place we must learn to separate a book's text from its format and illustrations. The untutored reviewer at once exposes his lack of critical judgment when he takes it for granted that, since a publisher has given us a lovely and distinguished book to handle, the text is equally distinguished. We must learn to examine the text itself, and we must do so with less timidity and more discernment. Before we can do this, we must know what elements enter into critical reviewing.

First, what do we know about fictional *forms?* Present-day children's books exhibit, curiously enough, the whole growth of fiction through the ages, from the simplest storyteller's tale to the highly complex modern novel. Our picture books (*Ping* and *Make Way for Ducklings*) are storyteller's tales, an ancient art form, the tale told aloud and then put down in writing in the same simple form. Our books for children of six to ten — these age groups, of course, are elastic — are sometimes a more complex storyteller's tale (*Call It Courage*), sometimes a pure short story (*The Match-*

lock Gun); and the true critic points this out. Books for the middle-aged group are sometimes a simplified form of the junior novel (*Blue Willow*), sometimes a mixture of the junior novel and the storyteller's tale (*The Little House on the Prairie*). For older boys and girls we have the junior novel, a form like the novel itself which is sometimes sprawling and picaresque (*The Codfish Musket*[1]), sometimes closely knit (*The Iron Doctor*[2]). The critical reviewer who knows young readers also knows that the closely-knit story with a rounded plot meets with more popular approval than the picaresque tale with a hero who moves on like Don Quixote through chapter after chapter to new adventures. A high percentage of our historical tales are picaresque in form; and it is this loose construction, I believe, which dampens the enthusiasm of so many young readers rather than the historical setting. Moreover, such tales are usually thin in plot, with the result that the young reader loses interest. On the other hand, the more popular, more tightly-knit story frequently reveals a weakness, at least to the adult reader. Unless the author is more skillful than most, his plot becomes mechanical, and thus his story lacks the sweep and breadth of life.

Of these fictional forms the most difficult from the writer's viewpoint, and therefore the one least often done with complete success, is the junior novel. This form demands of its author a far more sustained imaginative effort. It also calls for the knowledge and use of a far greater variety of literary methods of procedure. *Johnny Tremain,* for instance, receives from me much more applause than, say, *The Matchlock Gun.* Esther Forbes' junior novel is also much more tightly knit as to setting, characters, plot and time element than most historical tales of the same length.

Once we have decided upon the fictional form of a book, let us try to look at the elements within. We cannot tear a book apart, but we can look at it from different angles. Of prime importance in any work of fiction is the *story*. Our second question, then, is: Does this book tell a good story? Somerset Maugham says, " The novelist's essential gift is the

[1] By Agnes Danforth Hewes (Doubleday, 1936, o.p.)
[2] By Agnes Danforth Hewes (Houghton, 1940)

ability to carry the reader along from page to page by the desire to know what is going to happen next." The story must be one that's worth telling. Certainly Margaret Mitchell revealed that she could choose good material when she gave us *Gone With the Wind,* a novel that holds the interest of most readers through a thousand pages — a brilliant achievement. (We are not discussing here any other element in the book.)

Third, *characterization.* Are the characters alive? Are any of them memorable? This ability to create characters and make them live for the reader is, I sometimes believe, God-given. Jane Austen had this ability to the highest degree. Emma, Mr. Woodhouse, Miss Bates, all step right out of the pages of my favorite of Jane's six novels. Dickens gave us so many characters — Pickwick, Sam Weller, Mr. Micawber, Peggotty — that to list them all would become a parlor game. Conan Doyle created a great character in Sherlock Holmes. All these characters live as people; they live long after their stories are forgotten. Whenever I hear roller skates on my sidewalk I look up expecting to see Lucinda speeding round the corner, her ribbons flying on her navy-blue sailor hat, its rubber tight under her chin.

Fourth, does this book we are examining have a worthwhile *content?* Has it a theme, an idea, worth imparting to young people? The theme may be universal, or it may be timely and so perhaps transitory. Maupassant's *Une Vie* is universal in theme; it is the life story of an average woman. The same theme was used by Arnold Bennett in his great novel *The Old Wives' Tale,* and by Edna Ferber in her exceedingly American novel *So Big.* On the other hand, *Uncle Tom's Cabin* possessed a timely theme of great importance when it was published; and because it was not a work of art, it has become part of our history rather than part of our literature. Steinbeck's *The Grapes of Wrath* may be another *Uncle Tom's Cabin,* transitory because of its theme, though I believe it has more chance of survival as literature. In any case, young people are just as interested in books with timely themes as are adults. Such books are usually worth buying for our library shelves even if they are not worth replacing several years later. Their replacement will depend upon the other elements in the book. Many of Dickens' novels were written around timely themes no longer of interest to us; yet, because Dickens was a great novelist, we still read his books. Most stories of World War II will probably lose interest for young people soon after the war is ended. Some of John Tunis' books are written on timely themes; yet these same themes will no doubt be just as timely and pressing twenty years from now, and the stories still good reading.

Fifth, let us look at our book from the angle of *craftsmanship*. Does the author demonstrate skill in the craft of fiction? Does he know how to *tell* a story? Most of us are acquainted with at least one person who can ruin a good story by the way he tells it, and we can usually name another person who can take a mediocre story and yet somehow make it interesting to the very end. That is all, really, that craftsmanship means. Good craftsmanship eliminates hurdles for the reader, hurdles either mechanical or psychological. Good craftsmanship makes a book more readable, and with young people especially this is important.

Under this heading of craftsmanship we must list one fault now found increasingly often in some of our loveliest-looking books intended for children of nine to twelve. We must stop here and ask ourselves: Is the viewpoint in this book that of its young protagonist, or is it that of an adult, the author? For example, *Fog Magic*, in most ways a fine book, is adult both in conception and execution. Its appeal will therefore be to the adult and to the advanced youthful reader who in ability is much older than the age for which the story was obviously intended. The discerning reviewer will catch two hints of this adult viewpoint early in the story. First, Greta's mother, a farmwife, is usually referred to by the author as Gertrude; and second, Greta's conversation is as formally correct as the conversation found in a reading textbook for the fourth grade. Such books leave most young readers cold. Because the appeal here is chiefly to the adult who takes pleasure in looking back through a golden haze upon the days of his childhood, these books are known as " nostalgic " books. To be able to spot this type of book and point out its limited but grateful audience is the mark of a real critic.

Sixth, what of the *prose* in this book? Is it well written, or at least competently enough written so that we are not ashamed to put it on our shelves? The author, if he knows the craft of prose writing, should play with words directly upon the reader's mind, with the thought flowing on without interruption. A prose that demands of us as readers that we mentally jump back and forth and turn somersaults until the wear and tear upon our minds and patience leave us exhausted, is scarcely the kind to hold the interest of young people. Furthermore, does the prose style suit the story?

Seventh, and last, we come to an intangible, the *reaction* we have after completing the book. When the music stops playing, are we still charmed or uplifted or uneasy? If we have no reaction when we lay a book aside, we can be sure the book is a mediocre one. When I finish reading one of Eleanor Estes' stories about the Moffats I am all aglow. Something tells me that this is a real book, a work of the creative imagination. Very few books leave me with this reaction. Not many books, of course, are so alive, so real. A work of fiction, to be first-rate, must be more than a good story, more than characterization and craftsmanship and prose. It must succeed in creating the illusion of life itself. Eleanor Estes' stories about Rufus M. and his family possess this vital quality. This author is one of my enthusiasms, and as a result I am completely prejudiced in her favor.

Critical judgment applied to the work of any of our well-known novelists in the adult field will disclose fine qualities or blemishes, or gradations between, on all of the seven points here listed, though another critic may substitute a point or even add or subtract. The essential thing is to attempt precision. We have, for example, H. M. Tomlinson, who writes poor novels in a prose that is beautiful and even distinguished. We have Theodore Dreiser, a fine novelist at his best, whose prose is often very bad indeed, clumsy and tortuous and prolix. In Sinclair Lewis we have a journalist who gave us in *Main Street* a timely theme which justly caught the attention of the whole country; later in George F. Babbitt he created a character which has become a household name. Conrad was a novelist who admittedly lacked inventiveness; he was also a great artist whose lovely prose at times stops the reader because of its sheer beauty. Willa Cather, on the other hand, writes in a style so straightforward and limpid that it never comes between the reader and the story; she is an exquisite artist who works within narrow limits.

When we turn to writers of children's books and apply critical judgment to their work, we find it also standing up on one count and falling down on another. Let us take, then, a successful and important modern book for young people and look at it from this angle and that, even though we know we shall not all agree. Let us examine John Tunis' *All-American*. In *form* this is a junior novel, closely knit. Is it a good *story*? Yes, in interest it holds adults as well as young people. What of its *characterization*? So-so, I'd say; no character especially memorable. Has it *content*, a theme worthwhile? To the highest degree. Mr. Tunis is one of those rare authors who has something worthwhile to say about our modern world here at home. By boldly choosing his theme for *All-American* and by using it successfully he has enlarged the whole field of the junior novel. Next, what of his *craftsmanship*? Excellent, and that is a major reason why his book is so readable. The author's treatment of his material is unusual in that it is almost wholly subjective. In less expert hands this stream-of-thought manner might have become tiresome and wordy. Here the narrative is shorn of excess wordage, with the result that it has intensity and immediacy, two qualities of importance to the young reader. What of the *prose*? Is the book well written? I say it is, in spite of several adult readers who have said to me, " *All-American* is such a fine book otherwise, it's a pity it isn't better written." I always ask these critics how they would prefer to have it written. Would they find this story of present-day high school life better written if Mr. Tunis had used the poetic prose of a Walter de la Mare? Nonsense. Mr. Tunis used the sinewy and forceful student idiom because he chose to handle his narrative in a subjective manner. The story is presented, not from the viewpoint of an adult who is proficient in formal academic English, but from the viewpoint of a high school athlete who

102

speaks the language of the football field. For this book, the prose is perfect, as perfect in its way as the prose of *Huckleberry Finn*. I can think of no other modern writer for young people who could have written *All-American* so well. And last, what of our *reaction* when we have read this book and put it aside? Do we forget it? We do not. Its story rings and echoes in our minds for weeks and months afterwards. I myself found *All-American* one of the most exciting junior novels I have ever read. To me it remains a milestone in juvenile book publication. Yet I am aware that many readers do not agree with me.

This is not surprising. Since our minds are not stocked with identical goods like chain drug stores, we can expect few critics to agree on every point. Still, we can all help to develop our own critical judgment if we look at the text of a book from different angles. Take any new or doubtful book and submit it to these tests. You will be sure to discover fine qualities as well as blemishes, and you can then balance the former against the latter and decide whether or not the book is worthwhile — for you. And if other critics do not agree, perhaps that is all to the good. So long as we can discuss our books and disagree, and have a good time while doing so, there is hope for the future.

From *The Horn Book* for May, 1946

TWENTY YEARS
OF CHILDREN'S BOOKS

By Bertha Mahony Miller

O NE day as I was looking over proofs of beautiful lithographs with a famous illustrator, she said sadly, " It is
discouraging sometimes, this making of beautiful
books for children. So few are sold! A friend of mine with
plenty of money and a little girl of six told me recently that
while eventually she wanted her little girl to own all my
picture books, just now it was a question of quantity, not
quality, and so she went to the Five and Ten for her books."

Meanwhile another friend related how much her little boy
of six loved Dorothy Lathrop's *Snail Who Ran;* so much that
he almost knew it by heart; and how excited he had been over
the word " invisible " as he met it in that book. You remember that when the fairy in the story offers each of the three
tiny creatures of the wood a wish, the mouse asks to become
" invisible." For days Rockie was heard murmuring the
word. Then came a night when his mother read him a poem
about " the mercy and goodness of God." When the poem was
finished, Rockie repeated " The mercy and goodness of God "
— and then with such an air of triumph at having put words
to an idea of his own, he said: " 'The mercy and goodness of
God ' — it is invisible."

My friend, Rockie's mother, has two other boys, one four
and one nine. She uses the very finest verse and prose with
them; a great deal of Bible, ever so much poetry, mostly
from Walter de la Mare's *Come Hither.* Her small boys can
recite the Christmas story as told in the book of Luke, although they have not been asked to learn it. She begrudges
no money for the finest books for them. Rockie's mother is

a young woman who discovered in college under Hervey Allen a passion for English. She believes that we in America do not care deeply enough for our mother tongue and do not take pains to give our little children the chance at a large vocabulary and all the wonder which lies in words and their meaning. She believes, too, that little children must have the best from the beginning.

Which mother is the more usual, the first or the second? In the answer lies the core of my theme. Instead of being entitled "Twenty Years of Children's Books," perhaps it should be called "The Next Twenty Years of Children's Books." These past two decades have seen much accomplishment in the world of books for the young here in America. Influences have been at work to create an insistent demand for more books of excellent quality for children; public libraries have increased the number of their children's rooms in charge of trained librarians, or have given more attention to the buying of books for children; more schools have added libraries and librarians. Beginning with the reviews of Miss Anne Carroll Moore in *The Bookman* and her Three Owls Page, which ran for ten years in the *New York Herald Tribune,* newspapers and journals over the country have given increasing space to the subject. Normal schools and the teacher-training departments of colleges have added courses. Bookstores give special attention to these books. In response to the growth of this critical and interested public, more publishers have placed their children's book departments in the hands of properly qualified editors, following the example of Macmillan, who appointed Louise Seaman in 1919, and Doubleday, Doran, who appointed May Massee in 1922.

The result has been a steadily enlarging stream of good books, beautifully illustrated and well made. Any one who is interested may gain for himself some idea of this output by examining the bound volumes of *The Horn Book* as they may be seen in many public libraries, or by looking over *Realms of Gold in Children's Books* and its sequel, *Five Years of Children's Books.* A glance at these two volumes reveals the number of books now being published for boys and girls as compared with twenty years ago, for *Five Years of Chil-*

105

dren's Books (1930 to 1935) is almost as large a volume as *Realms,* which recommended good books in print from the beginning through 1929.

It may be seen swiftly, too, either from *The Horn Book* or from the two volumes mentioned above, that good books are appearing on almost every subject. There is a growing list of notable stories of life in the widely different sections of this country. The books reveal, too, the cultures from other parts of the world which have gone into the making of this country and which have contributed so largely to the art in our children's books. Yes, the past twenty years have brought us the books. But the production of the books is far ahead of their distribution at this moment. The books are not yet reaching the children. I don't mean just that they are not reaching the children in those sections of the country where poverty is rife. They are not reaching the children in those sections where the standard of living is high. The well-to-do mother mentioned at the opening of this paper who goes to the Five and Ten for quantity rather than quality is not an isolated instance. She represents a very large group indeed.

It is true that certain cities over the country, and here and there a large town, have splendid library systems which send books regularly into the school rooms for pleasure reading. For the past eight years even these systems have had a great shortage of books. When the whole country is considered, the children who have the opportunity to see fine fresh books, in all their individuality and beauty, are few indeed. Just the other day in a Massachusetts town of eight thousand people, a new school superintendent found no books for pleasure reading anywhere in the rooms of the seven large school buildings. A public library in a Massachusetts city of 40,000 has only recently reorganized an incredibly antiquated system and has not yet nearly enough books for its children's room and could not possibly consider stations in the schools. I know an academy to which children from various parts of the country are sent to prepare for college which does not have a library worthy the name. The instances can be repeated indefinitely.

Courses in children's literature in teacher-training schools are worth little if a good library of the books themselves is not available to the students. From my own observation and experience I judge, too, that many teachers today have themselves never had the real *experience* of reading, that enlargement of life and enhancement of living which comes through the understanding and enjoyment of the printed page. Immediately upon its publication, I circulated a copy of Monica Shannon's *Dobry* to eight teachers. During the several months while the book was traveling among them, and after its return, no teacher ever spoke of it to me. When, some months later, a storyteller told the Christmas chapter from the book in one of the schools, a teacher said to her wonderingly, " Why, I read that book but I didn't know all that was in it. " And what is most amazing of all, so far as I know no reading whatever was done from the book to the children.

We know that in the present conditions of home life those influences which used to prepare children naturally and unconsciously for the experience of reading no longer exist to any great extent. I mean reading aloud, informal storytelling of old tales or of what happened when father and mother were young, and attendance at church or church schools where the Bible or other sacred books are listened to regularly. Walter de la Mare in his *Early One Morning in the Spring* quotes John Dewey as saying, " One can pick out the children who learned to read at home. They read naturally." On the other hand such tremendous modern innovations as the movies and the radio, which might really take the place of earlier home encouragment of reading and go hand in hand with books, serve today only too often to break down children's interest in books and despoil it and, along with the automobile, create a restlessness and inability to concentrate.

My theme is meant to be challenging, not depressing. Our world of today is small and full of wonders. Nothing in it is more wonderful and beautiful and full of dynamic power to inspire toward understanding and well-doing than our children's books.

The past twenty years have brought us the books. What

shall we do in the next twenty years to take them to more children? Frederic Melcher initiated the idea of Children's Book Week back in 1918 to make an annual occasion when the books might be so emphasized as to win new friends for them. Nothing is more fun than to have a yearly festival over children's books, but the books need our attention every day.

We need to work much more actively for better programs on the radio. We need to provide excellent storytelling in the library and school as well as on the radio. Young mothers could do a great deal for their own increased pleasure and that of their children if they would form small study clubs to make the acquaintance of the books. They have a wonderful opportunity to work for the books and the children through their woman's club. I know a club which has had now for almost ten years a committee to conduct a special exhibition of books from early fall to Christmas, to advise and to take orders and even to deliver the orders. This committee holds itself ready to answer questions about books throughout the year.

In most small towns we need to take a fresh look at our public library service to the children. In times like these public funds should be made to give their fullest return especially for children. Where a small town public library has the life and the interest, it will be found possible to persuade an editor of children's books to come and talk about her books and their makers. Publishers will often lend the original drawings of their book illustrations.

Children and grown-ups alike love celebrations and the fresher and more different the occasion, the happier those who share in it. I shall never forget the day when I heard Kate Douglas Wiggin speak in a certain Children's Room of a public library. I remember, too, a bookshop dinner which fairly sparkled with the gaiety of the authors and illustrators who were gathered there along with children's editors and many other guests. *And books were sold as a result.*

No bookshop specially interested in children's books can be worthy the name if it considers its work done when it has stocked the books and sent out occasional publicity about them. It must take the books outside and show them to prospective buyers. It must arrange special occasions to bring children and grown-ups in. One grand occasion for bookshops to go out to schools is when children are having to choose their books for summer reading. The school may have as much to do with the choice of books to be shown as it formerly did when offering a printed list of " must be reads," but the feeling of the boys and girls toward the books which they have themselves chosen after having tasted and handled them is different indeed.

There will be in the future, undoubtedly, some plan by which large libraries and small in the same region coöperate for better service. The Library Commissions of the States may find new ways to work with such regional groups.

The *Saturday Review of Literature** published a paper by the President of the Julius Rosenwald Fund, Edwin R. Embree, entitled " Can College Graduates Read? " Mr. Embree commented upon the sad conclusions drawn by a Carnegie Foundation study of high school and college students over a ten-year period in Pennsylvania. In the course of his paper he wrote as follows:

" The present tendency to provide all schools with at least small collections of supplementary texts and stories is probably the most effective movement in modern education."

He also wrote, " My own belief is that a major aspect of sound education is reading. If children will learn to read fluently and understandingly, they have acquired the finest of the intellectual tools. If these young people will then proceed to read, they will take care of the greater part of their own education." I thought as I read this of the words of an English Dean from a great university when he was asked what learning he would consider essential for a boy who must leave school and go to work at fourteen. After a long moment of thought, the Dean replied, " A good reading knowledge of his mother tongue and the ability to sing and draw."

Walter de la Mare says in *Early One Morning in the Spring* that it was John Milton's view that " the knowledge of words

*Issue of July 16, 1938.

109

is best obtained in union with the knowledge of things. Language, he wrote, is but the instrument conveying to us *things* useful to be known; and he maintained that all true methods of learning must begin from the objects of sense. From life and nature to words, from words to life and nature again. It is chiefly because we so poorly see, observe and distinguish, that our words are wanting or feeble in a personal content."

Now it is upon just this view that the French proceed to make the reading and writing of their language the very heart of study in every year of a primary and secondary school child's life. They encourage the very little child to observe what interests him in the world about him and to find the exact word to express what he sees. And they are not afraid to expose him to the very best words of prose and of poetry in his earliest years.

The next twenty years of children's books — let us express our appreciation of their beauty and magic by giving them to the children.

From *The Horn Book* for Christmas, 1938

TO CHILDHOOD AND BEYOND

By Frances Clarke Sayers

I N this century of war and havoc to have experienced a golden age in any art is to have lived through a miracle. The last twenty years have produced such a miracle, since during that time, between tyrannies and fantastic horror in the world, the art of children's reading came to a golden bloom in America.

The recognition of any art as a vital and living force is the demand for critical estimate of it, and of those who produce it. It was the war year of 1918 which brought forth the first demand for sustained and serious criticism of children's books, on the same level of dignity and intensity as was allotted to literature for adults. The demand was made by Eugene F. Saxton, then of *The Bookman*, a monthly magazine of literary criticism, published by George H. Doran.

It was Anne Carroll Moore who rose to the demand, not only upholding its implied challenge, but bringing to it such a body of gifts as to make the articles appearing in *The Bookman* above her signature a distinguished contribution to critical writing in general, and an enduring influence on the writing, illustrating, and publishing of children's books in particular. She brought to the assignment intuitive insight, an exciting freshness of vision, and deep experience in life as well as in books.

The views and reviews of children's books appeared in *The Bookman* from 1918 until 1926. It is these essays which form the three books we know as *Roads to Childhood* (1918-1920), *New Roads to Childhood* (1920-1923), and *Cross Roads to Childhood* (1923-1926). The present volume, *My Roads to Childhood* (Doubleday), includes the material of the first

111

three volumes, and in addition two new essays. The first essay, rich in remembrance of a Maine background and Maine people, serves as an introduction to the book. The second accompanies the superb " Lists of Books Published 1926-1938, " which brings the survey up to date.

" I have chosen for this list," says Miss Moore, " those books which seem to me to have special values of originality, beauty or spontaneous appeal to children, and I have made the choice largely from the imaginative rather than the realistic field."

The annotations of this list reflect the wide experience of the annotator, books and authors being mentioned in fine association with each other, a gay web of cross reference, which enriches the list beyond its original scope.

Here, then, is a survey of twenty years in children's books; a guide so informed by a keen critical mind, so rich in humor, so warm with life, and so illuminated by an understanding of children in their world today, and in those inner, timeless worlds of their own, as far to exceed the margins of the twenty years with which it is concerned.

One has only to compare the new edition with the previously published books to find proof of the universal and enduring quality of these essays. How little there was that needed to be changed, twenty years or less after it was written. In this case, " time has not withered " what was written, because time was incidental to lasting principles of selection. Yet these years were fruitful years for children's books. Miss Moore herself acclaims in particular the years between 1926 and 1930 for " vigor and variety." She says of the last twelve years:

" It is the clear recognition of the great variety of children's tastes and interests and the extent to which these ever-changing interests have been taken into account in the information field, as well as in the higher reaches of the imagination, that is the distinctive contribution to American children's books of the past twelve years."

This period, too, is significant for the great progress that was made in the feeling of the publishers for the book itself as a work of art, in relation to the text and mood of the author. The golden age of graphic art in children's books accom-

112

panied this development, and there were signs, too, of strength in the critical judgment of that time. From this survey of accomplishment we may, then, take wisdom, as well as pride. One thinks of the future, the twenty years ahead, as one reads so keen an analysis and judgment of the past. Miss Moore's roads are roads that face two ways. The years ahead bid fair to be perilous beyond our imagination.

Looking down the dim roads of tomorrow, one feels the need for informed criticism, balanced judgment, and a renewal of faith in children's books as the very wellspring of our literature. Children and children's reading have been subjected to fads, theories, fashions and devices. They will be again, and there will be the added threat of propaganda. The level head and the clear vision will be our need. We will have need, too, of the truth which Anne Carroll Moore proclaims, a truth so simple that, like freedom, it must be regained for each succeeding generation.

" I would remind you," says Miss Moore, " that although children's books may come and go, children's reading is not a problem to be solved by any one. It is, or may be, a very wonderful, rich and free experience which should never be cheapened by artificial stimulation or reward.

" Reading is an art. It cannot be measured by graphs or statistics. The glow of enthusiasm a boy or girl brings to the first reading of a book — whether old or new — to which he feels spiritual kinship is an infinitely precious thing to be cherished and respected on its own terms."

As I read the long, unwieldy galleys of *My Roads to Childhood*, the old, accustomed excitement and exhilaration took hold of me, as it does year after year when I read these books or present them to my classes at the University of California. I remembered, too, a teacher from Colusa County, one hundred miles away, who said to me, " Do you know what those books mean to me? I've never met Miss Moore, and if I could have known that she was in San Francisco, I would gladly have walked here to see her."

What is there in this book on children's reading which takes so great a hold on the minds of those who read it, so that thereafter each slight encounter with a child comes to have special significance? There is in it the reflection of a

113

spirit which has greatly embraced experience. There is the essence of a deeply realized New England childhood, lived in companionship with tolerant and humor-loving parents. There is the revelation of a young woman finding herself in relation to her work, and her work in relation to the world, with moving tribute to men and women in many and varied walks of life who gave her wisdom of their own — Arthur E. Bostwick; John Shaw Billings; Caroline M. Hewins; Mary Wright Plummer — living names, as well as names of books and their authors. There is the reflection of a mind that enjoys the process of living, as well as the accomplishments of life; gardens, horses and cattle, sheep and dogs; the silence of sunsets, and the turbulence of city towers and subways; strawberries from Utah, and lobsters from Maine. Across the pages of this book there is the happy shadow of a person who approaches her reading through life, as well as "approaching life through an imagination charged with the passionate response of the great artists," which she has gathered from reading.

Above all, there is, in this book, a fine and splendid array of children, their books within their hands and hearts. The procession leads off with the same three children who started down the Roads to Childhood in 1918. They now return, to the appropriate joyousness of Edward Lear's *The Jumblies*, which forms the heading for the first chapter of this book:

" And in twenty years they all came back, —
    In twenty years or more:
And every one said, ' How tall they've grown!
    For they've been to the lakes and the Torrible Zone,
And the hills of the Chankly Bore.'
And they drank their health, and gave them a feast
Of dumplings made of beautiful yeast;
And every one said, ' if we only live,
We, too, will go to sea in a sieve
To the hills of the Chankly Bore.' "

There follow the children of Brooklyn at Pratt Institute, and the children of New York; and children of Utah, reading *Floating Island*, as a festival, under the Wasatch Mountains. The children of Iowa and California. The children of Denmark, and Norway and Sweden. The children of England,

and the little smocked children of France, devastated France of 1918.

All these have met and touched the person whose book this is, and they have been touched by her. The exhilaration of reading *My Roads to Childhood* is the exhilaration of encountering a mind as open to experience as the sieve of the Jumblies was to the sea.

" ' Are you a citizen of New York? ' " Miss Moore reports this conversation between herself and a London street waif, in a chapter of her book, "The Romance of the Streets" (p. 111), one of the most beautiful tributes to books in childhood to be encountered anywhere. " ' I am,' I admitted joyfully," the report continues. Had the question been "Are you a citizen of the world? " the answer could have been given as joyfully, " I am." For this New England citizen of the world believes with another New Englander who lived at Walden Pond, " not by constraint or severity shall you have access to true wisdom, but by abandonment and childlike mirthfulness. If you would know aught, be gay before it."

The wisdom of this book is inherited from New England, by the author's own confession; from the " social silences " she shared with her father on long drives through the country.

" Out of these moving silences it was to come to me quite clearly in later years that civilization has always rested and will continue to rest on the dreams and fancies of a few men and women and their power to persuade others of the truth of what they see and feel."

If now the roads of civilization appear to be sinking — as did the Cornish road of Anne Carroll Moore's childhood — beneath the bogs of greed and darkness, there yet remain these roads to childhood. In such a book as this, in the mind that conceived it, and in all the range and beauty of its subject matter, there lies the hope for survival of all that is glorious in the human spirit.

From *The Horn Book* for November, 1939

Selections from

THE THREE OWLS' NOTEBOOK

By Anne Carroll Moore

~~~~~~

ONE or two lines which arouse curiosity, the desire to see and test the book's quality for one's self, are worth columns of words which lead to nothing except boredom.   *March, 1937*

When I begin to find books of the year lacking in strength of background, in appeal to the imagination, in skill in the choice of words, I turn to *The Treasure of the Isle of Mist.* *September, 1937*

The Owls have felt uneasy ever since the publication of children's books became profitable. There is grave danger lest American children's books become a commodity rather than a creative contribution to literature for children in all countries. They saw this danger very clearly while in England and France last spring. Prizes and medals have started something, something not always easy to reconcile with creative art. Prizes and medals are good only so long as judgments remain sound and untouched by adventitious circumstances .... Integrities of the arts remain. It is the artist, the critic, the publisher and the public who are challenged and never, as it seems to me, has there been a more imperative call to defend our real treasures among children's books than in the year 1938.   *January, 1938*

Tolerance can neither be put on nor assumed at the command of anyone. It springs to life from the human heart and grows by what a child finds to feed upon in his family life and natural social contacts. The one chance the school has is to build habits of observation and of clear thinking in all fields and hope by the very lack of emphasis of what is an abstract term to children that it is demonstrating its own claim to *being tolerant* at all times, not merely making a futile gesture when war seems imminent. The same holds I think for "democracy." One has to be a recognizable democrat at all times if one would teach the essential principles of democracy in a crisis. "All my good is magnetic, and I educate not by lessons but by going about my daily business," said Socrates.   *May, 1939*

Beauty, harmony and humor are the birthright of children of every land. I have always felt it to be so and the present state of the world doesn't shake my faith one iota. Not even when Russian children are reported to be taking an oath they can't possibly keep. That too will pass as did the decree banishing fairy tales from their land.

Our little systems of education have their day and cease to be, but our folk-stuff, the poetry and music at the heart of life, the age-old longings and aspirations which rise afresh in every generation do not pass. They merely take on new colors and shapes and vitality — whether in terms of reality or of pure imagination will depend, in the future as in the past, on the interpreter's gift. No artist or author can hope to please children who has forgotten his or her own childhood. *Christmas, 1943*

EDITORIAL

By Bertha E. Mahony (Miller)

TIR-NAN-OGE, Tir Tairngire — Land of Youth, Land of Wonders — these were two very real worlds in ancient Gaelic folk lore, and they live in the hearts of some people today as shown in the two books reviewed in this issue. There is an instinctive wisdom that has nothing to do with schools. The American Indian had this wisdom. He recognized himself as a part of the universe. He was sensitive to his rhythmic brotherhood with animals and his sharing of life with the plants and trees. He knew, too, that as he stood upon the earth and was in every way a part of the universe, drawing his life breath from it, so he could draw his spiritual energy from it, too.

The spiritual power was there. He must discover the way to let it flow deeply and freely into his own personality and express itself anew through him. He developed a special kind of communion with the great spiritual forces, a way of opening his soul to the power he needed. Did he understand the forces? No. Nor does any one today. But he was filled with wonder and reverence before them. Wonder and reverence are rights of childhood. And prayer, too, because it is this last which is the soul's communion with the spirit of the universe, and it is by means of this that each works out for himself the way to spiritual power.

That is why it is so foolish to say " we ought only to give the child conceptions it can understand." His soul grows by its wonder over things it cannot understand.

It is the spirit which guides the personality. If the spirit has never had a chance to find itself, and has had no nourish-

118

ment or exercise, then we have just the kind of people we do have now in such numbers. Homesick people longing for they know not what. Real vision comes from the spirit. And human life is like a plant. The future is within itself. If we can only find the way to help young human beings to develop themselves fully — body, mind and spirit —in far simpler, more genuine ways than at present pursued! Then shall we have a true sense of values. Then we shall insist upon an adventurous, creative life; recognize superiority in its essence and choose for ourselves leaders who have it.

From *The Horn Book* for January, 1934

TIR-NAN-OGE
AND TIR TAIRNGIRE

By Bertha E. Mahony (Miller)

T HE coming of the Evening Grosbeaks to our garden
seemed a fitting climax to the end of Dunsany's book,
The Curse of the Wise Woman (Little). For a week
of evenings we had been reading it aloud; and our days had
been filled with wonder, — wonder about the cry of the
curlew, — what was it like? Wonder about that Land of Tir-
nan-Oge, that Land of Youth, so real in the literature of
Ireland and so real to Marlin, Master Charles's friend and
adviser in sport, bog-watcher for his father.

Marlin lived in a white cottage with a thatched roof beside
the red bog of Lisronagh, and with him there lived his mother,
the *wise* woman. Master Charles Perigore was home for the
holidays from Eton. The night after Christmas he and his
father were in the library. The boy wanted to go to Lisronagh
to shoot geese with Marlin, but his father had said, " Not
this week," so that Charles's holiday task might be finished
before sport. The housemaid had brought in a glass of milk
for his father's whiskey. His father, " the duke," lifted the
tumbler, set it down and said quietly the words which for
years he had warned he might sometime say, and when said
Charles was to act instantly and without question:— " Look at
the picture."

Charles moved at once and looked at the Dutch picture.
As he stood looking at the picture, he stood also near the one
door in the library. The door was closed. In the half minute
of looking at the picture, his father had left the room, but

not by the door. Then four men came in, demanding Charles's father. He led them a slow search over the house. It was not until after they had sworn him on a crystal Cross in which was a piece of the true Cross, the four kneeling the while with their pistols all pointing at the boy's stomach, that they heard the galloping of Mr. Perigore's horse beyond the last gate. But Charles had heard and followed the horse's step from the moment he stepped out of the stable.

So Charles went to Lisronagh the next day after all for his shooting and at evening the great gray lags came to the bog as Marlin's mother said they would come. And it is thus that the principal character, the red bog, comes into this story of mystery and wonder and stays until the end, when, like " the wood that came to Dunsinane," the bog resisted the efforts of commerce to subdue it, to dry it and drain it with engines, and itself moved, covering all that stood in its way. But before that happened Master Charles had spent some glorious days of hunting with Marlin for snipe and teal and the great gray geese, and Marlin had talked to him of the bog and of the Land of Tir-nan-Oge. Commerce had come and Marlin had passed to Tir-nan-Oge by way of the bog. Mrs. Marlin's prophecies were fulfilled. But Master Charles's father never came back.

Here then is a rare book to read aloud, and then to read over to one's self. When read aloud the words seem fairly to flow from one's tongue. It is for those who like the silences, the wild lonely places, and the mystery of Ireland and an Irish tale. It is for those who liked Siegfried Sassoon's *Memoirs of a Fox-Hunting Man*. " If you neared World's End, and fairyland were close to you, some such appearance might be seen in the earth and the light, and the people you passed on the way." That is the look that things took on for Charles as he neared the bog at Lisronagh, and that is the feeling some readers will have with the book.

We were sad to have the book end and then two things happened to relieve our sadness. First, there suddenly appeared in our trees a flock of beautiful, clear yellow birds almost as large as robins. Their beaks were large, strong and yellow, too. Their wings were bordered with black and so were their tails and in the triangle of wings and tail was soft swansdown. Well, Ireland might have its curlew and we probably should never hear it, but we were seeing the Evening Grosbeaks for the first time.

The second piece of cheer was that as an interlude to postpone the conclusion of *The Curse of the Wise Woman* we began the reading of Padraic Colum's *The Big Tree of Bunlahy* (Macmillan), and so with the close of Dunsany's book we did not have to leave Ireland for a while.

The Big Tree of Bunlahy is a collection of stories of the Irish countryside told by the people of the village as they sit on the seat of earth and stone under the great elm. It is strange — or perhaps it isn't — how much it means to imagine hearing these stories in a place like Bunlahy. It " calls itself a village, but it isn't a village at all." It is " just a single row of houses facing a wall that shuts in the wood and pastures belonging to an old, deserted mansion." But it's because Bunlahy has but one row of houses that it came to fame. For they used to say of anything one-sided: " It's all on one side, like the town of Bunlahy." The Big Tree added to its fame, too, and men referred to it all over the world.

Padraic Colum's book is a wonderfully varied collection and can be read aloud to a group widely mixed as to ages. One longs to know more about the Little Baron and his sister the Lady Sabrina in the story called " The Peacocks of Baron's Hall." Are they legendary people? Does the old, deserted mansion, Baron's Hall, still exist? And are the peacocks there still?

" Once upon a time, and if it wasn't upon my time nor upon your time, it was upon a good time, anyway, when jackdaws built their nests in old men's beards, and turkeys went up and down the laneways smoking pipes of tobacco, and the roofs of the houses of Bunlahy were thatched with pancakes, and ponies, saddled and all, went along the roadways, saying, 'Who's for a ride, who's for a ride?' Well, in those times there were two brothers whose names were Jack Sea and John Sea " — so begins the tale of " The Two Youths Whose Father Was Under the Sea," and if any one can withhold his interest after such a beginning, he's a strange one.

The Land of Youth, Tir-nan-Oge, is in the first of these tales. Old Simon the Huntsman told of it as his hound lay on the ground beside him and the recorder of the tales had finished reading a letter to him from his son Jack. " One harvest and another harvest," Old Simon said, " but I'll be as old as Usheen and as lonesome by the time I see any of my children again." And then he told " The Story of Usheen."

Usheen married Niav, daughter of the King of Tir-nan-Oge, the Land of Youth, and went with her to live in that land. But one day he felt a great longing to see Eirinn-O again. He wanted to see his father, the Great Captain Finn, and his friends of the Fianna. So though three hundred years had passed he returned on the steed that could travel the waves but from which he must not dismount nor let his foot touch the ground of Eirinn. He rode to the hiding place of the Fianna's great trumpet, the Borabu. None would help him raise it, and he in his eagerness let his hand touch the earth.

There is the story of " The First Harp " which the Clock-Mender told. " Upon a time that was neither your time nor my time," a man and his wife came always to be quarreling and finally " each put a hand in the cold ashes of their hearth " and left the house. But they happened to meet on a great beach and listened in amazement to the music that the wind made through the bones of a whale's skeleton. Forgetful of all that had passed they went home together, talking always of the music they had heard and how it was made. And from one experiment to another the man finally evolved the harp.

" Our Hen," that conscientious soul who mothered the brood of pheasants; and " The Three Companions," a story not unlike The Bremen Town Musicians, — of William, a retired Circus Horse, Kate-Ann, the Apple Woman's Donkey, and Billy the Goat who belonged to the Lodge of Loyal and Independent Men — are tales of Colum's own invention.

The others are retold from Irish legend and folk lore by this master storyteller. " When the Luprachauns came to Ireland," the tale of the tiny Eisirt's victory over the boastful King of the Luprachauns* and how that King Iubdaun was ransomed from Fergus the King of Ireland has been told

*Mr. Colum does spell it with a *u* after the L.

by Norreys O'Conor in the book *There Was Magic in Those Days*. " King Cormac's Cup " has been told in poetry by Æ in his " Nuts of Wisdom," and by Ella Young in " The Tangle-Coated Horse." It is a memorable story of Tir Tairngire, the Land of Wonders, sometimes called the Land of Promise, and the Well of Wisdom.

The Big Tree of Bunlahy is a splendid collection of stories to read not once but many times, and a beautifully made book with pen and ink drawings and one water color by Jack Yeats. Perhaps sometime the publisher will make as lovely a book of *The Curse of the Wise Woman*. In the hands of the right artist, it could become as complete a book treasure as is *The Big Tree of Bunlahy* and as permanent.

From *The Horn Book* for January, 1934

HOMER PRICE

Comment by Eric Gugler and James Daugherty

WHEN I thumb through this decidedly provocative bunch of illustrations made by Bob McCloskey for his new book, *Homer Price* (Viking), hundreds of tangent thoughts pop up. Memories are stirred and along comes the early stages of a smile and a crinkling at the corners of the eyes. What a universal and delightful brat, this Homer Price! Brats like him do belly-flops on icy hillsides and rip their pants in apple trees. They hook rides with the milkman and hitch on to the back of street cars. They play run-sheep-run and they hate girls — sometimes they begin to like girls when they are very, very old, around fifteen. They ring bells at front doors; when maids answer they snitch ice cream and cakes from the kitchen door and run away with bubbling glee; and they know they are never going to amount to much in the future unless they sell newspapers.

That upturned nose and the freckles, the impudent, quizzical, honest little look remind you of so many things. How much more than anything else in the world, even to be rich or powerful, even to be President, even to be anything ever so much more than anything else in the world, they wanted to be able to whistle very, very loud with two fingers stuffed in their mouths.

How you envied the boy with the perfect arrangement of teeth that made it possible for him to spit a thin jet of water in a high arched stream — the duffer could make it land where he said he would. No ambitions in later life will ever equal these, and you feel that Homer Price could do them all. Do you remember the half-friendly " chases " from Mr. Mooney, the policeman, and his dog, Dilly? Mr. Mooney would have loved Homer.

The older boys on the various teams were gods, and their pranks beyond fancy, but they certainly would have taken Homer with them to the football game one hundred miles away, hidden between two seats, back to back, covering him with their overcoats, so that the conductor would never see him — just because he was Homer!

As for Bob McCloskey — he is, and was, another better Homer Price than Homer Price himself. His book has given me a two-fold pleasure — deep enjoyment of his story and pictures and deep enjoyment of the accompanying reminiscences of other boys I knew very well indeed, — and one I knew the best of all.   — ERIC GUGLER

THIS is to welcome Homer Price to Tom Sawyer's gang, that immortal and formidable band of boys of American fiction. For this boy is a real boy, thinking out loud and living out these rich and hilarious dilemmas with solemn and devastating humor. The way Homer and his friends of Centerburg cope with, and master, such surprising emergencies with implications as radio robbers, Superman, musical mousetraps, ferocious doughnut machines, housing problems, and mass production is the American comic genius in top form. The stories, too, have all the excitment of the fantastic and incredible, so convincingly woven into the daily life of the Mid-Western small town as to seem as true as the front page of the *Westport Town Crier*.

What I want to speak about especially is the pictures. This guy McCloskey can draw and I don't mean just good academy. The way these boys fit into their pants, wear their shirts, and the way the folds of their clothes pull with every movement is all there to intensify vivid humor and real character. This humorous reality pervades even the objects in each scene so that you get the full delicious flavor out of every detail of Homer's room and the unforgettable barber shop. The double-page drawing of the historical pageant is a classic of small-town celebration. One goes over these drawings again and again with renewed delight in all their details. The doughnut counter, the ice cream parlor, and above all the impossible machines and gadgets that operate so convincingly, must not only be copyrighted but patented!

The satire is warm and genial and tolerant so that you feel these pictures are the autobiography of a generous mind as well as a shrewd and witty recording of familiar scenes. It is the true comedy of democracy in the great American tradition of A. B. Frost, of Kemble, and of Peter Newell, all the more so that McCloskey is entirely unaware of it. The laughter is in the drawing itself; you get the fun of the thing visually and even especially without the words.

It is America laughing at itself with a broad and genial humanity, without bitterness or sourness or sophistication. The whole thing culminates magnificently in the final story when " the wheels of Progress " come to Centerburg, and here McCloskey puts on a full philharmonic of fun and satire. One closes the book with the comforting feeling that although Centerburg can and does take the machine age in its stride, the salt and character, the humanities and individualism of Our Town remain triumphant and that democracy will keep her rendezvous with destiny, musical mousetraps, and all.

— JAMES DAUGHERTY

From *The Horn Book* for November, 1943

GERTRUDE STEIN FOR CHILDREN

By Louise Seaman Bechtel

ERE is a new book that is a new kind of book*, and I like it very much. It is rather a job to tell you why because it has to be read aloud. You and I should be taking turns, chapter by chapter, laughing and seizing the book from each other. For of course it is fun to find out how well one reads it. Inevitably one wants to see how much better one does the next bit, in spite of the lack of punctuation; how, in fact, one produces punctuation oneself with so little trouble.

But I must not talk about style before I tell you why you will like Rose.

> I am Rose my eyes are blue
> I am Rose and who are you
> I am Rose and when I sing
> I am Rose like anything.

For me, that verse is enough. And you, too, perhaps can easily remember — or have you never lost it? — that peculiar, frightening sense of being yourself, and, at times, of being almost too much yourself. " The World Is Round," says the title, yes, that is another appalling fact, the refrain of this book. Also the sun, moon, and alas, even the stars we once thought five-pointed, are round, and keep going round and round. Where do I come in? Please make someone stop it all and listen to *me*.

Taking this so obvious and simple a spiritual sensation, Miss Stein has explored it, tenderly, gaily, in her usual rhythmic flow of words. The story is subtle; to some it will seem no story at all, to others a thoughtful and entirely new ex-

128

ploration of the moods of childhood. Here is the child's quick apperception, his vivid sensation, his playing with words and ideas, then tossing them away forever. As for the story, Rose's part is clear. She tries to find the something that is not going round, that is always there. So at last she climbs a mountain, all alone — except, for comfort, she takes her blue chair. Willie's part is not quite so clear, but he will seem funnier to children — drowning (or almost), buying a lion, going to save Rose, and in a postscript, marrying Rose! But to an adult it does become clear, the difference between them, and Willie's sense of his apartness from Rose, yet his likeness to her.

I see I am becoming complicated, so I shall begin again, for the book page by page is ridiculously simple. Rose, we learn, had a very usual home and two dogs. She sang to herself a great deal, and it made her cry. (Her dog, Love, cried, too, when she did.) Willie, too, had a sense of himself as unique, and he too sang of it, but it didn't make him cry, it made him more excited.

> My name is Willie I am not like Rose
> I would be Willie whatever arose
> I would be Willie if Henry was my name
> I would be Willie always Willie just the same.

Well, Rose went away to school near the mountains (and all the time the world was going round). And Willie went to stay in the country, and sang of the lizard that lost its tail, and the " frogs and pigeons, butter and crackers, flowers and windows."

" It was time Willie did something, why not when the world was all so full anywhere." So he went to a place where they sold wild animals and chose a lion which he wanted to give to Rose. After several chapters of one sentence each, recapitulating facts about this lion, there comes a floating-off-the-page picture of noise with a drum in the middle. That was when Rose, listening to the band at the door, knew that there was a lion, but it was not a real lion. This idea made Willie laugh very much and — " Billie the lion never was anywhere. The end of Billie the lion."

Now comes Rose on her trip. Before she went, she sang:

" Dear mountain, tall mountain real mountain blue mountain yes mountain, high mountain all mountain my mountain. I will with my chair come climbing and once there mountain once there I will be thinking, mountain so high, who cares for the sky yes mountain no mountain yes I will be there."

So — she goes. And there is a night of fear, but not half so fearsome as the woods in the Snow White movie. And was she lost? " She never had been lost and so how could she be found even if everything did go around and around."

Is it all utter nonsense? Well, lots of it is purposely playful, so that the author catches herself up with a " well, anyway!" For some children it will actually ring true to their half-spoken inner feelings. For some older ones Miss Stein's real meaning, that it is all imaginary, will be clear. For some adults it will carry a deep nostalgia for the dreams and fears and never-told impressions of childhood, and the sorrowful moments of consciously growing older. For others, it will be too much of a shock; they will recognize the line by line landmarks of sensation, but will be impatient of so much " stream of consciousness."

Because Miss Stein has such a personal conception of style, still others will be " put off." For me, this is the first time that her style has spoken truly and artistically as perfectly fitted to her thought.

" But mountains yes Rose did think about mountains and about blue when it was on the mountains and feathers when clouds like feathers were on the mountains and birds when one little bird and two little birds and three and four and six and seven and ten and seventeen and thirty or forty little birds all came flying and a big bird came flying and the little birds came flying and they flew higher than the big bird and they came down and one and then two and then five and then fifty of them came picking down on the head of the big bird and slowly the big bird came falling down between the mountain and the little birds all went home again. Little birds do go home again after they have scared off the big bird."

For me, the whole is an unforgettable creative experience. It may be too esoteric to have a fair chance with the average child. But it is so new in its pattern, so interesting in its word rhythms, so " different " in its humor, that the person of any age who reads it gets several necessary jolts to his literary taste. Only a true artist could have written so charming a book as *The World Is Round*.

The publishers have tried it out on many children, all of whom were "surprised and attentive." The response was perhaps most intelligent and cordial in girls of about twelve to fourteen. But with such a style, it is true, as it has been true with so many modern artists working for children, that the actual age limit cannot be guessed and should not be defined. There may be some psychologically-minded who do not believe at all in fantasy or in the encouragement of a child's own increased self-analysis. One could assure them that such books have not any other effect than the deepening of their poetic consciousness. And, in this material age, such books come seldom in the course of their reading.

The most acutely honest comment the publishers received came from a boy of twelve: "It is more relaxing than anything I ever heard of." Another said, "It is much more *human* than most books." Another, "The use of words have you laughing till your sides ache." A thirteen-year-old girl said, "I think Rose and Willie are wonderful. I like people who really feel things inside, and I adore the way they express themselves in their wonderful songs." Another girl the same age: "The story is simple and dreamy. You can forget yourself and live in a separate world while you are reading it." A younger child writes, "I love the new style writing because it is the way I, or any other child, would think and write." Of course there also were children who thought Rose, Willie and Miss Stein were just "dumb."

The book is printed in large blue type on pink paper. Clement Hurd has done modern, flowing, symbolic pictures. His clever use of white is nicely balanced by large white numbers for each chapter. The whole make-up suits the material very well.

For a postscript may I add that it is no world-shaking matter to be "for" or "against" this book. But to those who honestly enjoy it, let me say it should be used, none too solemnly, with the most varied sorts of children. We don't want them all to write like Miss Stein! We do want to jog them out of the horribly ordinary prose that engulfs them.

131

In the big inclusive volumes of Mother Goose we used to find strong rhythms and endless variety of word patterns, but our modern, emasculated, carefully selected and word-counted material has lost that strong tang. Miss Stein is not "tops" even in her own field; she cannot touch the Joyce of *Ulysses*, for instance, or Virginia Woolf. But she is one freeing agent who was peculiarly fitted to do her good piece for modern children.

The World Is Round by Gertrude Stein, with illustrations by Clement Hurd. Copyright 1939 by Gertrude Stein. Published by William R. Scott, Inc.

From *The Horn Book* for October, 1939

I GIVE YOU THE END OF
A GOLDEN STRING

By Marcia Dalphin

D OES it seem futile to write of the beauty and delight to be found in a handful of children's books with the world apparently falling in pieces about our ears, and the country from which some of these very books come preparing feverishly for war, and fitting gas masks to its babies? No. It was never more worthwhile. For never were the values of imaginative writing more evident; never, in all the world, the imponderables more precious.

I am thinking of four books — books which, amid all the roar of the presses disgorging new books, should never be allowed to drop out of sight. They might, if we are not careful. For make no mistake, these are not popular books as the word is currently understood: not, like *Tom Sawyer* and *Little Women*, bought eagerly for birthdays and Christmas gifts, not in great demand in libraries by the boys and girls themselves. Yet eternally fresh and treasurable to those who know and love them are *The Three Mulla Mulgars*[1], *Tal*[2], *The Treasure of the Isle of Mist*[3] and *A Little Boy Lost*[4].

While each is set definitely in its own climate, they yet have points in common. They are highly imaginative: they are " quest " books, in each a search is going forward: and they are alike in a certain reputation with young readers; they are what is known as " a little hard to get into."

Who can explain why one book captures interest easily and quickly while another is slow to do so? One thing that I have often found puzzling to unimaginative children is the use of

133

strange, fantastic proper names. *Tal* and *The Three Mulla Mulgars* have this characteristic. *The Treasure of the Isle of Mist* has an uninviting page and one character whose humorously pedantic tone is entertaining to adults, reminding them of the Philosopher in *The Crock of Gold,* but to young people this must seem to hold up the action. Every one of these books fares better, probably, for being introduced, either by reading aloud or brief description, or, best of all, by the contagion of an evident enthusiasm for the story.

One would think that *Tal,* that gorgeously imaginative story of Paul Fenimore Cooper's, would not need much introduction. It is a truly marvelous tale of that type — old as the hills — the story within a story. The argument is simple. In the kingdom of Troom rules a king named Tazzarin, and in his throne room is a golden door on which is carved the head of a beautiful woman. When a king of Troom needs advice he seeks it here, but often her lips remain closed and nothing will move her to speak. One day the baby son of Tazzarin disappears under the strangest circumstances, and when the golden door is consulted the head speaks and tells the king that his son has been carried away by a Djinn; that he is safe, but will never be brought back until a story shall be told before the door that will please it.

When the story opens eight years have passed and forty storytellers have told their stories in vain. Far away from Troom in a little village by the sea Tal, a child of mysterious origin, is living. One day an old, old man with long white beard and green eyes walks into the village accompanied by a snow-white donkey with long pink ears, in each of which is fastened a golden bell. This is Noom-Zor-Noom and his Millitinkle. They come from Troom, and the whole book is the story of what happens when Tal goes with them on the long adventurous journey back to Troom, listening to the stories which Noom-Zor-Noom has been collecting to tell before the door when his turn comes, and helping to choose the one he shall tell, for the story must be such as would please a child.

In these fourteen short tales, as well as in the story of the return to Troom, one is conscious all the time of the apparently inexhaustible reserves of fancy and invention upon which

134

this author has to draw. As I read I have over and over again the impulse to exclaim aloud in surprise and delight as the writer's fancy takes some new and unpredictable turn. A charming vein of nonsense runs through it and a homely matter-of-factness. This is especially true of the terse remarks of Millitinkle, who is a character in her own right, in direct descent, moreover, from Mrs. Molesworth's Cuckoo and the creatures in *Alice*.

The enchanted land of Paul Cooper is not that land of Faery in which the elusive spirits of Yeats and de la Mare dwell; it is a land of magic where the wildest things happen quite plausibly, where barks are worse than bites, and nice helpful things are done for one by the unlikeliest people. One closes the book with a comfortable memory of Tal twirling a comet by the tail. Just a small comet, the author assures us.

> The old man caught hold of it and gave it to Tal to play with. He held it by its tail and swung it around so that it made a great circle of light. Then he let it go and watched it disappear in the distance.

W. W. Tarn's *The Treasure of the Isle of Mist* is laid in one of the Western Isles of Scotland. Against a background of misty, rocky shore, honeycombed with caves which were once the haunt of Spaniard and sea rover, where the boom of the surf sounds unceasingly and the salt spray is chill on the face, Fiona, the lovely girl-heroine, goes her way; Fiona, the " long-legged creature of fifteen . . . with a warm heart and a largish size in shoes," who is the delight of this book.

It is a haunting tale, reminding me as I re-read it just now of Chesterton's play, *Magic*. There is in both such a sense of the near presence of the strange elemental beings who influence the action. Who that ever saw O. P. Heggie as the Conjurer can forget that lean, tall figure with the magic-weaving hands: and who that reads this story can forget the old hawker, old as Time himself, who gives to Fiona the promise, not of the Treasure itself, but of the *Search* for the Treasure, a very different thing.

The element of mystery and suspense is very present in this book. Even the experienced reader may feel a chill hand laid on his heart when Fiona and the Urchin row away in haste from their exploration of the great West Cave, the haunted cave that no islander will enter, where lies hidden, they believe, that treasure of doubloons once brought here on a great Venetian. They row in haste and in fear, and neither dares speak of what each has heard — " in the utter darkness of the unvisited cave, the sound of heavy footsteps." And there is that other moment, too, when Fiona, hearing the old hawker's shout of warning, looks up and sees what no one else does — the little brown elfin hand pushing the rock which a second after stretches Jeconiah senseless on the floor of the cave.

It is after the Urchin's mysterious disappearance that Fiona's real search begins. She is the only one who can find him and release him from his strange captivity. And she must do it all alone. How one obstacle after another falls before her beautiful simplicity and courage the reader must discover for himself. To the sweet, soulless Oread who advises her to give up the search Fiona replies: " Oh, don't you understand? Don't you see that there are some things one *can't* do, whatever anybody says? It's not the reason of the thing; it's only just because I am I, and he is lost. You are so beautiful; haven't you any heart? "

Yes, Fiona finds her treasure — and the reader has found it, too, when he comes to the end. " The old lost loves, the old impossible loyalties, the old forgotten heroisms and tendernesses; all these are yours; and yours are the songs that were sung long ago, and the tales which were told by the fireside. . . ."

When William Henry Hudson was a child he found in books only rarely, he tells us, the beauty and wonder and terror that he sensed so keenly in the world of Nature about him. So when he was quite an old man, living in England, he wrote *A Little Boy Lost,* consciously intent on making it such a story as he would have liked in that far-off boyhood in South America, and embodying in it legends of the pampas and remembered actions and impressions of his own.

Certain adjectives occur inevitably to the reader of Hudson — simple, crystal-clear, pellucid. If they apply to his other books they apply a hundred times more to this book about the child, Martin. The recapturing of the emotions of a sensitive child receiving his earliest impressions of Nature, of sky and water, plain and tree, birds and flowers, has never been done better. Reading it, one is again of the very stature of a child. The overlayings of experience fall away like husks, and people and things take on again their relative proportions. Sunflowers, mustard, giant thistles, foxgloves are as trees, and it is only when we fight our way through this jungle that we get our first wide glimpse of the world. No one had told us that a stream of water goes somewhere; we find it out because a leaf drops in the water and it mysteriously hurries away out of sight.

It is in essence a book of first impressions, and it is Hudson's art (or, as I suspect, his lack of it) that makes it seem the memories of all childhood — yours, mine, not Martin's merely. Pictures from it rise up so clear and fresh as we close the book. The child with the snake in his pinafore; the tragedy of the rosy spoonbill (a child's initiation into death); the way in which Nature alternately torments and comforts her lovers, shown in Martin's pursuit of the mirage; and the delicious episode of the little dusty beetle eagerly drinking up the tear that runs down the grass blade, " waving its little horns up and down like donkey's ears, apparently very much pleased at its good fortune in finding water and having such a good drink in such a dry, thirsty place."

There is great beauty, as you would expect, in the book — beauty of the wide plains and the forest, of bird-haunted lake, of the flight of great birds across the sky, of all the manifestations of Nature. Yet it is not a book of beauty alone; there is humor in it and a keen sense of the grotesque. Martin's night in the hut with old Jacob makes children, as they read it, laugh aloud, and so does his ridiculous conversation with the Indian woman. And what a chapter is that called " The Black People of the Sky." I never read it without alternating between repulsion and amusement, nor without the keenest admiration for Hudson's skill in setting the scene and inventing a dialogue for those people which is absolutely *right*.

A Little Boy Lost is far too little known. It is not every day that a great naturalist and one of the greatest prose writers of his day writes a book for children, and we should be properly grateful.

And now we come to the last — Walter de la Mare's *Three Mulla Mulgars*. Fresh from the reading of it, no praise seems to me too extravagant. All compact of poetry, of the magic of strange, beautiful words: dramatic to a degree, employing every art of suspense, yet never falsely or cheaply: instinct with high qualities of loyalty and courage: full of a tenderness that never degenerates into sentimentality: constantly surprising the reader with its touches of a sly and pawky humor: how one wishes that every one might have his imagination kindled by it!

No one should miss the experience of sharing this book with some sensitive child. And be sure that any one who has read and loved it as a child will have it in his heart forever. I know a young scientist, now studying for his doctorate, who says that he "remembers with particular delight Nod's wonderstone, and with real desolation the burning of the hut." And whenever I read the story I find myself hearing his delighted chuckles in places where as we read it aloud some combination of word sounds or some turn of the plot took his fancy.

It is impossible in a few paragraphs to do any justice to this wonderful story of the three royal monkeys' search for the valleys of Tishnar. One might better hand it to a friend and say, "Read it for yourself and see what a poet can do when he turns his hand to prose, and what a father can do when he is writing a story under the peculiar stimulation that must come from reading it chapter by chapter to his children at bedtime." Or read him that page which tells of Nod and his brothers toiling up a dizzy mountain ledge on Arakkaboa and suddenly come to the end of the path that drops away into nothingness around a corner of the cliff. And as they stand there aghast, hoping to devise some means by which little Nod at least may turn back in safety, suddenly comes on Thumb's head a touch light as thistledown and he looks up into the hairy face of a Mountain Mulgar dangling at the end of a long living rope of his fellows, up which they may climb ladderwise to safety. Or bid him turn to those delightful chapters that tell of Nod's capture by Andy Battle and of

138

the friendship that grew up between the sailor and the little wanderer. Will he not have always clearly etched in his memory a picture of Andy and Nod in their little space of firelight surrounded on all sides by darkness and enemies, the sailor thrumming on his old lute while Nod dances a Mulgar jig on the log beside him? Through the frosty night of Munza echoes thinly the chorus:

> He sits 'neath the Cross in the cankering snow,
> And waits for his sorrowful end,
> Yeo ho!
> And waits for his sorrowful end.

[1] By Walter de la Mare (Knopf, 1910, 1948)

[2] By Paul Fenimore Cooper (Stephen Daye, 1929, 1957)

[3] By W. W. Tarn (Putnam, 1934, o.p.)

[4] By W. H. Hudson (Knopf, 1918)

From *The Horn Book* for May, 1938

Part IV

What Fairy Tales Mean to a Child

CINDERELLA IN IRELAND

By R. A. Warren

'TWAS one of the wee folk themselves that told me about it, sitting under a hawthorn bush last night by the light of the moon. The ins and outs of the whole story, mind you; for although Cinderella roamed hither and yon, so they say, over this wide earth, 'twas in Erin she really belonged.

Her father, Hugh of Tir Conal, was a great lord who ruled all the country round. She had two sisters, besides, who behaved themselves in Ireland pretty much as we've heard they did everywhere else, and led poor Cinderella a sorry dance indeed. As scullery maid in her father's own castle, she tended the spit before the blazing peat fire, redded up the floor with a rough twig besom, and endured the slights and abuses of the same wicked sisters for a weary seven years or more.

But Fate was not quite so blind as you may suppose. In the neighborhood dwelt a famous old witch who had been keeping her eye on Conal affairs, and now thought it high time to interfere. So bright and early one Sunday morning, as the poor girl was bending over her daily tasks, the witch suddenly appeared at her very elbow.

" How now, Cinderella! Why aren't you at church with your sisters? "

" Sure, my sisters would kill me if ever I dared set foot outside the house," was the sorrowful reply. " Besides, I have nothing to wear."

" What style dress would you have?" asked the witch.

"A snow-white gown," answered Cinderella, " with a pair of green shoes for my feet."

143

Then the old witch wrapped herself up in her cloak of darkness and solemnly wished a wish. In the twinkling of an eye Cinderella was robed like a princess, the most beautiful ever you saw. On her shoulder perched a bright honeybird, and beside her stood a milk-white pony with a shining gold saddle on his back.

With a joyous spring Cinderella mounted her palfrey and was off on her way to church; with strict orders, however, not to enter the edifice but to hurry back home when she heard the last Amen. So, like the obedient girl that she was, the first of the worshippers had scarcely emerged from the portal when she quickly wheeled her prancing steed and scurried from sight like wind over the heather before the congregation could catch more than the merest glimpse of her.

Next Sunday 'twas the same thing all over again, only the second time she wore shiny black satin just touching the tiny green shoes, and mounted a glossy black mare. A third Sunday came, and this time she rode boldly up to the very church door. The green velvet frock she was dressed in was the match of the shamrock itself. The honey-bird sang like the trill of the fountain, and the diamonds in her horse's dappled gray mane sparkled like dew in the sunlight.

By this time, as you well may imagine, a crowd used to gather in front of the church to await her. Among them was the handsome young King of Emania. Since first he caught sight of her he determined to win her, but he never could catch her, ride as he might. Today, when she sought to elude him, he made one desperate leap for her bridle, but missed it, and so laid hold on her foot. A moment later, and she had escaped him again, but left in his grasp one little green slipper.

Then the King of Emania set forth on his travels in search of its owner. She only, he vowed, should ever be queen of his realm. With him on his journey went several other fine chieftains, his rivals in love as in war. Not a spot did they overlook, whether in Ulster, Munster, Leinster or Connaught; and sad were the attempts of every girl throughout Ireland to fit to her foot the lone shoe that he carried; or rather,

144

you might say, her foot to the shoe, for plenty of cripples there were limping about in every townland afterwards.

At last the royal party arrived at the fine castle of Tir Conal. Great was the fluster among the two sisters at sight of these splendid knights in glistening armor, with banners flying and bagpipes skreeling, as they galloped across the drawbridge and dismounted before the castle keep. News of their errand had preceded them, and the sisters fairly burned with desire to try on the shoe. Wriggle as they might, however, one could get but a toe and the other a heel inside.

"Is there any other woman in the house?" demanded the king.

"No!" retorted the sisters.

"Yes!" called Cinderella from the dark closet where they had locked her.

So out she was had at once. From her tattered old pocket she produced the mate of the slipper, and with both on her feet stood up so slim and tall. Then entered the witch, again wrapped in her cloak of darkness, and before you could wink, Cinderella was robed in first one and then another of all the rich gowns she had worn. The ponies came too, while the honey-bird fairly outsang himself with delight.

The king was for marrying her immediately; but "No, you must fight for her!" it was declared.

"I'm ready," said the king, like the real Irishman that he was; and so the battle was on. There was the Prince of Lochlin and the Prince of Myerfui, and many another brave warrior, with quarter neither asked nor given. But of course, in the end, Emania got her. The wedding lasted a year and a day, and then they settled down for good on Irish soil.

And what became of the little green slipper? Stoop your head just a bit and I'll whisper. Go out softly some fine morning, just at the break of the dawn — mind where you tread lest you trample the pearls of the fairies — and take a sly peep under the nearest four-leaved clover.

From *The Horn Book* for February, 1932

ANIMALS IN FAIRYLAND

By Alice M. Jordan

<hr/>

RESH from re-reading Walter de la Mare's stimulating Introduction to *Animal Stories** I looked again at the newer books which have to do with animals seen through the eyes of imagination, wondering how far the authors have kept the sense of man's age-old beliefs concerning the animal world.

Let no one think that the distinguished collection, chosen and arranged by Mr. de la Mare, is just another compilation of true animal stories. There are many such collections, but here in generous measure are his own versions of the stories he loved as a child. Couched in the sure language of a master of words, they are set down in a more arresting form than that in which we often find them.

While the substance of the stories is not unfamiliar, the arrangement is new, displaying the variety and richness of animal folk tales, from the simple but gay nursery tales, like the "Three Little Pigs" and "Henny Penny," to the more complicated stories of magic and enchantment, such as " The Frog Bride," and to those sadder legends with the wistful eerie quality of " The Seal Man."

But the great treasure trove of this book is found in the Introduction in which Walter de la Mare illuminates the origins of fairy tale, myth and saga, tracing their developing pattern from the remote past of human history, to the creative imagination of our own time.

He emphasizes, too, the closeness of the old storytellers to the animal kingdom as shown in their interpretation of animal conduct in terms of the motives governing human actions. Believing them to have the power of speech and the

*Scribner, 1940

146

capability of acting like man, the storytellers found in these familiar creatures an ideal medium for the working out of marvelous literary inventions, more elaborate, less moralistic than the fable form.

When we compare our instincts and intelligence with the endowment of the other animals we do not always shine as superior. More acute in certain respects than we, they perceive things beyond our reach, they are sensitive to influences that do not affect us.

As I considered these convictions of primitive man, I asked myself how far writers today are accepting this racial inheritance for their stories of real animals in an unreal world. Nor was it wholly a surprise to find that the best storytellers of today can still convince readers of the ability and diversity of animal personalities, while they entertain us with their flights of fancy about a world unknown to man but known to his household pets and work companions.

Who are the animals lately arrived from the Garden Behind the Moon? More of them have names than in the old stories, although folk tales show exceptions. The cat's imaginary godchildren in "All Gone " were given names of double significance, the princess's horse, too, in " The Goose-Girl " goes by the name of Fallada, but Dick Whittington's cat was called simply, Miss Puss.

Eight creatures, insects, birds and four-footed animals dominate Padraic Colum's gentle tale, *Where the Winds Never Blew and the Cocks Never Crew.** From Krak-krak the cricket, whose song, all his own, was " about the cobwebs and the shadows on the wall and the bubbling of the pot while the Old Woman was stirring it," to Tibbie the cat, who also loved a warm place on the hearth, this group of friends is as individual as any group of friends could be. Yet, domestic in their tastes, they are all made restless and unhappy by the sight of a cold hearth and a lonely house.

Old Mother Gabble, the goose who spoke in a sensible way because she had a wise grandmother, Gruff the dog who took at last the trail to the place where there were tall white stags and tall white hounds, Croodie the lone pigeon, Speckie

*Macmillan, 1940, o.p.

the guinea hen and Droileen the tiny wren, if they are not actually of Fairyland they must have been well acquainted there. As they move from one place to another in a serene, quiet land on the edge of the world, their amusing conversation is full of bird and animal comment on the strange happenings they have seen.

No animal has had a closer association with witchcraft and magic than the cat, so it is only natural that many modern writers follow folklore in choosing this animal as leading character in their fanciful tales. One might say that the cat himself, with his inscrutable mien and lordly independence, demands it. But these are mostly kindly creatures, far removed from the black familiars of broom-riding witches.

Mr. Tidy Paws[1] is, to be sure, a black cat, but what an engaging one! Christopher was right in naming him, "Secret," for he wore a knowing air of mystery when he stepped softly into the village of Bean Blossom. We can see him as Christopher did, dancing with laughter alone in the moonlight, or marching in circles to the sound of tiny invisible hands, clapping an accompaniment. Only good grew out of the welcome given Secret by a boy and his grandmother.

Straight out of Fairyland came the white cat who brought good luck to Old John and his family of pets in Mairin Cregan's story.[2] Bairin, for that was her name, was a fairy doctor under an enchantment. Like many a human hero, this brave cat had to perform three good deeds for other animals before she could return to fairy form and these acts must be unknown to others. When her task was finished Bairin was allowed to return to her own country where ceremonious conduct was of great importance to the different ranks in the fairy kingdom.

Fairyland, it seems, has rulers as different one from the other as are those to be found above ground. The little black hen in Eileen O'Faolain's captivating story[3] had the misfortune to be hatched in a fairy fort, so she was at the beck and call of

[1] *Mr. Tidy Paws,* by Frances Clarke Sayers (Viking, 1935, o.p.)
[2] *Old John,* by Mairin Cregan (Macmillan, 1936, o.p.)
[3] *The Little Black Hen,* by Eileen O'Faolain (Random House, 1940, o.p.)

the arrogant queen, Cliona, whenever there was a new moon. Poor Cossey Dearg with her endearing ways was never allowed to stay long on her perch in the chicken house, without hearing the commanding call of the fairy cock. Written with the charm and flavor inherent in an Irish folktale, this story of warring fairy factions gives color to the belief that it is safer in Ireland to speak of the fairies as the " Good People."

Padre Porko[4] is a Benevolent Fairy in disguise. He might be said to belong to the executive type of animals like Puss in Boots. In reality, he is a figure from the folklore of Northern Spain where the peasants often recount tales of his helpful deeds. Wise and kindly, witty as well as courteous, he straightens out the difficulties and cures the ills of animals for miles around. All readers of fairy tales know how one kind of animal can understand the speech of another, how they confer together and often set right the stupid mistakes of men. So Padre Porko can, with equal ease, call the tribes of rats to help him draw a spike from a horse's hoof or send his bee messengers on errands of mercy.

The real world and that of make-believe come close together in the pages of Smoky House.[5] Here are two wonderful dogs who are respected by the fairies. Spot was " a very great gentleman." Sausage was of humbler birth but he had a fund of common sense. Between them they struggled to make their human family understand the true nature of the wandering Fiddler, so hospitably accepted in the household. It was Spot, too, who could talk to the pointy-eared Good People living under the roots of the trees. It was his nobility that called them to help his beloved family of children and grown-ups when disaster threatened. Laid in the beautiful West Country of England, this blending of magic and reality holds high courage within its charming romance.

Echo of dancing feet, tinkling of fairy bells, fairy rings in the pasture, gold under the tree roots — who knows if the animals do not hear and see them when they respond to a summons too elusive for our dull senses?

[4] *Padre Porko,* by Robert Davis (Holiday House, 1948)
[5] *Smoky House,* by Elizabeth Goudge (Coward-McCann, 1940, o.p.)

From *The Horn Book* for November, 1941

WHAT FAIRY TALES MEANT TO A TURKISH CHILD

By Selma Ekrem

I GREW up in the enchanted world of " once there was and once there was not," with fairies and ogres prancing into my dreams. Before I could read or write, I had mastered my nurse's repertory and was imbued with that fatal disease known as " love of fairy tales " from which I have not recovered and hope, never will.

The old nurse, who guided my faltering steps, awakened this love with her first stories. She was an elderly, kindly woman, ignorant of the modern methods of child care and hygiene and had never heard of vitamins; but she had a rare gift: a tongue for storytelling. It was not an art she had deliberately cultivated but had mastered unconsciously. No matter how wonderful the story, the wonder was doubly enhanced by the way she related the tale, never forgetting the proper introduction and the quaint expressions just as essential to a fairy tale as the fairies themselves.

It is now that I realize how fortunate a child I was. My old nurse was not a disciplinarian. She often slipped forbidden tidbits into my mouth and allowed me to drink from her coffee cup at the tender age when sipping milk was required. She carefully closed all bedroom windows at night for fear that the night air would bring in malaria. I was not brought up according to the best American method. I probably owe her occasional stomach aches and an excessive liking for coffee, but also the love of books and the desire to learn foreign languages.

There were days when nurse was not in the mood to open

150

the treasure house of her imagination; days when she sighed and said, " I am a fairy tale myself."

At such times, coaxing would not move her nor a sharp blade open her tightly sealed lips. Then I was filled with the desire to be " grown up " and plunge my nose into the many books in my father's extensive library. Volume after volume lined those shelves, some so old that their leather covers had been worn smooth with handling and their tattered pages drooped limply from the edges. But learning how to read Turkish did not help me. These books were utterly beyond my comprehension. I asked my father if there were none that children could read and understand and he answered that children's books did not exist; a lack of foresight he sadly deplored.

My elder brother attended a French school and in his room were gilt-edged volumes of Jules Verne and Bibliothèque Rose given to him as prizes for good scholarship — books filled with enticing pictures and a script totally different from the Turkish one I had learned. Alas, I could not read French although I could speak and understand it through hearing it spoken at home. Here was a new and vast treasure house whose key was still beyond my reach. Eager for more and new stories, I went to my mother and begged her to teach me how to read French. The alphabet was easily acquired but it was another matter to put these curving letters together into words making sense. How well I remember the endless hours spent over a page as if through sheer concentration it would yield its mystery. A word, here and there, would strike a bell with a familiar tune and I discovered that the letters gathered by the eyes formed the same words as those picked up by the ears. It was by this constant poring over my brother's books that I finally learned how to read French.

When my parents decided to send me to the American Preparatory School in Istanbul, my first reaction was, " Now I'll learn English and will read new stories."

Before I had mastered half a dozen English words, I had taken a book from the school library and concentrated on that as I had on the French books.

For years, the only samples of Turkish literature I tasted

were the same fairy tales my old nurse had told me prior to my school days. This was due not only to the lack of children's books but to the difficult and complicated language used by our writers. We had two languages, essentially the same, but poles apart. At home we spoke the simple everyday Turkish, colorful with quaint expressions which my father derisively called " a woman's language," but which he, too, used in our family conversation. When he picked up his reed pen to write his poems, he turned to the literary and classical Turkish, mentally slipping from his old bathrobe into his frock coat.

Literary Turkish was the monopoly of the writers, the scholars and the chosen few, not necessarily that of the upper classes or the government hierarchy. A writer who had spent years to master three grammars and three languages (Persian, Arabic and Turkish) was not going to waste his time writing for children and the masses. If he used the spoken Turkish, needed to reach these juvenile minds, he would be dubbed an ignoramus. A scholar was he who filled his books with the most obscure and often obsolete Arabic and Persian words; words which only ten people out of a million could understand. If the reader was baffled, so much the better, the author was then deemed a super-scholar.

While our writers rhapsodized over nightingales or transcended to mystical heights with their sober stanzas, the Turkish nation clung to its own limited literature made up of folklore, fairy tales and Nasreddin Hodja anecdotes. These were handed down from one generation to the other but never published. The scholar of this literary school was not the writer but the storyteller. Storytelling was an ancient and honored profession and one of the few open to Turkish women in the past.

Every village, town and city had its professionals who went from house to house, spending in each a few days and entertaining the women with their numerous tales. The men held sway in the village coffee house and favored more robust tales. In the cities, these men and women had their purses filled with gold; in the humble villages, they received gifts and went away with their baskets loaded with home-made delicacies. The arrival of a storyteller was eagerly awaited by every one, especially during the long winter nights.

My old nurse had amassed her assortment of fairy tales from one of the famous Istanbul storytellers, a woman whose honeyed tongue delighted the ladies of the upper classes, even those who had indulged in an education. As a child, nurse had been brought up in the home of my great-grandmother who was considered a remarkable woman for her time. Her education had not only consisted in mastering sewing, embroidering and cooking, although she excelled in these, but in a thorough schooling of Turkish literature. She could recite hundreds of Persian and Turkish poems and often discussed these with my father when he was a young man. The same great-grandmother had also a passion for fairy tales and her house was always open to one of Istanbul's famous woman storytellers who was much in demand at the palace of the Sultan and his viziers.

Her arrival was an event which sent a wave of excitement from the parlor to the kitchen. She came in the evening, had dinner with the family where her favorite dishes were served. The maids hurried with their work and one by one came discreetly to the sitting room. Leaving their slippers by the door, they crouched on the thick rugs and were silent as shadows. Old retainers, their children, the woman cook, all the women of that busy household were presently assembled in the room where great-grandmother and her guests sat on low couches covered with shawls and strewn with pillows. Nurse, then a little girl, had been the first to enter the room and sat close to the brazier near which, on a specially fat cushion, the famed storyteller had made herself comfortable. In winter, the brazier heaped with glowing charcoal threw a warm glow while the many candles flickered and danced with joy. Tale after tale unfolded in the dim candlelight as princesses " fair as the fourteenth of the moon " were wooed by brave shehzades. Nurse must have listened with her two ears and two eyes, drawing in her breath sharply as the tale reached peaks of suspense while noting every expression and gesture used by the woman.

" They had the wish of their hearts and may we climb the

153

ladder of ours." With these words, the woman was silent, the fairies hurried to their nests and the candles, dwarfed by the sharp edge of the flame, drooped with sleep. The maids woke up from this trance and hurried out only to return with trays loaded with the fruits of the season: figs, raisins, nuts and red-cheeked apples. Every one ate, guests, retainers and maids alike, only the latter nibbled shyly out of deference.

Nurse had told me about these nightly gatherings at great-grandmother's house and each time she had added, " There was one story, the most beautiful of all, but I can't remember it now." She drew her brows, trying to force her mind to pick the scattered threads of the yarn. But she never succeeded in luring that fairy tale out of its hiding place and to this day I have not gotten over my disappointment.

When I came to America, I translated these Turkish fairy tales into English and took them to the editor of a well-known publishing house. At the very word " fairy " I could feel her bristling. She did not care to see or read them. For the first time I realized that children could sneer at fairies and elder people handle them with a pair of tongs.

" Children are not interested in them," the editor explained. " Today, the trend is for practical stories. Why not write about a modern Turkish girl and her life?"

I was shocked and hurt. The lovely fairies of my childhood, who had guided my steps to the world of books, had been insulted. I put away the manuscript, realizing that these fragile ladies and their magic wand could not stand the wear and tear of our machine age or the stolid scrutiny of our practical era.

Fairy tales played an important rôle in my life, as I have attempted to show, due to the lack of children's books. Quite apart from their usefulness to me, I believe they are essential reading for children. Their appeal to the imagination, to the fanciful and wistful side of our nature is doubly needed today. Besides, a fairy tale is a distinct literary masterpiece with a musical rhythm, a refrain of repetition which delights any child.

From *The Horn Book* for March, 1941

154

Part V

Particularly for Parents

R. S V. P.

By Irma E. Webber

SOME invitations are precisely worded, beautifully engraved, and even gilt embossed. They generally come in two envelopes. Less elegant invitations, to perhaps more pleasurable affairs, are sometimes painstakingly penned or hastily scrawled. Others are casually extended over the phone or over the fence. Still others come to us in such camouflaged form we may not heed them because we do not readily recognize them.

Some of my most memorable invitations have been worded simply, " Mommy, come see! " They were first extended to me when my husband, son Herbert, and I were living at the foot of Mt. Rubidoux, Riverside, California. In those days, I frequently whizzed through the housework in order to study the anatomy of plants while Herbert played. My converted breakfast-nook laboratory overlooked the large, completely fenced backyard playground, so I could alternate studious gazing into the microscope with motherly glancing out the window. While this arrangement permitted some botanical progress, the periods of study were frequently shortened by Herbert's eager invitation, " Mommy, come see!" In the years since, I've been thankful that I sensed this was an invitation, rather than a mere interruption, and that I so often went to see what Herbert wanted me to see.

What was I invited to see? Nothing the newspapers considered newsworthy. Nothing my adult friends picked as topics for conversation. Just matters of genuine interest to a small boy: little, crooked plants that pushed up the soil; taller, straighter plants that spread out new leaves; the California poppy bud that doffed its dunce cap; the tomato

157

that was red enough to pick; the honey bees that buzzed about the rambler roses; the birds that pecked the figs; the glistening trail left by a snail; the lizard that climbed the pergola; the water that gurgled out of a gopher hole; the ants that labored with their loads; the worms that wiggled in the mud; the clouds that floated in the sky; the shadows that changed shape. These are but a few of the things I was invited to see in Herbert's backyard world.

I soon learned that, as far as Herbert was concerned, " Mommy, come see!" didn't always mean " see " in the visual sense. Often the invitation was really to touch, or smell, or listen. Herbert soon discovered that different parts of a rose bush don't all feel and smell alike, and that there is no more similarity in the feel of *stickery* rose leaves and sticky petunia leaves than there is in the fragrance of roses and petunias, or the song of jays and canaries, or the flavor of carrots and spinach. As Herbert, without assistance, repeatedly discovered significant similarities and differences in the things about him, I was repeatedly struck with the contrast between the sharp observations of a young child anxious to learn, and some of the perfunctory, slipshod observations I had encountered among college students who admittedly enrolled in science courses solely because some science was required for graduation.

When Herbert was nearly four, Irma Jean was born. By the time she was two, she also invited me to " see " many things. Her interests in backyard matters were as varied, and her observations as keen as Herbert's had been in his pre-school years. Moreover, they clearly indicated a lack of any inborn, feminine dislike of mice, grubs, spiders, or mud.

When Irma Jean was not quite three, I enrolled her in a small, but very good, nursery school. She was delighted with the idea of going to school as Herbert did, and she thoroughly enjoyed the school activities. With both children in school five mornings a week, I once again found a good deal of time for intensive work on plant anatomy. The whole family was very happy until the nursery school director moved away and the school closed. This meant that after having experienced the companionship of children her age and the assorted

158

activities of school, Irma Jean couldn't go to school because she had suddenly grown too young. It also meant that I had a broken-hearted youngster who knew she was old enough for school because she had gone to school for about a year. I couldn't stand seeing her so forlorn, and felt that the least I could do was to supply some of the activities that she craved. Accordingly, for the next year, a large share of my time and energy was devoted to running a sort of one-child school.

Fortunately, the backyard still invited a great many observations and activities. The near-by rocky slopes of Mt. Rubidoux invited hikes midst chaparral and its dwellers. The house invited mastery of simple tasks. Clay, blackboard and chalk, paints, crayons and paper invited artistic expression. And fortunately, the junior branch of the public library invited even those who were " too young " for school.

Our junior branch library doesn't extend its invitation in the most modern or elegant housing in town. No, its invitation is just an unpretentious, genuine welcome to all, betokened by good books, a comfortable place in which to peruse them, and a cheerful librarian with helpful suggestions. Its invitation is restfully quiet yet audible. Generally there is a soft shuffling of books. The canary is apt to sing, or splash, or crack seeds. The phonograph plays opera on occasion. The librarian sometimes reads aloud to groups. And once in a while, a book, too cumbersome for little hands, falls with a resounding thud.

In this little library for little folks, I found friends of my own childhood along with the latest in children's literature. There were books that invited song and laughter, books that invited enjoyment of beauty, books that invited journeys to real and imaginary places, and books that invited a better understanding of things close at hand. There were books that one felt lucky to discover. There were also some that made me wonder why anybody ever bothered to print them, and some that made me wish they could have been printed in larger type, or better illustrated, or put together in more durable form.

Even with the many types of books to appeal to many tastes, I found great gaps in available material that invited other books for other needs. My own training in botany, combined with the great pleasure I have seen many people derive from an interest in nature, and my own children's early interest in nature, perhaps made the gaps in factual plant literature for youngsters seem disproportionately large. After bothering me for some time, these gaps seemed to invite me to divert some time from technical botany into an effort to bridge a few gaps in children's plant literature.

I believe the response to the little books resulting from this effort should partially answer the often-asked question of whether my children's early interest in nature wasn't an atypical one induced mostly by heredity, or by association with botanical parents, a botanical grandfather, and their botanical friends. Basically the children of scientists seem to be as human as those of plumbers or poets. All children normally want to acquaint themselves with their surroundings, whatever their environment. Unfortunately, all children don't have sunny, backyard playgrounds where they can become acquainted with plants and the animals the plants attract. Yet whatever their environment, children are little human beings, and, as such, inescapably concerned with living things and the forces of nature that influence all life.

Modern children often have their early natural desire to learn about nature's marvels curbed or crushed by parents or teachers. There are homes where children are told in very positive terms to refrain from ever again picking up those ghastly, disgusting grubs; those horrid, slimy snails; those awful, wiggly worms; or those dirty, sticky pine cones. There are homes so overcrowded, or so full of parents' priceless bric-a-brac, that they lack any space for a sparkly rock, a curiously shaped seed pod, or a beautiful shell that a child finds and yearns to keep. There are homes where a child's questions about the sky, the earth, a plant, or any animal are always answered, " Don't know," in a manner that implies, " And don't care!"

A young child that has had his desire to learn something about nature nearly squelched at home, may have the squelching completed in his early school years. Where the teacher has a huge class and a schedule that must be rigidly followed,

160

there is apt to be little time to look at nature materials children bring to school, and no time to answer questions about them. Even where there is a nature study period, something so rare as a Southern California hail storm may pass unnoticed by the teacher because the hail signals its invitation to look out-of-doors during the arithmetic period. It takes an earthquake to awaken an awareness in some adults of greater things than personal schedules.

Important as plans and schedules are, unexpected events often make changes in them necessary or desirable. How often the acceptance of a sudden invitation to the unfamiliar seems doubly pleasurable because we hadn't scheduled it! Yet the fact that children's interests so often are aroused without reference to the schedules of their parents and teachers too often means that early interests worth developing are persistently ignored or repeatedly rebuffed until they perish.

Fortunate are the children who learn early that their interests, regardless of when they are aroused, are always invited to develop and expand at the library. Yet even at the library, development of interests is occasionally curbed by lack of information in assimilable form. That is why I feel that inviting, intelligible books about matters that interest young children are every bit as important as technical works for specialists.

From *The Horn Book* for October, 1947

A FATHER'S MINORITY REPORT

By Edward Eager

THIS is a minority report because in most families I know the father doesn't do the reading-aloud; the mother does. In our house it's different. My wife Jane doesn't like children's books, apparently never did. Except for a burning interest in the doings of one Flaxie Frizzle (unknown to the lists of Miss Moore and Miss Eaton) her formative years seem to have been spent absorbing the complete works of Shaw, Sheridan and Thackeray.

On the other hand I like children's books, remember all those I knew, and still have most of them. So when our son Fritz was three and had outgrown linen picture books, I took over. At first it was easy, because I owned all the Beatrix Potters, and these, with a few side excursions into Lear and Laura E. Richards and the well-known fairy tales, took up the next year. Then I found that too many of the other books in my own collection, while their pictures might still hold a nostalgic charm for me, were disillusioningly empty as to text. Unaided and unadvised, I started fighting my way through the accumulated nursery literature of the past twenty-five years (also dipping into some older books that had somehow never come my way).

Fritz is six now, I've found out about *The Horn Book*, *Treasure for the Taking* and *The Three Owls* volumes, and I feel competent to take on the field. But in the meantime we've made a few discoveries that, inexplicably to me, are passed by in the recommended lists. In some other cases we disagree with the learned ladies. So this is a minority report in another sense.

162

Take *The Fairy Caravan*. Miss Anne Eaton praises it. So does Miss Anne Carroll Moore. Then why did reviewers, in considering Margaret Lane's fine biography of Beatrix Potter, so meekly submit to her dictum that the book " cannot be enjoyed in a critical sense at all "? *The Fairy Caravan* is a work of genius and as such understandably uneven. Fritz and I are on our sixth reading of the book now, and by mutual agreement we pass over The Sheep (whom he finds too slow) and skip some of Charles and the Turkey* (who bore me). But nine-tenths of the book represents, to me, the fullest flowering of Beatrix Potter's art, a kind of apotheosis of all that had gone before. As for Fritz, the too-motherly cat Mary Ellen was his first great comic character, and remains loved. To continue my quarrel with Miss Lane, *Little Pig Robinson* may be dull — I don't think so — but certainly it is far less so than *Johnny Townmouse,* of which Miss Lane apparently quite approves. This was the one Potter failure in our house. Neither Fritz nor I ever showed enough interest to suggest a second reading.

Now to quarrel with some other people. Why, in the Wanda Gág Memorial issue of *The Horn Book* did everyone try to pass off *The Funny Thing* as though it were a bad smell, something best forgotten? Fritz and I discovered Miss Gág only this year, but went rapidly through everything of hers we could find. The other books are charming, yes; fine art, yes. But only in *The Funny Thing* does the actual text rise to heights of true nonsense. " I'm not an animal; I'm an aminal," is a truly Thurberian pronouncement which has become a password in this household.

Two major discoveries Fritz and I made are, unaccountably, overlooked by all the best authorities. One is Enid Bagnold's classic *Alice and Thomas and Jane,* the best " realistic " story for young children I know of. The irresistibly comic illustrations — some by the author, some by her young daughter, Laurian Jones, — the refreshing informality of the style, the charming relationship between the children and their parents combine to make this a must for every family. A picture on page 79 (" The cook began the trouble next morning quite

*Chapter XIII, "Codlin Croft Farm."

early ") showing the cook flinging spoons about in the base-
ment, while a miasma-like cloud sweeps upwards through
the house to envelop and carry away three protesting children — this is all that a discerning parent will need as proof
of this book's quality.

Then there is M. D. Hillyard's *The Exciting Family,* an
almost perfect nonsense story written to provide a text for a
group of pictures painted by two young Russian children.
Here is a book which speaks directly to a child in a child's own
language. E. M. Delafield, in one of the *Provincial Lady*
books, pronounces it " enchanting," which is how we found
out about it, but I've run across no mention of it by American
authorities. It was Fritz's first " long book," and two years'
rereading hasn't dimmed its charm for him — or for me.

I believe these last two books are both out of print at the
moment, but that shouldn't discourage an ingenious parent.
Both turn up frequently if one will look about — unlike the
magnificent works of E. Nesbit which I am now vainly
chasing through New York's thrift shops and secondhand
bookstores. A copy of *Alice and Thomas and Jane* has been
sitting unsold on the children's shelf of one New York bookshop (on East Forty-ninth Street, if anyone wants a clue)
for the past year, and I have myself bought two copies of
The Exciting Family since last summer, — one at a fire sale in
Toledo, Ohio. This lent it added charm for Fritz, as he can
still smell the smoke in the slightly singed binding.

Fritz and I have other idiosyncrasies in our reading. We
like *The Admiral's Caravan* much better than *Davy and the
Goblin,* finding the humor less forced, more Carrollesque.
Maybe in my case the Reginald Birch illustrations for *The
Admiral's Caravan* are a contributing factor, for they take
me straight back to days in my grandmother's attic with my
father's old copies of *St. Nicholas.* I must never have been
exposed to Bensell in my youth, for his pictures for *Davy and
the Goblin,* while I admire them, haven't at all the same
impact.

We like *Racketty Packetty House,* which the booklists
don't mention any more. And we like some Oz books. Miss
Caroline Hewins, the famous children's librarian, has been

praised by Anne Carroll Moore for being able to distinguish good Henty books from bad. I make a rasher claim: I can tell one *Oz* book from another.

I'm well aware that the best authorities on children's reading turn the other way when an *Oz* book goes by. But these were so much the favorites of my youth that I couldn't forbear trying them again on Fritz. I found the earliest volumes — *The Wizard of Oz, The Land of Oz, Ozma of Oz* — to have a certain homely American charm which in a way compensates for their lack of literary distinction. As L. Frank Baum continued to expand the series, his writing deteriorated, and some of his later books really typify all one doesn't like about the America of the World War One period. When Ruth Plumly Thompson took over the series, a startling change took place. If Mr. Baum's writing was labored, Miss Thompson's was obviously a labor of pure love. All too soon the law of diminishing returns set in for her, too, but in her earlier books she shows a fine ear for a pun, a real feeling for nonsense and, in lieu of style, a contagious zest and pace that sweep the reader beyond criticism. I still maintain that *Kabumpo in Oz*, her best effort, is a fine book, and Fritz thinks so, too.

This concludes the combative part of this minority report. Don't think that we aren't grateful to all you ladies, — Miss Moore, Miss Eaton, Mrs. Becker, Miss Mahony and the rest. Some of your recommendations, *The Hobbit, Floating Island* and *Rabbit Hill*, we already knew. But your enthusiasm has given us *Miss Hickory*, that true classic, and *Noah and Rabbit* and *Tomson's Hallowe'en* and Alicia Aspinwall's *Short Stories for Short People*, William Pène du Bois's books, and Eliza Orne White's really delightful *Enchanted Mountain*. And you've started us on the stories of E. Nesbit, the best children's books, I am quite sure, in the world!

I hear mothers in the park complaining about the dullness of reading to small children and the difficulty of finding good books for First Graders. These mothers just haven't looked. I've never let an " age-group " rating deter me from trying a book I think Fritz will like. I've made mistakes — *The Wind in the Willows* and *The Wonderful Adventures of*

165

Nils proved hard going and I stopped both at once rather than turn him against books I know he will want to read some day. On the other hand, at six Fritz counts *The White Deer* and *Stuart Little* among his greatest treasures. Someone gave him St. Exupéry's *The Little Prince,* and I read it to him. He loved it. I'm not sure he understood it; but then, *I* loved it and I'm not sure I understood it either.

I've learned one important thing in three years. It's possible to read to a young child without boring either child or parent. I think the parent's boredom is just as important as the child's. I'd like to take all the empty, pedestrian picture books away from all the beginning fathers and mothers in the world, give them copies of *The Enchanted Castle* or *Peter Churchmouse* or *Timothy Turtle* instead, and watch the difference — to the parents now, to their children eventually. A mother yawning over *Cunning Cunning and His Feathered Comrades* (and I'm not sure I made that one up) isn't going to " bring up " her child half so well as a mother laughing with *Mr. Popper's Penguins* or *Kersti and Saint Nicholas.*

BOOKS RECOMMENDED BY EDWARD EAGER

Treasure for the Taking by Anne Eaton (Viking, 1946)
The Fairy Caravan by Beatrix Potter (Warne, 1929, 1951)
Tale of Little Pig Robinson by Beatrix Potter (Warne, 1930)
The Funny Thing by Wanda Gág (Coward, 1929)
Alice and Thomas and Jane by Enid Bagnold (Heinemann, 1946, o.p.)
The Exciting Family by M. D. Hillyard (Coward, 1936, o.p.)
The Admiral's Caravan by Charles E. Carryl (Houghton, 1892, o.p.)
Racketty Packetty House by Frances Hodgson Burnett (Century, 1914, o.p.)
The Wizard of Oz by L. Frank Baum (George M. Hill, 1900)
The Land of Oz by L. Frank Baum (Reilly & Britton, 1904 [now Reilly & Lee])
Ozma of Oz by L. Frank Baum (Reilly & Britton, 1907 [now Reilly & Lee])
Kabumpo in Oz by Ruth Plumly Thompson (Reilly & Lee, 1922)
The Hobbit by J. R. R. Tolkien (Houghton, 1938)
Floating Island by Anne Parrish (Harper, 1930)
Rabbit Hill by Robert Lawson (Viking, 1944)
Miss Hickory by Carolyn Sherwin Bailey (Viking 1946)
Noah and Rabbit by Herbert McKay (Dutton, 1932, o.p.)
Tomson's Hallowe'en by Margaret and Mary Baker (Dodd, 1929, o.p.)
Short Stories for Short People by Alicia Aspinwall (Dutton, 1896)
Enchanted Mountain by Eliza Orne White (Houghton, 1911, o.p.)

166

The White Deer by James Thurber (Harcourt, 1945)
Stuart Little by E. B. White (Harper, 1945)
The Little Prince by Antoine de Saint Exupéry (Harcourt, 1943)
The Enchanted Castle by E. Nesbit (Coward, 1933)
Peter Churchmouse by Margot Austin (Dutton, 1941)
Timothy Turtle by Al Graham (Viking, 1949)
Mr. Popper's Penguins by Richard T. Atwater and Florence H. Atwater (Little, 1938)
Kersti and Saint Nicholas by Hilda van Stockum (Viking, 1940, o.p.)

From *The Horn Book* for March, 1948

Ed. Note: E. Nesbit's books were brought back into print in the United States in 1958 by Coward-McCann.

ON READING THE BIBLE ALOUD

By Ruth Sawyer

"And in that day shall the deaf hear the words of the book, and the eyes of the blind shall see out of obscurity, and out of darkness."
— ISAIAH 29, 18.

~~~~~~

FROM my hilltop as I look over the neighboring houses at dusk I wish I knew that inside those where children are growing up there might be a wise and loving person to gather them together and read the Bible aloud to them for a few intimate moments. This would be a comforting thought: to think that the children of today, faced with the world of tomorrow, might be experiencing this daily fellowship with that book which, above all others, can strengthen faith in God and mankind. We need this strengthening if ever peace is to endure, if we are to have world unity.

For some time now I have been asking groups of parents, teachers and students, to which I have been speaking about children's books and reading, if any of them have been reading the Bible in their homes — or if they can remember having the Bible read to them when they were children. Sometimes a single hand goes up; usually none. Afterwards a few may gather around for discussion. Usually explanations follow, justifications, excuses. Some put forth ignorance of the Bible. Some are embarrassed by it. Some dread their children's reaction to anything religious. But in the main I feel it is a matter of indifference. Who cares? The idea of reading the Bible strikes most young people of today as rather quaint and too old-fashioned.

The truth appears self-evident. Fifty years ago the Bible was seen in nearly every American home, in country or city;

it had its part in family daily life. The essential history of the family was carefully entered on the fly-leaf. Gradually it has been discarded, moved into obscurity. " Have you a Bible in your home? " I asked a young mother I know. At first she looked blank, then her face showed comprehension: " Why, yes. Of course we must have a Bible somewhere. I think it must be in the attic."

It is long since a German poet, Heinrich Heine, wrote:

The Bible, what a book. Large and wise as the world itself, based on abysses of creation, towering aloft in the blue secrets of heaven. Sunrise and sunset, promise and fulfillment, birth and death, the whole drama of humanity are contained in this one book. The Book of Books.

It is too long since the Christian world took the Bible to its heart to read, to revere, to draw from it solace in times of trouble, to build more firmly the good standards of living from its wisdom and precepts. To know it — the full compass of its beauty and greatness.

Let me share something vivid and compelling from my own childhood. At dusk every evening we met in the library, my younger brother and I, where our mother read to us from the Bible. Read, mind you; she did not teach it. There was warm, soft radiance in those old kerosene lamps. The one over my mother's head was an ancient altar lamp from somewhere in France. Two sides of the room were banked with books; against a third wall stood our *prie-dieus,* also from France, reupholstered in deep red, ecclesiastical brocade. Over our heads hung a tremendous steel engraving of the Sistine Holy Family, framed in magnificence. To us it seemed right that we should read the Bible in the room dedicated to books. Unconsciously we felt the dignity and wide spacing of that room. It did not seem strange to us, Unitarian born, to have *prie-dieus.* They spoke mutely of worship; and it was in that spirit we gathered.

I can see my mother's hands, so small, so indicative of loving concern as she opened the big Bible. I can see her face illuminated with a kind of joyful expectancy. My feeling for the Bible stems from hers. She died many years ago; I knew her longest and best as an old woman; but I remember her best as she sat with us, reading at dusk, her face young and very exquisite.

In time, " Family Prayers " ran seldom beyond the quarter hour; but what it held! The courage and majesty of the tribes of Israel in their everlasting wanderings; the lilt and power of the songs of David and the other Psalm-singers; the solid, hopeful words, swung to a gentle cadence, and spoken by the prophets Isaiah and Micah; the tremendous drama in the stories of the Creation, of Noah, of Daniel; the quiet wisdom in the parables spoken by Jotham, of the trees choosing their king; spoken by Christ, of a mustard seed, of a house built upon the sand, of the master of a vineyard; pictures — moving and unforgettable — of Christ feeding the multitudes, quieting the storm, healing, bidding this one and that to be of good cheer, and that day of days when, speaking from the hill near Galilee, He began: " Blessed are the poor in spirit; for theirs is the kingdom of heaven." She read to us of John, preaching in the wilderness, of Paul taking time from his journeyings to write to those far away, in need of counsel, and what he wrote:

Finally, brethren, whatsoever things are true, whatsoever things are honest, whatsoever things are just, whatsoever things are pure, whatsoever things are lovely, whatsoever things are of good report; if there be any virtue and if there be any praise, think on these things.

I remember I believed that in some mysterious way God was always present, enjoying the reading as we did. We had watched our mother welcome both friends and strangers into our home with that same gladness she accorded God. It was not until I was older that I came to know that those who worship in spirit and truth always worship with God.

There was nothing of sour piety, nothing of dour compulsion about our Family Prayers. Often there was hilarity. In my small, red diary there are frequent entries: " Laughed too much at Prayers." My mother must have judged that laughter was as acceptable to God as song or thanksgiving.

I know of no other way in which I would have come to know the Bible had my mother not wanted to read it to us, and had she not put aside those few minutes in a busy life, every day, to bring it to us. In Sunday School the Bible was taught out of pamphlets, question and answer method, which we learned by heart. Such pamphlets are still being used, not only in Unitarian Sunday Schools, but in many others. Only with rare exceptions do children hear the Bible read in schools. Where will they hear it, then; how will they come to be in fellowship with it? Unless the Bible again comes back into homes, another generation will grow up in ignorance, and so much of richness, of spirit and of truth, will be lost to them. What grew out of those quarter-hours in the library in the old house has been enduring — of incalculable value and inspiration. I have lived by it; and I am convinced such a heritage belongs to all childhood. The world must continue so much the poorer, so much more stupid and blundering until it comes again into this heritage.

Because my own familiarity and pleasure grew out of the King James' Authorized Version, I would have the reading from this at the beginning. Later, after fellowship has been established and the time is ripe, I would share other Bibles. Those of modern translations and arrangements, those abridged and selected especially for younger readers, make good supplementary reading. I should like every boy and girl to see a copy of the old Vulgate; and another of a polyglot Bible, with its parallel columns of Aramaic and Greek, Latin and English. Here is substance to wonder at. It does not take much time for the reader, granted there is a love and propensity for this Book of Books, to talk about the Bible before the readings, to tell of the centuries of gathering the books together, of the discarding and rearranging of material, of the translations from one language to another; to tell of the great struggle to put it finally into English so the common folk could read it. And finally — to tell of the men who gave their lives in this struggle. One does not have to be a scholar to do this.

I would have the Bible presented in its relationship to all living matter: the study of civilization itself, the growth of ethical consciousness, the immediate concern of personal behavior. How can we teach history without the Bible? How can we come to an understanding of literature without it; how appreciate the varied forms of art? How, in short, can a person be truly educated who does not know the Bible? And this, as my Irish nurse, Johanna, would say, is " the small, littlest part of it." For if our education is concerned only with the development of mind, reason and feeling, then we remain but half-grown, stunted as those children of medieval times, thrust into earthen jars to grow crippled, the better to become mountebanks or beggars.

Not long ago I heard Archibald MacLeish speak on the power of the spoken word. It was a fine, scholarly speech. He pointed out the good and bad effects of radio, the increased delight in poetry, read aloud, the carrying power of great speeches — such as the Gettysburg speech. But he never spoke of the Bible, of the sweeping power of its spoken word.

There is an effort being made by ministers and some educators to bring the Bible back to common usage; but I think this will not go far until all concerned with books, education and young people join in this effort and make the reading of the Bible of primary importance. Even then it will not succeed if the reading is not done wisely, if it is not attuned to the ears that are listening, if the approach is not made with intelligence, reverence and pleasure. And it must be the Bible that is read, not stories taken from the Bible and rewritten in simplified words, supposed to be on the " reading level " of the average child. All great literature makes its honest demand on both reader and listener. Who expects to read *The Odyssey* with ease, or *The Nibelungenlied* or Stephen Benét's *Western Star?* Yet here is stuff we would share with boys and girls. Good reading means challenge. The automatic tick-tock of the mind may take easily in its swing a mystery yarn; but it takes the will to read as well as something of the art of reading to appreciate what is great and enduring.

I think there can be no question in anybody's mind as to the greater value of what is read aloud, or told, the spoken word as against the silent word. For words spoken capture the imagination, reach an emotional depth, and satisfy even before there is a full comprehension of the substance read.

172

The glorious sound of words, the rhythm of words spoken together, the clarion or the hushed quality of the voice — all these can hold the attention of a young mind while it grows in understanding. There is the additional value of two or more people sharing something that is good. I have often wondered if the tales of King Arthur would not have been missed by the boys and girls of our modern world had they not largely been told or read aloud. Had the story of *Alice* not been first told to a little girl in England, would it ever have been written down for three generations to adore? And if Allison Grahame's nurse had not read aloud to him those letters from his father, setting forth a ditty about Mr. Toad, would we ever have had that immortal book, *The Wind in the Willows?* That is why I feel the Bible must be read aloud if it is to survive as a living text — the " word made flesh."

About stories written from the Bible I feel as I do about Lamb's *Tales from Shakespeare;* I want none of them. But there are many excellent books of selection and good revision with the text taken from the " Authorized Version." Let it not be thought for a moment that all the Bible must be read. There is much that is dull, much that is better left out. For young children *Seventy Stories from the Old Testament* is particularly recommended. It is a great pity that Helen Slocum Estabrook did not live to finish her work. Here is an unforgettable book, of rare beauty, with the fine woodcuts from Holbein and Dürer, Jean de Tournes and many others; with clear, large type, wide spacing and margins. It is a book to invite reading.

I like the slim book of *David,* with text arranged and illustrations made by Elizabeth Orton Jones. The story of David belongs to youth; and very little children have drawn much from the ancient frieze-like quality of the figures; the feeling in the double-spread of the host of Israel meeting the Philistines I think is superb. *Small Rain,* a book done last year by Elizabeth and her mother, is a less pretentious book, far more everydayish; but it is definitely a book in the right direction. Here are short and lovely things taken from the Bible, and pictured through children of today. It is a small, intimate book. What child would not feel deep wonder at

173

" The heavens declare the glory of God," or the simple reverence and quietness in those figures which accompany the " Lord's Prayer."

A new book, of great distinction, for older boys and girls has been published this fall: *The Book of Books*, by Dr. Sypherd of the University of Delaware. Here again is good bookmaking and wise selection. The introduction for both reader and listener is excellent; and the brief and concise commentaries make good appetizers for the text which follows. The author gives but one Gospel, that according to St. Luke. I like that. It is far the best piece of biographical writing done in the New Testament. It gives the canticle of Mary, which none of the other Gospels give; and the Christmas story is told with a beauty and cadence that are only found in Luke. How much more vivid the Gospels could be made if the little that is known of their authors was told in connection with the reading. Matthew, held forcefully down by the human angle of the story he had to tell. St. Mark, concerned more about Christ as the Messiah. Luke, presumably the Greek physician, coming years after Christ, eager to make a living narrative about the man who performed miracles and raised up disciples to follow Him and teach what He had taught. And finally St. John, the mystic, concerned mainly with the spiritual and eternal values of the life he was reporting. The Gospels read in the light of those personalities who created them become far more compelling.

Mary Ellen Chase has written a new book. She calls it *The Bible and the Common Reader*, a good, rendering title. Here she presents the outcome of her work with the Bible and the students at Smith College. I think the first and strongest impression one has is of the complete and delightful companioning the author has had with the Bible. It is a keen, invigorating book that belongs within easy reach of all thinking persons, a good book to read aloud and an exceptional book to share with young people. In the author's foreword and the four chapters of introduction she has presented a great deal to ground the reader and student in the history of the Bible, of the Hebrew people, their character and their literature. For the rest she talks of the Bible itself, and does it with great simplicity and moving effect. I have never read a finer interpretation of the Book of Job than hers. It left me longing to hear her talk about Job, read Job, to those nineteen- and twenty-year-olders in her class. She marks that which is human — human, and that which is divine — divine. In her foreword she writes: " The Bible belongs among the noblest and most indispensable of our humanistic and literary traditions. No liberal education is truly liberal without it." Here surely is a book to build background and a closer fellowship with the Bible.

Another book for background is Hendrik van Loon's *Story of the Bible*. Not a book that can measure up to his *Story of Mankind;* but a book, nevertheless, that has a great deal to give. I know of no other writer who has given his readers a picture of the wanderings of the tribes of Israel in terms of such weariness, endlessness, steadfastness and faith. For all their brevity I know of no one who has brought the traditional tales of the Old Testament into such strong, clear focus.

Those who know the three lectures, *On Reading the Bible,* delivered by Sir Arthur Quiller-Couch to his students at Cambridge long ago, know how much in them is both provocative and worth treasuring. I go back to these often, for fresh evaluation and inspiration. While he discusses it as literature and in its relationship to all literature, one is always conscious of the fact that to Sir Arthur it remains the " Holy Bible." Literature, yes; but literature with the creative impulse of the Divine moving through it.

There are many modern Bibles that must not be forgotten. The Goodspeed *New Testament* and the later *Complete Bible,* with its text in good, work-a-day English, is liked by a great many, scholars and common readers. How it is liked by young people I do not know. But I am convinced that much of majesty and beauty are lost out of the text through this modernizing treatment. We have enough great literature in good, plain English.

The St. Anthony Press brought out in 1941 a Catholic New Testament which I like very much. I keep a copy by my bed-side, and read it often for the pleasure the clear type and arrangement give me. There is no confusion of marginal

175

notes; and I think this might well be the answer to those who would like to see the Bible read in every school. Catholic and Protestant children together could surely listen to its reading with reverence and with grace.

I should like to see a copy of *The Bible, Designed to be Read as Great Literature,* in those homes where there are older boys and girls. The arrangement of prose and verse is well done; and the subject matter well classified. It is a far bulkier volume than *The Book of Books;* but it gives a greater selection, and could be used advantageously for the more adult.

I wish classes of children, or a single child with its parent, might visit the library just to see Bibles — shelves upon shelves of Bibles, lettered and illuminated by hand on parchment, printed in every country, in every tongue, bound in vellum, carved boards and leather — more Bibles than any other book in the world. And after such a visit I wish the children might have the home Bible taken from shelf or table, that loving hands might open it, that a voice rich with understanding might read, for the hope and the promise of a better world to come, these words written by that great mystic and prophet — St. John:

And I saw a new heaven and a new earth: for the first heaven and the first earth were passed away; ... And I heard a great voice out of heaven saying, Behold, the tabernacle of God is with men, and he will dwell with them and they shall be his people, and God himself shall be with them, and be their God. ... And there shall in no wise enter into it any thing that defileth, neither whatsoever worketh abomination or maketh a lie: but they which are written in the Lamb's book of life.

BOOKS MENTIONED

Seventy Stories of the Old Testament, compiled by Helen Slocum Estabrook (The Bradford Press, Portland, Maine, 1938, o.p.)

David, by Elizabeth Orton Jones (Macmillan, 1937, o.p.)

Small Rain, chosen by Jessie Orton Jones. Illustrated by Elizabeth Orton Jones (Viking, 1943)

The Book of Books. The King James Version of the Bible, Abridged and Arranged with Editorial Comments for Young Readers, by Wilbur Owen Sypherd (Knopf, 1944)

The Bible and the Common Reader, by Mary Ellen Chase (Macmillan, 1944)

The Story of the Bible, by Hendrik van Loon (Boni and Liveright, 1923, o.p., Rev. ed. 1946, Liveright)

On the Art of Reading, by Sir Arthur Quiller-Couch (Cambridge University Press, 1920)

The Bible, Designed to be Read as Living Literature. Text arranged from the King James Authorized Version. Ed. by Ernest Sutherland Bates (Simon and Schuster, 1936)

The Complete Bible — with the Apocrypha. American translation by Smith and Goodspeed (Chicago University Press, 1939)

The New Testament, ed. by Catholic Scholars, Confraternity of Christian Doctrine (St. Anthony Guild Press, Paterson, N. J., 1941)

From *The Horn Book* for March, 1945

LATER ADDITIONS FOR THIS SAMPLER

The Great Story — From the Douay Version. Illustrated with woodcuts from the old masters (Harcourt, 1938, o.p.)

The First Bible. Illustrated by Helen Sewell. Selected and arranged by Jean West Maury (Oxford, 1934)

Many Mansions, by Jessie Orton Jones. Illustrated by Lynd Ward (Viking, 1947)

Joseph, arranged by Elizabeth Yates. Illustrated by Nora Unwin (Knopf, 1947)

A VILLAGE SUNDAY SCHOOL

By Caroline Dale Snedeker

A SUNDAY School class is generally considered a prosaic affair; and teaching one a dull duty, but mine is of vivid interest to me Sunday after Sunday. It is a small class, five boys and three girls. They are from fourteen to seventeen years of age and growing so fast that they seem new individuals every week. One of them is the son of a prominent lawyer. When he returned from a visit to New York I had him tell what he had seen. One is an Italian — the most enthusiastic. One a city boy whose parents are here for the War-duration. Two brothers live outside the town. The father commutes to New Orleans, so most of the activities of the little farm rest on the two boys and their mother. They have chickens, vegetables, three cows and pigs. They even sell bacon and pork, which entails work I hardly like to think of. These two boys milk the three cows before they arrive at Sunday School at 9.30 in the morning. Yet they always come neatly and even charmingly dressed.

The Gulf and the Bayous round about are a great temptation to Sunday fishing. The place is famous for it. The lesson must be vivid enough to compete with this. But in spite of the cows, the fishing, the early hour of school, I have an almost perfect record of attendance.

Our tiny church, with its spire, faces the Gulf. It is set in the midst of green yards with a live-oak nearby. The congregation is small but intimate and devoted.

In my teaching I have never learned to promote discussion and get expression out of my pupils. It is a bad fault which I am still trying to correct. We have studied the Life of

Christ, the Life of St. Paul and some of the Old Testament. I do not make the pupils read Bible verses to me. I prefer to quote the Bible myself often, and I never do so without a deep thrill of joy in its lofty beauty and meaning. I think this gets over to them. I think the boys love best the Life of Christ, as I do. And I try every way to make Jesus real and present to them. When I tell of his ancient miracles, I match them up with a miracle of today: our fliers in their planes who, when the plane is completely beyond control, feel and know that God takes hold and brings them home. They call Him " The Divine Pilot " and are not afraid to talk about this at mess with their companions. I find such articles in the daily paper and bring them for the class to read.

I tell the class how in my girlhood it did not seem necessary to " stand up for Jesus." Everybody was Christian and went to church. But now it is very different. While we sit here, people are suffering and dying for their faith as they did in the early church. You boys must never miss an opportunity to declare and show your faith. Stand up for Jesus. He needs you now. He needs you as he has not for centuries past.

I notice one of the boys, who plays the piano for the hymns, chooses most often, " Stand up for Jesus."

I remind the boys that soon they will be citizens of the town, maybe on the School Board. I want them to fight for Bible teaching in the Public School. For a country which calls itself Christian to neglect utterly the study of Christ means the greatest possible loss in morals and integrity and a grave danger.

I bring all sorts of things to show to the class. When I get an interesting V-letter from a flier in India, I bring it. I brought a Crusader's lamp which was found by a relative of ours on Mount Carmel. It is authentic and must have been carried actually by a Crusader of the 13th century. I even brought a letter I received from Princess Elizabeth's lady in waiting. It was written on Buckingham Palace paper and stamped with a little crown. The boys were delighted. This had nothing to do with the lesson, but I love to share my interests with them.

When I find a significant book I bring it to the class. I

179

tell them of Rickenbacker's *Miraculous Voyage,* of Whittaker's *We Thought We Heard the Angels Sing.* These are thrilling and true stories.

When I was reading Mary Ellen Chase's *The Bible and the Common Reader,* I was fascinated with her chapter on the Book of Job. I determined to give Job to my class. I studied hard beforehand. First I told the class of the great problem of evil which the Book of Job opens up. Then I told them the story. It so happens that years ago I had heard Stuart Walker give Job as a play. It had moved me as almost no other play ever seen. I now told Job as a play. First there was the prelude given by two lovely angelic figures. Then the curtain went up, and there was Job, almost too terrible to look at. He cursed the day he was born and you did not wonder that he did. Then came the friends. Strangely enough the long discussions were emotional — never boring. Job answered accusation after accusation and when driven to the wall burst out with that most amazing prophecy of the whole Old Testament, " I know that my Redeemer liveth and shall stand at the latter day upon the earth." Slowly the stage began to darken — flashes of lightning, rolls of thunder. At last total darkness. Then suddenly a shaft of white light and the splendid voice of God.

" Gird up now thy loins like a man: for I will demand of thee, and answer thou me."

Then Job, speaking with great awe and joy, " I have heard of thee with the hearing of the ear; but now mine eye seeth thee."

I was thoroughly excited as I gave this and the class listened immovable throughout. I think they got something of the mystery and beauty of Job.

I talk a great deal about archeological finds — those that prove the accuracy of the Bible. Especially I have told of Sir William Ramsey, who started out very skeptical as to the writings of Luke, but when one find after another proved Luke absolutely correct in Acts and Gospel, Sir William turned right about face and asserted that Luke was as great a historian if not greater than Thucydides.

When we studied the dramatic riot at Ephesus (Life of St.

180

Paul) I told them of the English archeologist, John Turtle Wood, who by clever detective work discovered the great temple of Diana at the bottom of a lake. It had been completely lost for centuries.

The boys are exceedingly fond of the rector and they love to serve at the altar. This gives them an active part in the service. It makes them churchmen. We are not High Church, but have enough ritual to be dignified and reverent.

On Easter Day, as I rounded the corner of the church toward the front door, there I saw three of my boys in their white cottas. One carried the cross, one the church flag, one the American flag. A gale from the Gulf was whipping us almost off our feet. The boy with the American flag set it aside and came to help me up the steps, which is always necessary. Then he went back to the procession. My whole class attended service on Easter Day, and I sat in my pew feeling that, in spite of my years, I am still of some use in the world.

From *The Horn Book* for July-August, 1945

ALONG THE ROAD
TO CHILDHOOD

By Margaret Warren Brown

D URING the war, and before it, for many reasons, my
household moved so often there never was time to set
up housekeeping in any traditional sense. Then, just
as I had decided to change my classification from housewife
to migratory worker, we bought a house. This suggested a
more permanent way of life, the pleasant possibility of at last
gathering together some Family Belongings.

Since these arrived from the warehouse a few weeks ago, I
have been unpacking them, especially books — boxes and
boxes of books which had belonged to my sister, two brothers,
and me in our childhood. To me it has been an extraordinary
experience. Though I had seen and used copies of many of
these books from time to time, I had not seen my own books all
together since I set forth to college seventeen years ago. It is
true that in five years of library work with children, and more
recent experience with three small daughters, I had acquired a
firm conviction of the importance of good books for children.
Nevertheless, I was quite unprepared for the emotional impact
of these. Turning the familiar long-lost pages, I was over-
whelmed with sudden clear memories, and I re-experienced
feelings as immediately as if I were again a child reading for
the first time.

Like most mothers, I am constantly besieged for information about " What did you do when you were a little girl, what
was it like then? " In these books I found a direct road to my
childhood — not just my reading childhood, but the whole of
it. Adults may be able to compartmentalize their books into a

182

single section of their lives, placing them neatly under recreation, or self-improvement, or escape; but a child's reading embraces the whole of life — work, play, even dreams. And so my memories were whole memories.

On the top of the first box, a battered *Home Book of Verse for Young Folks* by Burton Stevenson — the furry-edged pages, hanging together with a few threads, still carry the frostiness of a December morning in New England, red checks of a blanket, surprise of an unexpected present. I was six-and-a-half that morning when waking, stretching my legs, I felt an unaccustomed weight. I found a thick square package, wrapped in tissue paper and bright ribbon, lying on the red blanket. Clearly a present, but why? Christmas, though crawling closer, was still weeks away.

I found the answer on the flyleaf. " St. Nicholas' Eve " was written in the familiar hand of my great-aunt. (From faraway New York, throughout our childhood, she brought festival and magic into our lives, as well as almost all our unusual collection of books.) The night before, by candlelight, she had told us of St. Nicholas in Holland. But I had not expected him to find his way to New England and the foot of my bed. From that year, Christmas in our family began on St. Nicholas' Eve and lasted all the way to Twelfth Night. *The Home Book of Verse* lasted long too; it was a good book just to read, and it played its part in school assignments right up to high school, supplying everything from " Mr. Finney's Turnip " for 4th grade Parents' Day to " My Favorite Poems " for Freshman English.

I suppose all children at some time conceive the enchanting idea that somewhere, if only they can find it, is a secret door or passageway or staircase leading to unimaginable adventure. David Blaize's adventures are confused and fragmentary in my mind, but I can never lose the completely satisfying quality of his finding a blue door banging back and forth under his pillow. Even more mysterious and satisfying to a child's yearning for secret passageways to secret worlds was *The Princess and the Goblin*. How clearly I can experience again the feeling of anticipation and excitement with which

I first followed the Princess Irene down the long door-lined corridors and up that promising secret staircase.

This book I treasured for another reason too. It was — and is — mine as no other book was. When I was ten, I went with my great-aunt to Boston. Any trip to Boston was interesting; any trip with my aunt was bound to be unusual. The combination offered unlimited possibilities and I set off with the highest hopes, which were more than realized. We went to The Bookshop for Boys and Girls, which was already a familiar place to us children. And, when we arrived, I was told that I could choose any book that I wanted . . . any book in that whole wonderful place. The possibilities were staggering; my stomach felt suddenly queasy. It was the *Princess* I chose, finally, and I have never regretted it.

This Bookshop provided many other gala occasions for the four of us. From the broad window looking over the Gardens, we watched Marshal Foch lead a parade up Boylston Street. Swanboat rides, which officially opened Spring, always ended at the Bookshop. Our dentist was kind enough to have his office nearby, on Arlington Street. The frequent visits to him during the long years of teeth-straightening were made almost attractive by follow-up purchases of books. Shopping expeditions usually included lunch at the Women's Educational down below, where, if you waited for a front table, you could watch people's feet passing by up above you, while you dredged up the stickiest, thickest, most delicious butterscotch sauce from the bottom of your ice-cream dish. At Christmas time, the Bookshop became a still more special sort of place, the most Christmasy part of Boston. Most of our books, as I look them over, have the Bookshop label in the front.

All too many of our early picture books have vanished, worn out physically. But in reading copies of them to my children I have everyday proof of their immortality as art. Every line of a Caldecott, Brooke, Greenaway, or Potter is familiar. (Incidentally, my daughter's copy of *Benjamin Bunny*, when compared with the few surviving pages of mine, shows a lamentable deterioration in the reproduction of line and color.)

184

I owe a double debt to Beatrix Potter for the pleasure she gave me as a child and for the haven she provides to a reading-aloud-parent. A book to which a child becomes attached has to have many readings. Standards being variable and often peculiar, what is delightful to a child can be distasteful to the parent on the first reading and torture thereafter. It is the great and rarely equaled gift of Beatrix Potter to be infinitely readable. I began reading *Peter Rabbit* aloud before my first child was two. I am still reading it, without boredom, to my second; and in a few months the third child will be introduced to the third copy.

The importance of the Potter books in my childhood is witnessed by several facts. It was with *Peter Rabbit* that I made the thrilling discovery that I really could read. No Christmas would have been complete without *The Tailor of Gloucester*. And the play we made from *The Roly Poly Pudding* and produced in our barn was by all odds the outstanding performance of the many which our drama-conscious neighborhood gave. (Surely, those rats are the most sinister in literature.)

Jerrold's *Big Book of Nursery Rhymes* emerges from a box as a big collection of loose sheets (all out of order but surprisingly few missing). " Christmas 1912 " is written on the title page — a gift, again from New York, to my brother, almost three at the time, and myself, a year and a half. What better cornerstone for a child's library could be found? It still seems to me the most thoroughly satisfactory Mother Goose. It is a perfect book for reading aloud to very small children, because it has so many pictures for them to look at while listening — at least one to every verse, frequently one for each line. Of the hundreds of pictures, every one is familiar to me. In fact, in looking over all the picture books, I discover that the pictures are permanently engraved in my memory even when the accompanying text has been forgotten. The verses in *Marigold Garden* and *Under the Window* awake not the slightest echo, but I recognize each delightful drawing.

To me this has been an interesting and most meaningful discovery. As a children's librarian I fully endorsed the general assumption that of course the best art in the earliest books is essential. But it was a rather theoretical conviction. I had not realized, until I recaptured my own experience, just how fully and permanently an artistically ungifted child of ordinary mental capacity can absorb good pictures. Before learning to read, a child necessarily relies on the pictures. Undistracted by the text, he gives them his full attention. A book is pictures, pictures are the book. No wonder the pictures stick, and stick fast. The best color work, the best drawing, and the most honest intelligence in concept are clearly required.

Some of our foreign picture books stirred up additional reflections. Two wonderful ones came to us from Sweden on Christmas Day of 1913 — Elsa Beskow's *Mors Lilla Olle* and the *Bilderbok* of Ottilia Adelborg. Later there were French books, including Anatole France's *Nos Enfants,* with its delicate pictures by Boutet de Monvel and, greatest prize of all, the same artist's *Jeanne d'Arc.* These became part of a small special collection, which my mother kept in a secret place and brought out only on most important occasions. This in itself gave them a definite attraction, and it occurs to me now that they had still another — that no one could read them to us (no one knew Swedish, and nobody's French was sufficiently sturdy) and so we were forced to rely on our eyes and free imagination.

Certain books have deep associations with our life together as a family. Through constant reading aloud, they became part of our pattern of living. *Perez the Mouse,* for instance, entered the family before the first of us lost his first tooth, and kept on leaving things under our pillows until the youngest came of dental age. *Dr. Dolittle's* Gub-Gub the Pig and the Pushmi-Pullyu became family characters. Everyone in *Winnie the Pooh* was adopted, though by this time my older brother and I had (according to statistics) outgrown them. In such cases younger children in the family are a distinct advantage — under the guise of reading to them, or just happening to be around when reading was going on, we could laugh our heads off at " little kids' books " and still not lose face.

Most deeply imbedded in our life as a family were Willebeek

LeMair's unsurpassed song books always open on the piano rack. They are every bit as beautiful as I remembered them, and I find they contain hardly a song which I haven't been singing to my children these past few years from memory. An extensive repertoire of songs is a great resource to a parent. Mine, I see, I owe to these books and to my mother, who played them to all of us so many times.

Then there are *Little Boy Lost;* Howard Pyle's *Robin Hood; Billy Barnicoat; Crossings* and *Down-a-Down-Derry; Old Peter's Russian Tales; East of the Sun,* with Kay Nielsen's exquisite illustrations; the *Mysterious Island* and all the other Wyeth-illustrated Scribner books which (technically) belonged to my brother; and so many more. Each carries a wealth of associations, a direct feeling of what I felt and what I was when I first read them.

Much as I loved them all, it is not hard to place at the very top, in my hierarchy of favorites, the plain simple books of Eliza Orne White, in particular *The Blue Aunt. The Blue Aunt* was given to me when I was seven, by my own great-aunt (who knew better than anyone else ever has what to give, and when). More than any other episode of my childhood reading, Evelyn's adventure with the plaid dress affected me. The dress was a present from a kind but imperceptive relative, and Evelyn hated it at sight with passion. So she snipped it up into tiny bits to fill a Red Cross pillow, with satisfaction far stronger that her feeling of guilt. I waited, anxiously, for the inevitable punishment to fall — and it never came. To be sure, the Blue Aunt did, in warmly human fashion, make it clear to Evelyn that the giver's feelings would be hurt if the deed should come to her attention. But she understood as completely as I did Evelyn's hatred of the dress, and even went so far as to buy a duplicate which Evelyn — without even wearing it — was able to bestow on a cousin who liked it. She felt a little bit guilty for the undeserved praise she received because of this generous act — " But there are some things which can never be explained," says the author. This was my first experience in literature (or life) of deliberate sin unpunished. It was an intensely relieving experience, and any competent psychiatrist would approve.

This summer I read *Ann Frances,* published only a few years ago, to my daughter, who, like Ann, had just had her fifth birthday. I read it several times, in fact, for Rachel liked it every bit as much as I did; the magic was as strong as ever. It is a foregone conclusion that the sixth birthday will be celebrated with *When Molly Was Six,* which contains as a chapter one of the most expert short stories (by any standards, adult or " juvenile ") that I have read — " How Molly Spent Her 10 cents."

Eliza Orne White is unique. Her world is tremendously real, the writing as lively and fresh to me today as when I first read her, and her genius — it is nothing less — for understanding children is evident throughout all her books.

From *The Horn Book* for November, 1946

SOPHIA'S BOOK

By Martha I. Johnson

S HE sat on the mulberry plush footstool with the book on her lap, her fat dark-brown curls decorated with a white satin bow. Yesterday had been her birthday, and although she had marked off only seven years of her life on that day, she knew intuitively that it was a Special Day, but not because it was her birthday.

It was the book. Her first one that was not a picture book. Her *Hans Andersen's Fairy Tales* was an unillustrated edition, with much print on each page, and 392 pages. She had looked at it solemnly when it had come miraculously new from its pretty pink-and-white wrappings. A sturdy, buff book with a toadstool outlined in green on its cover. A strange, overwhelming sense of grown-upness rushed through her body and mind. She was no longer a *little* girl. She could read now, without benefit of pictures, these lovely, magic words that were not like words in a reader, large, repeated, illustrated.

As usual, she had wakened early yesterday. Long before anyone else had roused. She had pulled on the light over her bed, and given herself to the complete luxury of last night's paper, which she had smuggled from her father's easy chair after he had gone to bed. She had been warned not to read the paper. Her father came into her room each night to be sure she was not reading. Somehow her father could not seem to understand that there was so much already printed in the world that had to be read. And the time seemed short to her. What if — oh, what if she did not have time to read everything that had been written? So in spite of remonstrance she had dug into everything she could find to read, ever since the

189

moment she realized she possessed the key to this magic door. Parts of Tennyson's *In Memoriam* were gulped down with the latest scandal (when she could filch the paper), Eugene Field was absorbed along with the "Views on Many Toothpicks" column in the daily paper. (It was not until a year later she discovered the pronunciation of "topics.")

On her birthday morning she had lain awake wondering if there might be a book among her gifts — certain there MUST be. She had heard Mother stirring in the raw, dark December morning. Time for her light to be out. They must not know she had been reading. A scolding would spoil her birthday.

She had turned over in her thoughts the names of books she would most like to own: *Alice in Wonderland, Peter Pan*. She did not own these. But most of all she wanted *Andersen's Fairy Tales*. And then suddenly, in the center of her dreaming, Mother, Father, and Small Brother had come into her little room, as was the birthday custom in her family. Father came first with the red-and-black candelabra bearing five white candles which lighted the room, with its yellow climbing-rose wallpaper, and shone mistily and golden on the white spread over her bed.

Mother followed with a silver tray holding her birthday cake and pink-and-white mysteriously wrapped gifts. Last of all was Nils, carrying another gift, wrapped primly, carefully. They recited in three voices, solemnly, as was their custom on birthdays, "We have the honor to congratulate you, little Sophia, and to wish you many happy returns of the day."

She slid up in bed against the white pillow, her face pink and shy. Father placed the candelabra on the oak chest beside her bed, while Nils came close so he would not miss the gift unwrapping. She looked at the cake frosted so whitely and crystally. She looked at the stiff, snow-clean cloth on the tray. The cocoa in her little pink-and-yellow cup looked good, but she was not hungry now. The gifts! She opened the first one, a squashy small package. Mittens! Gay, scarlet ones with white at the wrists. Then a tiny package. A purple velvet box. Father showed her how to press the small button. A little

190

golden locket, round and fat, on a delicate chain. Her heart shone tremulously and happily in her eyes. Then there was writing paper with a rabbit, a little brown rabbit, at the top of each sheet. Aunt Martha had sent a picture book from Sweden, *Olle I Trollskogen*. That would be fun. She looked joyously at the gay, strange illustrations. Nils slipped his package behind his back. He must tease her a little, even on her birthday.

"You have something for me, Nils," she reproved. Her heart was beating turbulently now. Could it be that there was no other book?

" Come, Nils," said Mother. " Give her the book."

At the word *book* the color came and went in her face. It was that important. It was terribly important. It was life or death nearly. Book, book, book! The word pounded within her at every beat of her heart.

Nils grinned and handed her the package he held, wrapped in pink-and-white striped paper, glistening with a white bow. She thought, I can never take off this ribbon and paper. But she did. And there it was. Her very-longed-for treasure. *Andersen's Fairy Tales*. New and buff-colored, with a toadstool outlined in green. She touched it gently, she stroked its cover. A book, a new book, her book, her very own new book!

" Thank you, thank you very much," she said softly to them all. After they left, she drank her breakfast cocoa and tasted the cake. While she dressed the book lay where she could see it. Finally, her bed made, and her small chores completed, she came to the mulberry ottoman with her book under her arm. She glanced at the titles of the stories: The Fir Tree, Little Tiny, The Daisy, The Brave Tin Soldier, The Ugly Duckling. She would read them all, she would read them and read them. If she never read another word elsewhere, she would read *this* book over and over. She could not have explained why. But she knew vaguely that this book was her passport out of babyhood into a mature and significant childhood. She was leaving something behind, gladly and with a strange relief. This she knew.

Her mother's friend Sadie had come to see her later in the day. Sadie had brought a really beautiful doll with eyes that

191

opened and closed, long-lashed; a doll dressed in a yellow coat and bonnet, wearing a lace and silk dress. She named the doll Marion for the little girl next door, but she did not play with the doll. She placed it, a little wistfully and resignedly, in her small caneseated rocker. Then she sat down solemnly again on the mulberry footstool and began her reading.

She had worn a bright red flannel dress, flecked with small white dots. It was in honor of her birthday. So were the black patent leather slippers and white stockings which had caused Sadie to exclaim, " My, the little brown-eyed one is dressed up today."

Max, who was a roomer with them, came in at dinner time and handed her a long, narrow, white box. Dark-red kid gloves. Her very first. " Oh, thank you very much, Max," she cried. She was still sitting on the ottoman with the *Hans Andersen* on her knees.

" Have you read all day, child? " Father came in swiftly with a rush of cold, cold air and a *Daily News* curled up in his hand. Mother replied for her. " Nearly all day," Mother had sighed. In the sigh Sophia lived too, for she knew her mother thought of all the books to come into Sophia's hands, but she thought proudly, lonesomely, " There will never be a book like this one." She outlined the green toadstool with her finger and turned to the next story.

From *The Horn Book* for January, 1947

Part VI

Youth in the War (1941-1946)

A PART OF VICTORY

By *Armstrong Sperry*

I T is my conviction that we who are parents or editors or
teachers or writers of books — people whose work in any
way influences the development of children — today have
a great opportunity, and perhaps also a great privilege. There
was a time (and not so long ago) when men and women could
look ahead. They could plan ahead and say: " When John is
twelve or thirteen years old we'll send him to such and such a
school. We'll choose this college or that. We'll help him prepare for law or medicine or one of the sciences or the arts. . . ."
It was as simple as that! But who today dares to plan with
such utter certainty, such blind conviction that by tomorrow
or the day after, the very institutions upon which our society
is grounded will not have crumbled like the walls of some city
that we fondly believed was invulnerable.

And please let no one imagine that in this I am sounding any
note of defeat, for nothing could be farther from my thought
or intention. There have always been troubled times, and the
future never has been wholly predictable. Yet men and women
still have looked ahead, they have trained their eye upon the
unattainable just exactly as the astronomer trains his tele-
scope upon the most distant star. Of course we have with us,
and I suppose always will have, those timid and faint-hearted
ones who declare that there is no solution to the problems that
perplex us. And we have as well those people whose attitude
of cynicism is, I believe, the very attitude that was basically
responsible for the downfall of France: that attitude of " *Je
m'en fiche* — what's the use? " And so here in America it is
well for us to remember, I think, that out of the most troubled

195

times in our history great leaders have always risen, and the common man himself has at such times seen human life with greatest clarity, not alone for what it *is*, but for what it may be.

How good a job have we made of this present-day world to bequeath to our children? Won't there be many of them who will turn upon us with scorn for this heritage? And if they do, what are we going to give to them that will help them meet and deal with this world of the future, which will be their present?

These children are going out into a world where the only certainty is the utter uncertainty of their future; a world where all the values by which you and I have grown are being challenged. Many of those values already have been overthrown. Some of them will not be reinstated in our time. How are we going to make those values important and vital and exciting to children? Therein, I believe, lies the opportunity of which I am speaking, and the privilege as well.

Our forefathers were individualists in a day when a man couldn't see the smoke from his nearest neighbor's chimney, and when he could, he pulled up stakes and moved along. Things were getting too crowded. He wanted more elbow room. More wing room. And above all he demanded the right to be let alone, that most comprehensive of rights and the right still most highly valued by civilized men. I think I am not blind to the fact that change is a part of the basic nature of all things, that that which doesn't change in one form or another becomes static — dies. Races either go forward, or they begin the long march to extinction. And today, when the whole of America has been welded into one great gregarious community, the particular kind of self-sufficiency which was our forefathers' no longer is possible. Now men must give and take, offer and receive, in a social sense, of themselves. There's not so much elbow room any more. But there's still wing room for anyone's spirit! And I believe that that ideal of personal integrity is our most precious inheritance. It is our genius. It is the thing about us that the European, with his totally different heritage, finds almost impossible to understand, yet it is as much a part of us as this air we breathe, this soil to which the bones of our fathers have returned.

196

How are we going to preserve that ideal of personal integrity for children? Perhaps, as one approach, through the medium of words. I am aware that, in these days of violent action, it may sound futile to talk about the power of mere words. And yet, surely, words are one of the weapons dictators have feared most of all. What better proof of that statement do we need than this — today, in the occupied countries of Europe, the dictators have made bonfires of the books written by the most constructive thinkers, by the wisest philosophers. They have hounded from nation to nation the courageous few who have held out publicly for that ideal of personal integrity. And they have threatened with death the man or woman who dares to listen to the words that come in over the short-waves of the air — those words spoken out of a free heritage by free men. Yet, in spite of these threats, what is the picture brought back to us by those who know the situation inside Europe? It is a picture of men and women shutting themselves into their cellars and garrets, darkening the windows, plugging up the keyholes, risking their lives to listen to those forbidden words of freedom. It appears that the *need* to believe in a man's right to choose a way of life for himself is a rather universal need. It dies hard. But it can die! And it is through this same medium of words that we, you and I, can help to keep that need alive — to keep for children that vision of personal integrity. It is as important as a victory on the field of battle. It is a part of victory. For what will it profit us to win a war if the things we fought for are forgotten?

We hear a great deal about " escapist " literature (even for children) and usually on a note of scorn — implying that any book which doesn't concern itself with immediate social and economic problems is a disgraceful flight from " reality." I believe this to be a false concept. For what can be more *real* than the great themes of literature — those themes by which the human race has climbed? Simple themes! Justice . . . Compassion . . . Integrity . . . Love. . . . The plight of Romeo and Juliet, the wisdom of Portia, the predicament of Macbeth (to choose but a few) have been translated into many tongues and understood by all who listened; because the themes themselves transcend time and changing fashion, and speak to something universal buried deep within the hearts of men.

When children in their books demand above all else a good story, a story where things happen and keep on happening, how are we going to get over to them these other, these intangible things? I can only tell you the way I tried it myself in a book. It is a story about a boy who lived on a small island in the South Pacific, yet who was profoundly afraid of the sea. So before his whole tribe of seafaring, warrior people, he was branded as a coward. He came to realize that the only way he could win his proper place in the tribe as the son of a chief, and win also his own integrity, was to go out to face this thing he feared — to face it and conquer it or else be destroyed by it. Well, he went out to face it. And those of you who have read *Call It Courage,* know what happened to that boy.

When I wrote that story I didn't concern myself with Age Groups or Word Lists, or any of those bugbears of the person striving to do a piece of creative work. I wanted only to tell my story as well as I could and with whatever distinction I could bring to the telling. But when I had finished it I *was* concerned that children themselves might find a concept of spiritual courage much less exciting than a tale of more obvious bravery and action. But I have received literally hundreds of letters from children in every State of this Union, telling me how much *Call It Courage* has meant to them. A fact which, I need scarcely add, has strengthened my deepseated conviction that there is no call for anyone to " write down " to children. Tell your story as well and as honestly as you can. Children will understand it, and they'll ask for more!

All of which brings me back to my starting-point — the great opportunity which is ours today. One of these days the United Nations will win the final battle of this war. And when men start in again at the beginning laboriously to rebuild, what is it that they'll remember? Will it be the deeds of conquerors or tyrants, or even of heroes? I don't think so! They'll remember the words that men have spoken and men have written that proclaim the ideal of freedom which is the inalienable right of all men. They'll remember such inspiring and incorruptible words as our own forefathers wrote into the Constitution of these United States. They'll remember such words as Lincoln spoke in his Second Inaugural Address, with the simple grandeur of those closing lines: "With malice toward none, with charity for all." They'll remember the words of the man who cried out his demand for liberty and gave as his alternative — death. Those are the things that they'll remember.

And so I say I think it is our great privilege—the privilege of all people who work in any way with children — to help to keep alive that vision of freedom, that these children of today may carry it with them into the world of tomorrow: that imperishable dream of the right to live, to work, and to worship, as free men — in peace.

From *The Horn Book* for May, 1943

THE VOICE OF POLISH YOUTH

By Kazimierz Wierzynski

W HAT is the attitude of the young people of Poland in the present war? What are they fighting for? Perhaps the best answers to these questions are to be found in words spoken by these young people themselves, words which were not spoken with the purpose of " making an impression " or even with the intention of consciously describing their attitude, words which are therefore all the more convincing. They were spoken over the Warsaw underground radio during the uprising which broke out there in August last year against the Germans.

As you know, Warsaw fought for sixty-three days. It is hard to imagine a battle inside a city numbering over 1,000,000 inhabitants, without water or electricity, where the population moved from district to district through underground corridors, was forced to eat dogs and cats for food and for two months continued to fight in spite of unceasing bombings and fires which raged day and night. Yet that is what happened. The whole world was terrified to learn of the details of that struggle; the Poles living outside of Poland in free countries trembled with horror. But in answer to words of praise and encouragement which reached the defenders of Warsaw from without, the radio of the underground Polish Army unexpectedly broadcast the poem of an unnamed young Warsaw poet. He expressed in his poem that attitude and hope of Polish youth to which I referred.

" None here weeps in despair," cries the unknown author of a city where hundreds of soldiers and civil population daily lost their lives. "And everyone, men, women, children, is

200

found fighting and bleeding for Poland, for home," continues the poet of the Warsaw barricades, as if the ruins of their individual homes and lives inspired greater love in them for their country. "Though we fight among graves, still our spirits are high," he sang. And he finished his song, "Give us not praise. Give us arms! Let us act!"

This poem gives us a key to the understanding of Polish youth. It is a cry for freedom, freedom at any price, freedom which is more important than life itself, freedom for which they die with a smile on their lips and which has only one purpose: victory.

This ideal may appear too generalized to some; others may not quite understand it. The young American, who lives a life of complete, unthreatened freedom, may find it difficult to realize what it means to lose one's freedom.

Polish youth, born in a free Poland, also lived in freedom, but they well understood what it would mean if their freedom were threatened. For 123 years, when Poland was partitioned between Germany, Russia and Austria, the life and activity of every Pole was directed towards the reëstablishment of Polish independence. It is not possible to forget those 123 years of slavery in a short twenty years of freedom. The blackout which had veiled Poland for over a century was constantly before the eyes of Polish youth — in their history, in their literature, in their own homes and the experience of their parents.

For example, they could not forget that during the partitions in the little town of Wrzesnia, near Poznan, there broke out a strike of Polish children in protest against the Prussian order requiring them to say their prayers and conduct their religious education in the German language, under penalty of heavy flogging. They could not forget how the Germans had forbidden Polish peasants to construct homes on their farms, and how a certain farmer by the name of Drzymala had got around it by buying a cart (something in the nature of an American trailer) and living in it. When he was brought to court he explained that he had not broken the law, since he was living in a cart and a cart was not a house. They could not forget the persecution of young people in Warsaw and in

Wilno whom agents of the Russian Tsar had torn from their homes in the night and sent to compulsory labor in the mines of Siberia or tortured to death in prisons — all because they had founded secret student organizations. They could not forget the three insurrections which broke out during the years of Poland's partition, in which the young people participated actively and in large numbers or the terrible reprisals which followed. They could not forget the gallows which dotted the country or the whole martyrdom of the nation, which earned for Poland the name " unfortunate."

Poland's slavery and persecution lasted many years until at last the change came for which four generations of Poles had struggled. After World War I a new free Polish state was established once again, the 13th point on the famous peace program of President Wilson.

The youth of reborn Poland rejected the " tradition of misfortune " of the earlier generations and began life proud of their freedom and confident in their strength. The former evil days had passed, it would seem, forever. There remained only the memory of their terror and a consequently still more impassioned love of freedom.

Our young people wished to create a modern Poland, to mend the insufficiencies inherited from the years of slavery. They wanted progress and development. Universities and technical schools were established, talents were multiplied among the young architects and engineers, the writers and the artists. Along our tiny seacoast the ambitions of our sailors waxed great and every new Polish ship brought joy to all Poles, but particularly to the young people. Sport had its world-famed stars, especially among our young women, while the sons of mountaineer-folk were among Europe's finest skiers. Our young doctors organized traveling clinics to bring medical care to the countryside. Rural theaters showed a fine development and just before the outbreak of the present war a new literary school of young peasant authors had come into existence.

It is not my intention to describe here a paradise on earth or to claim that our Polish youth were angels in disguise. Polish youth also had their faults and made mistakes, just as youth all

202

over the world; nevertheless, they contributed greatly in many fields of Polish life through their vitality and aroused energy.

That world of enthusiasm, ambition and hope begun in freedom, so different from the old world of misfortune, suddenly shook on its very foundations when bombs fell over Poland on September 1, 1939. At five o'clock in the morning Polish towns and villages began to burn and fall into ruin from explosives dropped from German planes all over Poland. War had begun, an undeclared war. Poland became the Pearl Harbor of Europe.

Our young people realized at once that they were fighting a war for freedom, for that freedom in which they had grown up as the first generation of a free Poland after thirteen decades of slavery. Our young people knew that without that freedom life was nothing, that life would become for them a nightmare terrorizing them as it had their parents, their grandparents, and their great-grandparents.

That is the source of the stubborn and fierce resistance of the Poles. When their country was occupied by the invaders, the young people began a veritable pilgrimage to France and later to England. There they volunteered in the re-formed Polish armies. These young pilgrims often traveled hundreds of miles, and they numbered tens of thousands. Each expedition was a unique experience. In Paris I met the son of an old friend, young Jacek Stryjenski, sixteen years of age, who had traveled alone across many countries with an arm crippled from wounds received during the war in Poland. He immediately volunteered for service in one of the Polish divisions formed in France, underwent an overdue operation on his arm and soon afterwards moved to the front. Another of my acquaintance, the young and universally talented Richard Bychowski, began his journey to the army from another part of the world. He went from Warsaw to Wilno, from Wilno to Sweden, from Sweden across all Russia to Japan and from Japan to Canada, where he enlisted in the Polish Army and was later sent to England as a Polish aviator. He flew many missions over Germany as a bomber navigator, and proved to be an excellent soldier. He died at last a hero's death and when he was buried, not only his rabbi (for he was of Jewish faith) but also the Catholic chaplain stood at his grave.

The longest and most tortuous road to the battle for freedom could not deter the young people of Poland. A Dutchman or a Belgian, if worst came to worst, could try his luck with boat and sail and make his way across the Channel to British shores. The Pole, in order to reach that stronghold of liberty, was forced to traverse at least four or five strange, often enemy countries — Slovakia, Hungary, Jugoslavia, Italy, and later even France, and then, reaching the coast, ask himself, "And now what? " But in spite of all this, the Polish armies, which have been fighting now for five years beyond the boundaries of Poland, have not diminished in size although casualties have been heavy. Indeed, the Polish Air Force and the Polish Navy are larger than they were before the war. The secret of this mathematical riddle lies in the fanatical love of freedom which inspires the young people of my country.

Still further examples of their spirit are revealed in the records of the underground struggle in Poland. There are two spheres of Polish life: the one on the surface created by the enemy and the second, the underground, which resists all orders issued by the occupying authorities. The Germans have closed all Polish universities and secondary schools, but in the underground these institutions flourish. Lectures are given, examinations take place regularly and diplomas are issued. Both professors and students often are put to death for their efforts. Several times this has happened when the Gestapo discovered such an underground school. The Germans have banned Polish newspapers, but the underground prints and distributes about 100 publications, some of them quite specialized, as, for instance, humorous magazines and children's papers. The young people themselves are in charge of distribution.

Life in the underground, too diverse to describe here, belongs primarily to youth. They undertake the most dangerous missions. Young girls most frequently play the part of couriers, smuggling orders from place to place. In Poland there exists a system of underground courts which pass the death sentence upon the German hangmen, and it is the young people who ordinarily volunteer for the work of executing these sentences. Certain of these acts of justice may only be executed in such a way that the executor perishes together with the accused. In Warsaw, for instance, a certain director of prisons was sentenced to death for his bestial cruelty. He proved to be exceptionally well guarded and the sentence could only be executed in a night club where the Gestapo officer often went for amusement after a day of crime. A young student, Jan Kryst, volunteered to do the deed. He knew that he was going, as well, to his own death. It was decided that he should shoot at close range in order to kill only the accused, so as to prove beyond a doubt that the hand of justice always reaches even the most carefully guarded. Kryst got into the night club, worked his way up to the table where the Gestapo officer was sitting, fired several well-aimed shots at him and then threw down some pamphlets explaining the reason for his deed. He had been given a guard to shield his retreat, but unfortunately, in spite of their assistance he was unable to get out alive.

During the last Warsaw uprising in August and September of 1944, Poland's young people took their place on the battle front, girls and boys alike. The underground radio in a broadcast on August the 18th stated that women comprised one-eighth of the underground army. They served as nurses and as *liaison* officers, they directed the field kitchens and fought in the ranks. The underground radio on August 19th broadcast the news that a fourteen-year-old girl destroyed two German tanks with grenades. On August 20th the radio reported that a twelve-year-old boy destroyed a German tank of the " Tiger " class, killing its crew; his comrades-in-arms have named the little soldier " Tiger Hank — *Henio-Tygrys.*"

These few details speak for themselves. They ably describe the part which the young people of Poland are playing in the war.

Polish youth have gone into this war to defend their freedom, the most priceless acquisition of man, and are confident that they will achieve their freedom in the war. United in face of the enemy without regard to station, origin or religion, they form today a united front, and place above all else the dignity of man and his rights. They confirm this not by words expressed in declarations or programs, but in their life-and-death struggle on the barricades. They wish to live in the future according to the same principles for which they are dying today.

The voice of the poet who spoke to the world from the depths of the Warsaw ruins is indeed the voice of Polish youth. " None here weeps in despair "— thus cry thousands of young Poles to all the free people of the world, assuring them that they will continue the struggle in spite of incalculable losses. " Give us not praise. Give us arms! Let us act! "

From *The Horn Book* for March, 1945

INCIDENT AT TEA TIME

By Grace Allen Hogarth

MACARONI and cheese: yes, in the oven. Baked apples, ditto. Spinach, boiling," I said over to myself as I looked at the clock and realized that it was nearly time for the children to come home from school. Even after six months back in London I never could manage to make my subconscious check over my responsibilities as cook, simple as they were. I had been too long at ease in America. I was thinking of this, and wondering whether or not the macaroni would be done in time, when I heard what sounded like a stampede of elephants at the back door and knew that David had arrived.

" Here's a note from the school," he said, as he burst into the kitchen, " and I don't want to wash my hands yet because I've got some things in my pockets I want to sort out first."

I made an effort to push him along and absent-mindedly took the note, wondering whether I had failed to put loops for hanging on coats or left name tapes off mittens. But this message had a different look. It was mimeographed, and I noticed that my name was written in pencil. This time, whatever the rebuke, I was to share it with the other mothers.

" Dear Mrs. Hogarth," I read, " you have doubtless heard of the tragic death on Wednesday of one of our pupils, John Abbot, at the incident in Ludlow Gardens. I am sending a wreath on behalf of John's schoolfellows, and you may care to give a contribution towards it — not more than one shilling, please.
" Yours sincerely,
" ————, Principal."

I read this over twice, not believing, and gasped, I expect, for I had not heard this news. David, who had taken advantage of my preoccupation to turn out his pockets, asked me what was the matter. I tried to tell him simply and without emotion that John had been killed.

" How? " he asked at once, interested.

" In an accident," I said, weakly.

" Oh," he said, apparently satisfied with my answer. " I expect he got run over. It's a good thing. He knocked me down last week."

I managed to be silent, even almost to envy his six-and-a-half-year-old complacence. I sent him off upstairs.

Two minutes later Caroline's sniffles announced her arrival. " David left me behind again," she wailed.

Hearing her, the culprit charged headlong down the stairs. " Caroline," he shrieked, " John's been killed in an accident."

" Oh," she said, grievance forgotten, " then I'll have to ask someone else to my birthday party," and then, underlining each word, " when I'm five years old next week."

For them the incident was closed. While they ate their macaroni and did sums across the kitchen table, my mind went back to that Wednesday.

We had just sat down to tea, as we were now, the three of us. David, leaning his elbow on the table, was saying, as he always did to preface each enormous meal, " I don't much like this, do you, Caroline? " I had learned that this was just by way of conversation and was about to turn his thoughts from the unsatisfactory jam onto what we would do between tea and bedtime, when it came — a blinding flash, a convulsion of the earth, and, in half a second, the deafening double report we had come to recognize as V-2's trademark. I waited for the long rumble — the sound of the rocket's fall which always came after the explosion of arrival — but it did not come. Then I knew terror. Talk in queues at the butcher's, bits of gossip from the char lady, hints from the radio and newspapers, pieced together, had warned us that those near a direct hit did not hear the roll of descent. All the open doors in the house banged shut; the windows rattled. Then silence, broken only by the sound of David's steady munching.

"What was that? " he asked, calmly enough. Caroline looked mildly interested.

"Oh," I said, lying, and trying to hide the shaking hand that poured my tea, "I expect it was a gun or a doodlebug." And even as I said it, I was conscious that in the light of this newer menace, I was turning last summer's lion into this winter's kitten. Satisfied, the children ploughed on through their tea, unaware of my fear, unmoved and incurious at the sound of cries outside, of people running, and cars dashing past at full speed.

At Ludlow Gardens, three-quarters of a mile away, John Abbot had been at tea, just as we had been. I knew this now as I struggled with my macaroni. It didn't bear thinking of, and yet it was impossible not to think. Wednesday's tea for David and Caroline had gone peacefully on to its end. Sums had been made and the message of health on the cod-liver oil bottle had been spelled out, as usual, letter by letter, and word by word. From the kitchen window I had watched, first the column of black smoke against the grey sky, and then, as night came on, the searchlights set for the rescue parties.

Now, weeks later, I cannot lose the memory of those two family meals, so like all the others, and so different. Someone has said that it was necessary to bear this last "terror by night and destruction wasting at noonday" in order fully to realize that annihilation is possible. The realization should be a preventive of future wars. But one wonders whether in their turn the high-explosive bomb, the incendiary and the V-1 have not meant as much to those who have known them. Whether, indeed, these civilian "weapons of war" have proved anything to any but those who have felt their dragon breath and have known fear strong enough to remember.

From *The Horn Book* for May, 1945

YOUNG PEOPLE IN A WORLD
AT WAR

By Margaret C. Scoggin

WHAT young people think of the war and its problems is a matter of profound importance to all of us. To discover their attitudes we could do worse than watch the books they read and listen to their comments. My observations are based upon such watching and listening over a period of two years in a library for young people.

War has come close to young people in many ways. We have told them, and they realize, this is a young man's war. The boys have seen their friends and contemporaries scattered to the corners of the earth where they expect soon to follow. The girls are aware of shrinking social circles and are faced at an early age with questions of work and marriage. This closeness of war gives them an alertness, a sensitivity to human problems, an awareness of their part in the crisis, and some feeling of tension and insecurity. And yet, despite the obvious surface effects of the times, young people's temperaments are still sanguine, their predominant attitude is one of calm, and their reading interests are as wide and as varied as ever.

Boys have always had a professional interest in vocational possibilities. Since they look now to the armed forces for their immediate careers, they ask for guides to qualifications and duties in the various branches of the services and for data on ships, aeroplanes and weapons. Books which give step-by-step training are popular because they are practically blueprints of what the boys themselves are soon to experience; their interest in them is as natural as their interest in college catalogues and career guides in normal times.

210

Since the Wright Brothers flew the first plane at Kittyhawk, aviation has been of prime interest to boys. The war which has compressed decades of plane development into a space of months seems also to have quickened these youngsters' grasp of the complicated science of flying. Books on combat fighting, navigation, meteorology, engine design and performance, and aerodynamics may seem strong meat for fourteen and fifteen-year-olds, but it *is* their meat. Said one fourteen-year-old after looking judicially at several books on aerodynamics, " But these are too elementary."

This precociousness extends to interest in, and grasp of, new applications of radio, chemistry, photography, electricity. So far as technological war and the future technological world are concerned, the young are ready. However, although these scientific interests are now directed toward wartime applications, war did not originate them. The boy who reads about chemical warfare today read books on chemical experiments yesterday and will just as happily read about industrial chemistry tomorrow.

Most popular of all war books are those which recount the daring of men in conflict. This, again, is not a new interest, for the lives of men who meet danger have always been popular reading. The fighter pilot matching his wits, his skill and his plane against a wily foe, the submarine commander coolly dodging depth charges, the battered but indomitable marines capturing inch after inch of steaming jungle may differ in uniforms and weapons from the knights at Roncesvalles, the men at Thermopylae, and the shivering hungry soldiers at Valley Forge, but the quality of their courage is the same.

But what of young people's attitudes toward the more subtle problems of our time —democracy, isolationism, international relations, the post-war world?

Young people do not think abstractly and they are little interested in blueprints of tomorrow's world. They are, however, well aware of the problem of democracy in human terms. All of them know that injustice is often meted out to boys and girls of other races and colors. There is indeed prejudice among our youngsters, but more of them than you might think are eager to right this injustice. Such books as *All-*

American and *Keystone Kids* by John Tunis put the specific problems of racial prejudice and intolerance in terms young people can understand. Here is what a thirteen-year-old boy wrote about *All-American:*

This is a very fine book for boys. It shows that even in such a great Democracy as the United States, people are still handicapped by color, race, or creed. Ned LeRoy, a colored boy who plays left-end for the high school team, wins a game single-handed but cannot attend the intersectional game because he is colored. Meyer Goldman wants to be a doctor but is afraid he won't succeed because he is Jewish.

Another boy says of it:

This book clearly shows the racial prejudice in this country. It combines sport with Americanism and brings out the fact that all men are equal regardless of race or creed. I would say to my friends, read it and you will see the idea we are fighting for today.

There is idealism here, idealism of the very best kind — a deep belief in democracy not as something vague or abstract but as equal opportunity for all people and an equally firm belief that we are fighting for that equality.

There are no isolationists among the young. They do not have to acquire a world outlook; they have grown up with it. The speed of the aeroplane is matter-of-fact to them and they take for granted the nearness of all continents. Their world outlook does not express itself in an interest in international and national planning. They have, rather, a genuine curiosity about other peoples. They read the books which show these peoples as human beings and center attention upon everyday life. Perhaps they are wise. No scholarly volume on Mexico could arouse the genuine understanding one girl got from Gertrude Diamant's *Days of Ofelia:*

This is a story of a normal everyday Mexican family. Till I read this book I can honestly say I never really thought of these people who live on our border but seem so far away. . . . As I read further and further, I was first amused, then interested, and finally completely absorbed. . . . Any one to whom Mexico is just a name would have a different idea after reading this.

China is real to boys and girls in the persons of understandable Chinese. Of Pearl Buck's *Good Earth* a boy wrote:

One of the finest books ever written. It is just as life-like as a typical Chinese family.

Of *Dragon Seed*, a girl said:

I learned a lot about the way the Chinese live. A very sad book but a very human one. I would tell my friends to read it and see how a courageous Chinese family struggled through the Japanese invasion.

And note the solicitude of the older toward the younger young person in this review:

Dragon Seed is a book I would not recommend to very young people. It is written in a very strong descriptive language and some of the things Miss Buck describes are not for the eyes of the very young. However, I heartily recommend it to those who are interested in China and her struggles, for I myself enjoyed it very much.

Perhaps this genuine warm interest in individuals of all races is part of the American gift. Americans have always been great travelers; as travelers they have been friendly, humanly curious and alert. At any rate, our young people like such personal accounts as Carl Glick's ingratiating stories of his Chinese acquaintances (*Three Times I Bow*), Maurice Hindus' report on the plain people of Russia (*Mother Russia*), Thomas Ybarra's recollections of a Latin-American family (*Young Man of Caracas*) and Sigrid Undset's charming reminiscences (*Happy Times in Norway*). Their interest embraces also the enemy and they read with understanding Nora Waln's *Reaching for the Stars*, which says the best that can be said for Germany, and Sugimoto's *Daughter of the Samurai*, the autobiography of a very human Japanese girl.

Though young people are willing to listen to every one's side, they are shrewd critics for all their sympathy. Here is a fifteen-year-old's remark about K. Shridharani's *Warning to the West*:

An informative book but with many shortcomings. The author takes a 100 per cent anti-British stand. He refuses to admit the English have ever helped India. . . . By this very one-sidedness, he almost makes you take the British point of view.

Young people understand the tragedy of countries overrun by the Nazis and they see the threat to us, but they do not always agree about the books they read. Age, temperament and

213

background give the spice of variety. Says one boy of Stein-beck's *The Moon Is Down:*

> The story about what would happen to a town if it were invaded by Nazis. It shows how the fifth column works. . . . I enjoyed it immediately upon reading the first page because of the simple yet direct way in which it was written. It's a good book for us to read because it shows us how the Nazis work but also how the invaded people kept their courage.

But another disagrees:

> I found this novel below par for two reasons. . . . First, the events that occur . . . are not new and exciting but are of the type one finds every day in his newspaper. Secondly, the language the author uses is dull for the simple reason we hear it so often. The dialogue and description follow the pattern of war propaganda. Much to my disappointment, John Steinbeck did not make this book as interesting as he did his *Grapes of Wrath* and his *Of Mice and Men.*

Incidentally, these books of countries and peoples upset by war are often strong and frank portrayals of cruelty and bru-tality. Sometimes worried adults ask whether young people should be exposed to such horrors. The only answer is, " Better let them read truthful accounts which are written with sin-cerity, courage, and restraint than suddenly meet the horrors upon the battlefield or in a bombed street." So long as they keep their own balance and perspective, young people will not be upset by the truth in current books any more than they have been harmed by the truth in classics of the past. Even more reassuring, perhaps, is the fact that those who are too young or immature for a book will probably skim through it untouched.

Young people are interested in the problems of human beings, in life and death and love and religion — but these interests have not originated with the war. One boy found in Douglas' *The Robe* a strengthening of his faith:

> For one who is in doubt about the reality of religion, let him read *The Robe.* . . . It revived the good in me and made me want to learn more about man in relation to God.

Despite the inevitable interest in professional books on war tools and current war experiences, there is reassuring continuity and variety in young people's reading. . . . They are still leading normal lives for the most part and are still reading widely. So far they have not felt the full impact of war as have the young people of Europe and Asia. So far they have been untouched by the bitterness and pessimism that swept over the young people of the last war. What will happen as the war goes on? This question is the challenge to us who watch young people and hope for them. . . .

They *are* idealistic, hopeful, and impressionable. We see their idealism in their wholehearted acceptance of the cause of democracy. But they are all the more susceptible to disillusionment. They need the stability that comes from realization that man's struggles, problems, ideals, laughter, courage, and triumphs have persisted through the ages. This contact with the ideals of other ages is of vast importance. "Man must have memory before he can have aspiration." We must see that young people get — along with the practical books of the times — the great books and the good books of humor, beauty, imagination, and courage. So shall we help them recognize enduring values which transcend momentary crises; so we shall give them stability.

Young people need security. What kind of security can we give them? Pearl Buck has answered that question:

The security, then, which we must somehow give [them] is not the security of house and garden, of home and community, of all the settled ways of peace. It is not safe to let them believe in such security, for it no longer exists. But there is a security deeper and bottom true. It is the security of the soul taught to believe in the worth of mankind, to the last individual, and so in its own worth.[1]

---

[1] Buck, Pearl S. *What America Means to Me,* " Children and the World," John Day, 1943. p. 150.

From *The Horn Book* for November, 1943

1959 COMMENT

As I look back over the post-war years, I note that young people have not succumbed to bitterness and disillusionment. In spite of " juvenile delinquency " and the " beat generation ", teen agers are reading more than ever. They still like suspense, adventure, humor, hobbies, science, biographies of daring and courageous people. They are still more interested in their contemporaries throughout the world than in the older generations in their own countries. They expect to conquer space. They face the future fresh, energetic, and optimistic.

MARGARET C. SCOGGIN

Part VII

Small Children and Books

SMALL CHILDREN AND BOOKS

By Alice Dalgliesh

~~~~~~

EVERY day of the school week I share books with four-
and five-year-old children. Every day they make their
own choices and come to me with favorite books
tucked under their arms. So violent are the arguments over
what is to be read that sometimes we have to make a " waiting list " or " count out." Naturally, the children have taught
me a good deal about their likes and dislikes. Under such circumstances one loses most (not all!) prejudices and learns
to put aside even the most cherished notions about books.
I was brought up on Kate Greenaway, but it doesn't hurt in
the least to find that her books are never among the *request*
readings. Four- and five-year-olds are very contemporary-
minded. Recognizing this, many of our " young " booklists
might well be taken out of camphor and thoroughly reno-
vated. We should really have two types of booklist, one for
the average child and one for the child with unusual apprecia-
tions.

What are the books that my children choose again and
again? *Peter Rabbit, Little Black Sambo, Karl's Wooden
Horse, Millions of Cats, Herbert the Lion, The Little Wooden
Farmer* (probably my influence!), the *Snipp Snapp Snurr*
books, the *Angus* books, *The Greedy Goat, Clever Bill,* and
others equally simple and child-like. It is no use saying that
a book is " artistic " or " unusual "; if it hasn't a well-written
childlike story *it won't live.* Many of our most elaborate picture books pass quietly on for this very reason. Good pictures
do not carry a poor story very far. If there is one outstanding
thing that our picture books need it is improvement in *text.*

If a book is to be a favorite with small children it must pass some severe tests. First of all, the content must be child-like and must concern itself with things in which children are really interested. Children like familiar things. A picture book which strains to be bizarre or " different," which wraps its story in too thick a fog of " atmosphere " is not for little children. I can see why five-year-olds should be vitally concerned with the doings of Angus, with the adventures of Peter Rabbit, with the naughtiness of the Greedy Goat, but I certainly can't see why they should be much concerned with the love affairs of a Spanish cockroach. And they are not!

Then, if a book is to be a favorite, it must also pass the test of being read aloud over and over. All those who make books for small children should read them aloud to a number of children to see if they have that clarity and smoothness that make for good reading aloud. When a book becomes a favorite, children make it their own by memorizing it partly or entirely, so picture-story books should be simple and clear enough to make this possible. This does not mean that colorful words should be omitted; children love to try the flavor of a new word. There is, however, a certain way of writing, a certain clear simplicity of phrase, a rhythm that makes books easy to read aloud and easy to remember. We find this easy, smooth-flowing writing in *Millions of Cats* and in *Little Black Sambo*. Almost any day I am likely to find four-year-old Georgiana, who cannot really read a word, with a group gathered around her while she " reads " fluently and with confidence.

> " ' If we only had a cat,' sighed the very old woman.
> " 'A cat? ' asked the very old man.
> " ' Yes, a sweet little fluffy cat,' said the very old woman.
> " ' I will get you a cat, my dear,' said the very old man."

It slips along so easily! There are not so very many books that do this. Too many of our picture-story books have carelessly written, wandering texts. Many foreign picture books suffer in translation. Elsa Beskow's books are examples of this, with *Pelle's New Suit* as an exception.

Our picture books also need to be more interesting, to make better use of surprise and suspense. *Peter Rabbit* and *Little Black Sambo* have lived through the years because they are real adventure stories. Will Little Black Sambo lose *all* his fine clothes? Will Peter ever get out of Mr. McGregor's garden? It is hard for us to realize that the suspense *holds* even in the twentieth reading. A supersensitive little girl asked me not to read *Angus Lost* " because he may not get home." " But you *know* he gets home," I said unintelligently. " I've read it to you several times." "Well," she said, " you never can tell. *Some day he might not get home!* " Some time Little Black Sambo might be eaten by a tiger. Who can tell? Most children enjoy the uncertainty. We do not need " nursery mysteries," but we do need a little wholesome excitement once in a while.

Another great need is for more books of real childlike humor. Books that children consider " funny " are few and far between. Their humor is so crude and so physical that it is hard for us to approximate it. It takes real courage to read Hugh Lofting's *Story of Mrs. Tubbs* aloud to a group of six-year-old children, so great is the hilarity over " Beefsteak-and-Onions " ! And some teachers are afraid of hilarity, or of any mob enthusiasm. One teacher told me that she had put *Angus and the Ducks* away in a cupboard because she was afraid to read it to her group of forty children. What was her fear? Why, the chorus of " Quacks " and " Woofs " that followed when the story became familiar, the laughter that came each time the ducks nipped Angus' tail!

Perhaps the weakest of our younger children's books are those that are intended to convey information. Most of them suffer from being deadly dull. It seems to me that someone is always pointing out to me some particularly ineffectual book of information with the caustic remark, " I suppose *you* like that because you are a teacher." As a matter of fact, being a teacher and using the book with children probably helps me to realize its failings. There is no reason why informative books should not be as attractive and as lively as other books. Some of those written for older children are far superior to the younger ones. I wonder why we have no American books that are like *Pelle's New Suit*, a charming book so full of pleasant gardens and flowery meadows that one scarcely suspects it of being " the story of wool." Little children are most eager to hear about trains and boats and airplanes and all the exciting events of this modern world. But it is very sad when stories are stuffed so full of information that they bulge obviously. Four- and five-year-olds prefer the thrill of an imaginary ride on an engine, with maybe a *little* information tucked in deftly here and there, to being told in cold print that an engine has so many wheels on each side. There is a great deal of room for experimentation in this field; at present there are no informative books for young children that are entirely satisfactory.

We are finding out a good deal about the interests of younger children. The next few years will probably bring a number of experimental books. The best thing that could happen to our picture-story books is that none of them should be reviewed until they have been tried with children. No sincere experiment should be condemned without trial simply because the book does not seem to measure up to certain preconceived adult standards. Some of our most popular children's books have had a slow and difficult start, but have found their way into the booklists because the children themselves have forced this recognition. Some of the books that have been on the booklists for many years might well make way for newcomers that are more childlike and more readable. There should be nothing static about books for the youngest children.

From *The Horn Book* for August, 1933

1959 COMMENT

This article was written a good many years ago when I was a teacher. Since then there have been many more books for young children, great changes in books, and a few changes in my point of view. However, the article is still valuable because it grew out of daily experience with children.

I'm amused at the comment on *Perez and Martina* (the love affairs of a Spanish cockroach) because last year I was the editor on Mary Little's *Ricardo and the Puppets*, which dealt with a puppet show based on *Perez and Martina*, a book that has lived a good many years in spite of me! However, it still wouldn't be my first choice for five-year-old children.

We *have* more amusing books now, some of them child-like, some adult in their humor, some leaning *too* far toward the cartoon. We have *many* more informative books, some charming, imaginative, rhythmic, others still " deadly dull."

Picture books have become more experimental, sometimes successfully so, sometimes not. I'd still hold fast to the rule that for young children a picture book *must* communicate. A young child " reads the pictures."

ALICE DALGLIESH

A CANADIAN TRIBUTE
TO LESLIE BROOKE

By Lillian H. Smith

LITTLE children's first reaction to pictures is always a literary one. They expect a picture to tell a story and to take the place of the words they cannot read. This ability for putting into pictures all that words imply is perfectly exemplified by Leslie Brooke and is immediately, if unconsciously, recognized by very little children, but because this artist addresses himself to people so new in the world that they can give no reason for the faith that is in them, they merely turn to his pictures as they would to the sun, less happy with any others. A three-year-old was shown a profusely illustrated Mother Goose at the house of a friend and when the book was opened before her, she pointed to a picture. " Who's 'at? " " That's Wee Willie Winkie." " No! " " But it *is*." " No! " repeated the three-year-old, "Wee Willie Winkie's in my *Ring o' Roses* at home."

When I ask myself what is this *living* quality in these classics of the nursery, timeless and ageless in their power to charm, my thoughts fly to Caldecott and Leslie Brooke. With both these men their lasting value is in the understanding that informs their pictorial interpretation of life in a topsy-turvy world when animals and inanimate objects assume the foibles of the human race. It is this understanding that gives strength to the artist's ideas expressed so perfectly picture by picture in " The frog he would a-wooing go " or in *Johnny Crow's Garden*. When Caldecott died, some one said, " The children will laugh less now," but children's laughter has always kept his books alive as it will those of Leslie Brooke.

224

Children are always attracted by the warmth and colour of Leslie Brooke's pictures but they are even more captivated by their droll humour. His line drawings in black and white are pored over as much as the coloured ones because of their action and their laughter-making situations, pictured in simple familiar detail. To the adult connoisseur his slightest line can beautify the page.

All Leslie Brooke's animals (and no one else draws pigs and bears so well) are carefully and humorously observed as well as decoratively rendered, and he never forgets for a moment the children's fondness for them. He had formed the habit of making his pictures under the eyes of his own children, and in a letter written after they were grown he explains how he had come to need the criticism and collaboration of a small child. " Now-a-days," he wrote, " I am not in constant touch with any small people, and it is almost ridiculous how much, when drawing for them, one misses the corroboration, as it were, of the rightness of one's half-formed idea, and still more the look of boredom which warned me when I was going off the line." That he heeded the warning and did not go " off the line " is seen in his ability to picture all sorts and degrees of emotion—jaunty self-confidence, bewilderment, anticipation or dejection. More than once children have been heard to say of " the beaver " who " was afraid he had a fever," " Oh, look how sick he feels! "

Year after year when dropping chestnuts and whirling maple leaves bring back the picture-book hour to the children's libraries, it is usually " Johnny Crow " who first appears, for as you turn the pages and show the pictures the jolly chant " in Johnny Crow's garden " that rises so spontaneously to the lips of boys and girls brings back into the room the fun and laughter so necessary for a happy winter's work. Indeed a library without " Johnny Crow " would seem sad and lonely like Hamelin Town after the worthy burghers lost their children for the sake of a thousand guilders.

In these days, so dark and fretted with care, we can ill spare for our children the jovial and kindly humour of Leslie Brooke. We can ill spare his light-hearted enjoyment of the animals and his sunny landscapes where the trees are always in blossom and daffodils, delphiniums and foxgloves scatter their fragrance around. It is true that without Leslie Brooke we would still have *The Three Bears,* but we would no longer see Father Bear smiling so benignly through his spectacles and no longer know that the Little Wee Small Bear had so impeccably chosen " Tom Bruin's Schooldays " for his bedside book. " It is the first time the Three Bears have looked like a family " was one child's comment as she gazed at the pictures. And what other pictures than Leslie Brooke's of *The Three Little Pigs* could convey the affable self-confident air of the little pigs as they set out into the world, and the final victory over the wolf of the third Little Pig who not only ate him but used his skin as a cosy hearthrug so that he could warm his hooves on the back of his ancient enemy?

A few weeks ago a group of children were playing " Here we go round the mulberry bush " and " Here stands a blue-bird." Among them was Joe, a small refugee from middle Europe. After the games, Leslie Brooke's *Three Little Pigs* was taken down from the shelf and the story told. Solemn little Joe came up and looked at the pictures. He had been miserable all morning. He wasn't a successful bluebird and now he didn't understand the story. He looked at the pig, a forlorn little outsider. The pig, successful and English, looked back at Joe. Joe smiled, looked again and laughed aloud.

There are probably no books that useful grown-ups are called upon to read aloud as often as those of Leslie Brooke. Little Pamela who peeks over the edge of the desk to say " Here's *Johnny Crow* — six times I have taken him home. Eighty times my daddy has read him " gives some hint of the endurance of parents in the cause of literature. Leslie Brooke, doubtless, had the resuscitation of tired daddies in mind when he placed on the cottage wall of the Three Bears the subtle motto: " Thyme is honey. Save it," and when he placed the morning paper, " The Bear Truth," on the breakfast table where Goldilocks tasted the Bear's porridge, and when he buried Mr. Toad of Albury Heath deep in the pages of his favourite tabloid, " The Weekly Croak." And surely it is for the enlightenment of the old rather than the edification of the young that the Tailor's Wife finally locates the brandy bottle in the lower workings of the great hall clock!

Leslie Brooke's humour stands with that of Tenniel and Lear and Mr. Punch. His country gardens of blossoming trees and perennial borders, low stone walls and trimmed hedges, link him with Kate Greenaway and Caldecott. His kindly yeoman folk, the jovial innkeeper, the parson, the sexton and the good-natured village simpleton are akin to Hardy's rustics making merry on the Heath.

Today even the old nursery rhyme

> Half-pence and farthings
> Say the bells of St. Martin's

> Oranges and lemons
> Say the bells of St. Clement's

sounds sad and mournful because we who are grown know that now all the bells of England are silent and many are broken, and I am afraid that the fairies that Leslie Brooke saw and painted as they gracefully danced to the tunes of the bells on the old grey roofs of London, must be gone.

But all who share with Leslie Brooke his English heritage, know that once more the children will sing

> Gay go up, and gay go down
> To ring the bells of London Town.

I hope " Johnny Crow " will hear the bells as he struts the paths of a sunlit garden.

From *The Horn Book* for May, 1941

BEATRIX POTTER AND HER
NURSERY CLASSICS

By Bertha Mahony Miller

TO Americans, the sufferings and the courage of England have epitomized the suffering and courage of the Spanish Loyalists, the Finns, the Chinese and the Greeks, and have brought the war close to us. They have brought it into our imaginations. Already people in America begin to raise their lives to a higher level under the stimulus of England. What is happening has made us turn with a new sense of appreciation and treasure to beloved books out of England. The places in these books have become doubly precious. What a magical wonder that they remain ours forever — if somewhere, somehow, the books can be preserved.

For myself I have been living with the books of Beatrix Potter among others. There is the small seaport town of Devonshire, as it appears with some of the artist's finest pen-and-ink drawings in *Little Pig Robinson*. There is the old town of Gloucester in the county of the same name, with its memorable drawings of streets and ancient buildings in *The Tailor of Gloucester*, and there is the beautiful region of the English Lakes in the twenty-two little Potter books; that region she has loved and the natural beauty of which she has worked hard to have preserved through the National Trust. It does not matter whether it is the country about Derwentwater, as in some of the earlier volumes, or the region near Windermere, as in later ones, we have it in all its lovely phases, for ourselves and our children, in the books.

No better fare will young parents find for their children than these volumes. Fanciful and humorous though they are, they contribute to the understanding of little children and

228

stimulate early and all unconsciously an interest in the child's own environment; for the characters, their joys, adventures and sorrows all center in their homes, the village and the country round about. They express, too, what is so common throughout folk literature, that old understanding among the so-called "dumb animals," their instinctive helpfulness and wisdom.

Once I stayed for a short time in a tiny village at the southern end of Derwentwater, the home of that gay and irrepressible, saucy character, Squirrel Nutkin. There and thereabouts, I saw the mountains as they are pictured in *Mrs. Tiggywinkle*. The author's own home, Castle Cottage, is drawn, I feel sure, on page 33 of *Pigling Bland*. All the action of *Tom Kitten* and *The Roly Poly Pudding* takes place in the author's own Hilltop Farm. Rooms are shown in both books exactly as they are. Not far from Hilltop Farm is the store from which Ginger and Pickles' shop was drawn.

Beatrix Potter's books are picture-story books, with the picture an integral part of the whole, and perfectly placed. There is a drawing in color reproduced from water colors for every page of text. However interesting to grown-ups backgrounds and details may be, each picture is thoroughly satisfying to the child for its close presentation of the story. *Peter Rabbit* and *Benjamin Bunny* are sometimes enjoyed by children as young as two. The young doctor in our town read *Peter Rabbit* over and over again to his little girl in the three months before she was two. Just the other day a lad of fourteen brought to his mother his childhood copy of *Jeremy Fisher* to be cleaned and mended, since he wanted it always to remain among his books. His mother told me it had been his first favorite. His laughter would begin just *ahead* of the place where Mr. Jeremy's galoshes were to be mentioned. The word "mackintosh" pleased him, but the word "galoshes" tickled him and his mirth was side-splitting when the trout swallowed them. The first four grades in the two schools of our town listen with delight each Christmas season to *The Tailor of Gloucester*. After looking at the pictures with the storyteller, they depart murmuring

"No more twist! No more twist! No more twist!"

These books are genuine classics because they have been written out of an environment known and loved, and to which they are true. They live for children because they are of those things which have given their author and illustrator infinite joy. There is a convincing matter-of-factness in their telling. Perhaps this is because so much in them is real. The places are real whether indoors or out. The furniture is real and always good. The cups and saucers, bowls, pitchers and plates are real, and lovely, too. The creatures are real. All have been passed through the imagination of Beatrix Potter in mysterious combination with things long remembered. Happily her imagination is thoroughly infused with humor. She has a genius, too, for knowing what will please very little children. The stories are not wishy-washy. There is plenty of nature and human nature in them and the salty commonsense that springs from the earth and life on a farm.

For nearly forty years Beatrix Potter's little books have been providing youngest children with volumes charming on three counts — story, drawings and style of book. Like all genuine artists, she has spared no pains either in writing or drawing. Some years ago she wrote us that her usual way of working was to scribble, and cut out, and write it again and again. "And read the Bible (un-revised version and Old Testament)" if she felt her "style needed chastening." She also wrote then that many of the dialect words of the Bible and Shakespeare — and the forcible direct language — are still in use in the rural part of Lancashire. Her own books partake of these things.

It is from Lancashire that Beatrix Potter springs. Naturally much of the folklore of her home county is in her books. She has said that she is descended from generations of yeomen and weavers; obstinate, hard-headed, *matter-of-fact* folk. She has also said that it was not the Lake District at all that inspired her to write children's books but mainly three things:—
1. The matter-of-fact ancestry. 2. The accidental circumstance of having spent a good deal of her childhood in the Highlands of Scotland, with a Highland nurse girl and a firm belief in witches, fairies and the creed of the terrible John Calvin. (" The creed rubbed off, but the fairies remained.")

230

3. A peculiarly precocious and tenacious memory. (She has been laughed at for what she says she can remember quite plainly from one and two years old; not only facts like learning to walk, but places and sentiments —the way things impressed a very young child.)

Beatrix Potter was born July 28, 1866. Sometime in the early 1900's she bought a home in the Lake District at Sawrey, near Ambleside in Westmorland. This place grew gradually into a large sheep farm. At forty-seven she married happily Mr. William Heelis, a solicitor.

A naturalist friend who has visited Mrs. Heelis tells me that he saw in her portfolios many exquisite drawings, accurate as well as beautiful, of mushrooms, toadstools, mosses, lichens, fungi.* Much of this work had been done from looking through a microscope, a great strain upon eyes. From her letters I have come to know of Mrs. Heelis's great interest in old cottages, old furniture, china and silver. It is only from a recent letter, however, that I have discovered how real an authority she is on old English furniture, especially oak. I am quoting a short paragraph from this letter because it shows the same vigorous interest and originality in the field of furniture as in other directions. The hand-written pages of it are beautiful with pencil drawings of ancient chests and chairs and details of carving, showing in one the round Norman arch and the pomegranate (" traditionally the symbol of Catherine of Aragon ") on a 17th century chest. I wish there was space to reproduce a page of it.

I have a theory (only my own) that the craftsmen who carved our designs were imitating the runic interlacing. It would be too much to say that their patterns were developed from the Scandinavian because there is a complete gap between the early civilization of High Furness and the return of prosperity after the Union. Everything was swept away by the Border Wars and by the Scottish free-booters' burnings. I do not claim that the patterns are traditional; but I do think some one of the old joiners and carvers must have been familiar with such patterns as those on the Gosfirth Cross. Our figure of ∞ when elaborated is not a heart (as shown in designs in Lockwood's *History of Colonial Furniture in America*), it is twists ⋈ and in one of the panels of a bedstead in a neighboring house there is " the Worm Misgurn " clear enough.

231

The letter closes with report of a bombing eight miles away caused by the lantern of a war-forgetting farmer going out to attend a calving cow. That letter and another received earlier speak of the difficulty of doing steady directed work under the war pre-occupation. " Only the active works that must be done " are easy, and " the hobbies like furniture and old china, which are in the sense of that tiresome new term ' escape.' " The following excerpts give evidence of the relief her hobbies provide.

One thing is certain, *I* shall not run far. I will retire into the nearest wood — the cellar of course for bombs; but it is one in a million risk. If there is invasion, I am afraid villages near the landings will be burnt. I look wistfully at my fine old furniture. I have a wonderful old bedstead too heavy to move in a hurry. Nevertheless I went to a sale at Coniston the other day and bought three chests and a coffin stool. Two of my chests are thin and long, like deed boxes. They might come in convenient in the wood for holding things, dry and solid.

I do love old furniture and old china — especially earthenware. I got a Bristol punch bowl, early eighteenth century, in the sale; it has written in the bottom " Fill every man his glass." It has been repaired, but it gives me pleasure; decorated in the Chinese style, in cobalt and manganese.

You tell me you find it difficult to concentrate so you took refuge in *Pig Robinson*. Well — he sailed away and away and found peace; but we will struggle on and find peace — some day — at home.

The Fairy Caravan — I don't know how many times I have read it since its publication in 1929. In the summer of 1939 I read it aloud to my granddaughter then aged seven. What fun we had! Most of the reading was done in the garden. That seemed just right, too. The text seemed fairly to flow off the reader's tongue in its musical charm and simplicity. As we advanced, the fear began to be felt that it would be too soon ended.

" Oh, we still have a lot to read, haven't we? I can't bear to have it end! "

The book seems to embody the wellspring out of which all Beatrix Potter's writing has sprung. " Through many changing seasons these tales have walked and talked with me," she writes in the Preface.

The Fairy Caravan is the story of a miniature circus —

William and Alexander's Travelling Circus. It is truly fairy, for the members all carry fernseed and are not only tiny but invisible to humans. William is Pony Billy who draws the Caravan and is the mainstay of the outfit. Alexander is Sandy, a white Highland terrier, and able assistant to Pony Billy. Paddy Pig pulls the gig and plays several parts in the Circus — " The Learned Pig that could read, in spectacles; the Irish Pig that could dance a jig; and the Clown in spotty calico "; the Pigmy Elephant, too. Xarifa, the Dormouse, rides in a howdah on the Elephant, and Tuppenny, the long-haired guinea pig, rides in front of the howdah on the elephant's neck. This, of course, is during Circus Shows. Jane Ferret is the housekeeper. The Circus performs only for audiences of animals. In fact, it has no contact with humans except on one or two occasions when fernseed is lost or forgotten.

It is spring when we first meet the Caravan with Tuppenny and it is spring when we leave it. We travel with it through the other seasons, and visit all its author's haunts on farm, in meadow, woodland or fell. As we follow the Caravan's journeyings and adventures, we listen to some fine old tales out of England's north country. There are stories of sheep, shepherds and sheep dogs, of flowers, mice and birds. What reader will ever forget the " Fairy Horseshoes " chapter and Mettle's lament at the Smithy over the passing of horses and carriages and the coming of " these here rattletraps," and his story of Mistress Heelis's madcap dancing clogs? The book closes with the story of " The Fairy in the Oak " as told by Xarifa, the dormouse.

One cannot help feeling that the principal characters in the story are all portraits of animals especially beloved, and that for the rest, the whole book is written to record the author's deep response to the beauty of the region and to Nature and her creatures.

Some time after the reading of *The Fairy Caravan*, Nancy was seen passing a chest on which the book lay. She gave it an affectionate stroke and said, " Oh, lovely *Fairy Caravan*, if only there were ten of you!"

*See *The Art of Beatrix Potter* (Warne, 1955)

From *The Horn Book* for May, 1941

Part VIII

Touching Poetry

ELLA YOUNG'S UNICORNS
AND KYELINS

By Anne T. Eaton

ELLA YOUNG, one reads in the brief sketches of her life that are available, is a graduate of Dublin Royal University where she took honours in history, jurisprudence and political economy. Yet her life has not followed the lines such an education would indicate. She has been associated for many years with the workers for an Irish state and an Irish culture, she has studied Gaelic, and for twenty years or more she has sought out the legends of her country, going to the far-away places, living with the country folk and listening to their tales, as she says, in brown-sailed fishing boats, on rocky hillsides and in cottages by turf fires.

In 1925 she came to America and has remained here ever since,* save for the four months in 1930-31 when she left California for British Columbia in order to re-enter the United States under the British quota.

The Wonder Smith and His Son (Longmans) was published in 1927. Before that, in 1923, Miss Young had published *Celtic Tales* in London (imported here by Dutton), *The Weird of Finovar* and *The Rose of Heaven. The Tangle-Coated Horse* and *The Unicorn With Silver Shoes* (both Longmans) followed in 1929 and 1932, respectively. In 1906 a volume of poems was published by Maunsell in London. In 1930, *To the Little Princess; An Epistle* was brought out in a limited edition in San Francisco, and her poems have appeared from time to time in *Poetry* magazine.

*This country was her home until her death in 1956.

Such, speaking matter-of-factly, is all the record we have of this author; her books tell us far more, for in them we find the clearest revelation of her life and work. More truly than any one else who has rewritten Irish folklore, Ella Young has gone back in spirit and understanding to those ancient days when gods and heroes walked in windy, starlit spaces, when the white horses of Faeryland might trample outside a king's doorway, when the Hidden Folk rode out of the green raths and there was laughter in the heart of the hills.

In a few short years she has managed to span the ages; more than that, for her, the barriers between the world of which she writes and the world of everyday, perpetually disappear, if, indeed, they have ever existed. She tells simply, and with no sense of strangeness, of the hearing of fairy music; she speaks, those who know her say, of ancient Celtic days as though they were a part of her personal memories. Many, if we may believe the poets, have visited Faeryland, or Tir-nan-Oge, the Land of Youth; few have been able to recount their experience; they are like Kilmeny, for

" Kilmeny had been she could not tell where,
And Kilmeny had seen what she could not declare,"

but Ella Young can tell of what she has seen and heard in a way that takes the reader back with her to this world of faery, of high romance, of beauty and courage and magic, as easily as Flame of Joy, in *The Unicorn With Silver Shoes,* could transport Ballor's son to the Wood of Pomegranates where adventure began.

In *Celtic Tales,* Miss Young seems to have been gathering impressions of an ancient, lovely universe, absorbing its beauty, its colour, its atmosphere. The gods, Angus, the Ever Young, Midyir, the Red Maned, Ogma, the Dagda, Brigit and Lugh, are figures of splendour, seen through the misty spaces between the worlds; Midyir drives away the blackness with the Sword of Light, Brigit unrolls her silver mantle on the earth, Angus leaps down and scatters greenness from the Caldron of Plenty. We feel elemental forces at work, we see the colour of dawn and sunrise, hear the song that the Earth sang when in darkness she dreamed of beauty, but the scene is too vast, the deeds too strange and mighty for the reader to grasp completely.

As she has continued to write, however, Miss Young has more and more surely found the way to take the reader with her across the boundaries of the Hidden Country. There are still magic and mystery and grandeur, but we can travel the world with Gubbaun, the Wonder Smith and his son, or feast like a king in Gubbaun's house when the two return safely from the country of the treacherous Fomor. The Wonder Smith, his son, the son's wife, Aunya, who has the fire of wisdom in her mind and who uses her magic with keen, practical commonsense, are not only characters from a cycle of Irish legends, they are at the same time simple folk who endear themselves to us by their humour and shrewd kindliness. There is still a strange wild loveliness, still skies with desolate lights in them, white bulls of the forest with moon-curved horns, young leaves in a beechwood with a greenness as of fire, but the human quality increases in each successive volume of tales.

In *The Tangle-Coated Horse* the author has used more familiar material than in *The Wonder Smith*. The story of Fionn or Finn McCool and his son Ossian, or Usheen, one of the oldest and loveliest of all cycles of legends, has been retold by many writers. Lady Gregory has given it very fully in *Gods and Fighting Men,* and James Stephens tells several stories of Finn's boyhood in *Irish Fairy Tales*. Standish O'Grady has written *Finn and His Companions,* and T. W. Rolleston *The High Deeds of Finn*. The book by Lady Gregory is meant for adult readers, and though the excellent versions by O'Grady and Rolleston were made with a youthful audience in mind, they have not the joyous spontaneity and wonder that make *The Tangle-Coated Horse* a delight to boys and girls. *The Tangle-Coated Horse* tells of Fionn's early life in the forest, how under the training of his woman guardian, Bovemall, he learned to run more swiftly than the deer; to track the forest creatures, but to make friends with them, too; to call the wind; to listen like a fawn for all the slightest sounds and to know their meaning, until at last he is fit to win back the Treasure Wallet with the talismans that had once

239

made his father the leader of the Fianna. Not all the book is about Fionn; Diarmid is often the central figure, brown-haired, slender Diarmid, the youngest of Fionn's followers. Connaun, the old warrior, adds the salty touch of humour. The title story has the joyousness of a jest; a stalwart fun, like a hearty clap on the shoulder, when seventeen of Fionn's war-riors tried to subdue the great, ugly horse, who is more than a match for them all; a moonlit twist of fantasy when Diar-mid, who is promised a fairy steed to bring him back some day to the Under Wave kingdom, bethinks him of unicorns, golden-eyed, milky-white, that had slipped between the trees with silver leaves, and leaning over his horse's neck whispered, " Send a unicorn for me! "

Was it perhaps her sympathy with Diarmid that led Ella Young to write *The Unicorn With Silver Shoes?* Of all her books this one has the most unity and beauty of form, and her style, always of a jewelled loveliness, is fitted to the subject like music to the words of a song. *The Unicorn With Silver Shoes* is also the most childlike of Miss Young's books. It grew, in fact, out of stories that were told to the children of George William Russell (Æ). For them, she says, in an unlucky hour she invented Ballor's son and could never be quit of him after; as she explains, " he especially delighted those children per-haps because he was not a model of all the seven deadly vir-tues." No wonder is it that Ballor's son could not be spared, for he supplies the human note that reaches both children and adults, and, descendant of the Kings of the Fomor as he is, we can all recognize in him something of ourselves. His play-fellows, Flame of Joy, the slender lad with pale gold hair and shining gray eyes, the Pooka who could take any shape it had a fancy for, please us by their beauty and magic arts, but their companionship with Ballor's son brings out the humour and kindly commonsense that win our hearts.

Mortals and the Ever Young mingle freely in this volume of tales. If adventures begin in the wood beyond the world, they continue in the fields around the little village and in the small house of Michael O'Hegerty. In the speech of the gods and the speech of the humble folk there is the same starry beauty. " The blessing of the sun and the colours of the day to

240

you," says the Wonder Smith. " We make of our thanks a bundle of good wishes at your feet. We make of our thanks a wind of good fortune to run before you. We make of our thanks a blossoming of luck in house and hearth and homestead," says the Pooka, disguised as the Fabulous Animal. " I learned the handicraft of the weaver," Michael O'Hegerty tells the three travellers in " Flower of the Moon," " because I wanted to sit quiet between four walls and think my own thoughts. I do be repeating old ranns to myself at times my hands are throwing the shuttle. I do be remembering old days and hours, and redness of dawn on the grass-blades and moon-whiteness in water. There's many a thing a man can be remembering when his eyes are on the threads of the loom."

Only in Ireland does the talk of the country people, with its " images of magnificence," echo the speech of the ancient gods and heroes. Characteristically Irish, too, is the sudden humourous turn, the contrast between high heroic deeds and more homely matters. Over the mountain of black obsidian that draws to itself the moon, over the mountain of chalcedony that blossoms against the stars, leaps the great Cat of Cruachan, carrying Ballor's son and Flame of Joy away from the scene of their " ploy " with the Kyelins, over Frondisande, the Mountain of the Silver Unicorns; but as he tumbles the boys to the ground he says simply, " It's small and innocent ye look, to have stirred up such a turmoil."

In the title story, Ballor's son tries, under Angus's instructions, to shoe the Unicorn with silver, only to find, as many another has found before him, that it takes more skill than he is master of to shoe a beast that melts into moonshine when he is unskillfully handled. " Flower of the Moon," the story in which Ballor's son, the Pooka and Flame of Joy go in search of Eblis, Ballor's Djinn, who fell into the Civilized World, is the most lovely tale in the book and into it is woven the high beauty of the old legends and the humour and courtesy and kindliness that also are Ireland. When we close the book we realize that we have seen " things wild and lovely, many wonders and many folk," and also that through a quickened understanding these experiences may be ours to keep, that, as another Irish poet has said,

" Oh, the great gates of the mountain have
    opened once again,
And the sound of song and dancing falls
    upon the ears of men,
And the Land of Youth lies gleaming, flushed
    with rainbow light and mirth,
And the old enchantment lingers in the
    honey-heart of earth."*

*"Carrowmore " by Æ. Quoted from *Collected Poems* by Æ, 1915, with kind permission of Mr. Diarmuid Russell; Macmillan & Co. Ltd., London; and St. Martin's Press, Inc., New York.

From *The Horn Book* for August, 1933

MEDALLIONS TO THE THUMB

By John A. Holmes

RCHIBALD MAC LEISH, more than most poets, is one of those rare persons who has grown up and found that what he thought about when he was younger is true, and valuable, and possible of expression. He has made words speak of the inarticulate mystery of being alive. According to his genius, every poet worth the name has kept that mystery's ache in him, and has offered the answer of which he is capable. But MacLeish more than most. It is the mystery of being alive at all as one of the race of men, and its essential quality is exactly that of being in-articulate. It is what men feel and after a while forget; for-getting even that it had been a mystery and that one had wished for words. When this poet does find words, he still uses them to tell of the feeling beyond words. On pages 12 and 13 of his book (*Poems, 1924-1933*, Houghton), in the long poem, " The Hamlet of A. MacLeish," he says:

> It is always as though some
> Smell of leaves had made me not quite remember;
> As though I had turned to look and there were no one.
> It has always been secret like that with me.
> Always something has not been said. Always
> The stones were there, the trees were there, the motionless
> Hills have appeared in the dusk to me, the moon
> Has stood a long time white and still in the window.
> Always the earth has been turned away from me hiding. . . .

MacLeish's work is what, on casual reading, seems to be diffi-cult poetry. But the real difficulty of his work is not one of line arrangement and lack of standard punctuation; that is only superficially difficult. The problem is one of following a mind

243

that has carried on this agonizing effort to put into words the feelings no one finds words for. Usually his cadences are so beautifully handled that the breath and the throat and the emotions of the reader put punctuation in the right places. But to understand the content it is necessary to recover an early aching wonder and questioning, and to follow with sensitive intuition the possibilities of its growth. It would be hard to find out from a child or a young person whether or not the thing is there to grow or die. It finds outlet infrequently and then not for long; but it must be possible to prove it by watching recognition come to young readers. And certain older readers will know that a poet has said what they once wanted to say. If we approach MacLeish's new book of collected poems in this way, perceiving this urgency behind them, then we feel that he is the most heartening reassurance we have that genuine poetic maturity is possible after a sapling fancy has shown itself. Think, then, that one American poet has reached the full leaf of which he was the seed, and achieved it without twist or blight. Think that it began as a strong sense of a secret withheld from him.

If the world is a stage, and people players on it, it seemed to him that they all played in front of the curtain, on a narrow stage, and could not or would not remember what was behind it, or who taught them their lines, or what convention had costumed them so. There was a little girl who thought that notes in music had a meaning as definite as words. She thought music was a pleasant thing as it was, but that when she grew up she would understand, as all grown-up people did, what it really was saying. MacLeish began by asking the question; now he seems to know the answer — or at least that the question must be asked again and again. Then think that his power of keeping the feeling has grown with the growth of his understanding of the mystery, and you will have a key to his poetic life and his poetry. No older person who has read Sir James Fraser's *Golden Bough* fails to know what the mystery is. Even the voice in which MacLeish's poems come out has the feeling. This he intends; he has said so in his "Ars Poetica":

244

A poem should be palpable and mute
As a globed fruit

Dumb
As old medallions to the thumb

Silent as the sleeveworn stone
Of casement ledges where the moss has grown —

A poem should not mean
But be

Thus, in perceiving the mystery and stating his "Ars Poetica," he first discovered himself. Then, as the strength of his mind and its outlet in poetry grew, he discovered the universe; then humanity. The poem, "You, Andrew Marvell," is his most moving testimony to the sense of infinity and awareness of being on the surface of a green globe spinning between the light and the dark. To a lesser degree (since that is one of the finest of modern poems) this awareness is attested in "The End of the World," "Immortal Helix," "Signature for Tempo," and "Seafarer." The first stanza of the latter poem reads:

And learn O voyager to walk
The roll of earth, the pitch and fall
That swings across these trees those stars:
And swings the sunlight up the wall.

It has that dizzy sense of riding the gale of stars on a small, tossing ship: the sense of the infinity of space. Einstein appealed to him as a fit hero for another poem, perhaps because Einstein helped teach him that feeling of infinity. That famous theory is stated in the poem, "Signature for Tempo":

Think that this world against the wind of time
Perpetually falls the way a hawk
Falls at the wind's edge but is motionless —

His discovery of humanity is a gradual extension of the poetry of himself, and the long poem, "The Hamlet of A. MacLeish," contains the essence of what he felt about it. Based on the Shakespearean story with familiar characters, Hamlet is the tragic prince, and the author in his own life, and the race of man in its tribal and tragic history. The King, his father's ghost, becomes the old compulsion that MacLeish has

245

always known, to find out the secret. Mankind is haunted by this ghost. The Uncle King is the sun, or the blind life force that goes on though men die, covering up their secrets and bringing other men into life and the play. The Queen is earth. Ophelia is woman, who cannot see far enough to comprehend Hamlet's quest. In the end the hero, MacLeish-Hamlet-mankind, will compromise with life, make the necessary acceptance, and act in the play within the play to the mortal end by the poisoned sword, knowing beforehand the outcome.

This poem is a dramatization and extension of the discovery of himself, written at the point in his growth where he could perceive man's long history reproduced in little in one life, his own. The other poems, even " Conquistador," fill in parts of the vast picture, particularizing the earlier and more sweeping strokes. This Pulitzer prize poem, instead of the anonymous and symbolic tribes in the shorter poems, tells of a known people, the Aztecs, conquered by another known people, the Spaniards. Everything inherently tragic and beautiful and mysterious in the material has been brought into the poem, and the fresh wonder of that lost civilization caught again. His protagonist, a Spanish soldier, gives us the story from a single point of view, that of a man among men, rather than the story given in the shorter poems by the omniscient poet. Technically, all his writing trained him for the urgent fullbreath line he uses with such hard strength in "Conquistador." For this reason, as well as the others so far suggested, it should be read last of all.

The shorter poems fall into what may be called a personal group, an American group, and a tribal group. The first two give us respectively some of his most beautiful and some of his most savage poems. The third repeats and varies the statement of the mystery of origins, perhaps his most characteristic addition to modern imagery. The American poems may be called the more specific statements of this group. " American Letter " shows where the two groups touch. Of the more personal poems the finest are "The Thirtieth Year of My Age," "Memory Green," " Not Marble Nor the Gilded Monuments," " Immortal Autumn," and " Lines for an Interment." The last is one of the most bitter war poems that has been written.

In this book it takes on a new bitterness: it was originally written on the tenth anniversary of his brother's death, and so titled; now it is for any soldier dead. The first version was ten years after; the second is fifteen. Best among the tribal poems are " Men," " Land's End," " Epistle to be Left in the Earth," and " 1933."

Several years ago I came upon the poem entitled " The Thirtieth Year of My Age " in one of the little Rittenhouse anthologies, and felt then as Keats felt on first looking into Homer, quite literally. The poem began:

> And I have come upon this place
> By lost ways, by a nod, by words,
> By faces, by an old man's face
> At Morlaix lifted to the birds.*

I was far on the young side of thirty, but I knew as I never knew by the sound of any other poem, that here was a poet, and that what more he wrote I would read. That may be the way to begin, after all. It leads through long collection of separate magazine publications; re-reading them silently and aloud; and his books; an inspired determination to master " The Hamlet of A. MacLeish "; and finally this introduction to the collected poems, consummating for the time being that early conviction that Archibald MacLeish is a poet worth any one's ten years of watching, reading, and understanding. Whichever way one takes, it is true of his poetry as of all the poetry of men of rare spirit and great vision, that it rolls the darkness back and sheds a light on all of man's anxious, brave endeavor — a light that will never go out.

---

*This poem under the title "L'An Trentiesme de mon Eage" appears in *Collected Poems,* 1917-1952, Houghton, and all quotations used in this article are used with permission of Houghton Mifflin Co.

From *The Horn Book* for March, 1934

DEFINITION OF A POET

By John Holmes

I F you see three men walking down the street together, and one of them happens to be a poet, although at the moment you do not know that, nothing the man does will reveal which one he is, and nothing about his look will set him apart. In these days, poets act, dress, and appear like any other normal human being, which is as it should be. They must be close to life, and share life equally with men and women of their times, and in their country. It is a cruel and stupid legend, persisting for the most part in comic strips, slapstick movies, and the minds of the less intelligent and in-formed majority that poets wear long, ragged hair, live in garrets, and are happier to be poor, happiest in the unreal world of their rhyming imagination.

There is an all-too-popular prejudice against poetry, because of this mistaken and old-fashioned conception of the poet. This prejudice sees poetry either as something too highbrow for the average citizen, or too obscure for easy understanding, or an occupation somehow unmanly, and certainly unprofit-able. All these matters must be taken into consideration by teachers and lecturers, and by poets themselves, and over-come if poetry is to occupy in this country in our lifetime the place of honor it once had. The common prejudices seem to be the last ignoble remnants of our pioneering age, when a right man certainly had not time to sit idling with words, and a weak or a lazy man could find only women and chil-dren to listen to him. Naturally, the vigorous and active and fortune-founding gentlemen were suspicious of poetry; it seemed to exclude them, and they resented the intimation that such inequality could exist, especially when it could not be bought, sold, or seen.

To the penetrating eye of the physician or psychologist or the literary critic, there would be a difference between the strolling poet and his two friends. Though they would appear to be active and alert, the poet would be even more eager and vigorous, awake and sensitive, observant and wondering. In a very literal sense of the word, the poet is more alive than other people, and it shows in his writing. Ordinarily we know the world around us through our five senses. We see red and green lights, smell wood-smoke, touch woolen cloth, hear the door slam, and taste the bread and cheese. Now the poet has all these senses, although in him they are much heightened, and in addition he is equipped with twice as many more, perhaps three times as many. This is where he differs. In some degree, it is where any creative artist differs.

It is, then, with the poet's unusually sharp senses of sight, touch, taste, smell and sound that we are here concerned, as well as with his extra and more subtle senses. Hearers and lovers of poetry are endlessly curious about this difference. Again and again they ask, How does a poet know the things he puts into a poem? Why do they come to him, and how? How is poetry written?

Here is the answer. When a poet looks at an object with the eyes in his head, he sees more than merely accurately. Most people do not see accurately, some do not see at all, and they are like the little monkey in the familiar group who puts his hands over his eyes. Sight is the sense that most enriches poetry; everywhere we read it, we come upon amazement exemplifying this fact. When Winifred Welles writes about the pale-colored caterpillars, she says that they are " pleating and unpleating," and that " Some wear dark spots, some have small dreary faces." The sense of sight, in the poet, is closely related to the sense of words, the sense of analogy, and the sense of curiosity. When first she saw pleats, she had the feeling it was a forming of matter not restricted to cloth; it was a shaping that also had a feeling. When she saw the caterpillar, she had the right word for it, and again when she looked ever so closely at the face. The sense of curiosity that made her examine even the crawling worm is one of the poet's most useful senses. To the poet, nothing happens, nothing exists in vain. Sometimes words excite him for their own sound or look on the page. He must have the sense of words, which is really a love for words, just as his sense of curiosity is really love. Then there is that second seeing which we call analogy. Let me quote again from Winifred Welles:

THE BODY OF THE ROOTS*

The hand, that up the dark and twisted stair,
   Carries the tulip's candle in its case,
The shoulder and the thigh, that, straining, bear
   Up to their shelf each gossamer urn and vase,
Are tense and knotted, lean and veined and spare.
   Not with deft swiftness nor with delicate grace,
But in slow agonies of strength and care,
   The burden of a flower's ephemeral face
Is lifted and unhooded in the air.

Seeing people stretch up to put something on a shelf, or urge the leaning body upstairs, she felt a quality in that motion, the quality of growth, slow and careful and upward. Probably the poem was made then and there, in her mind. That is what we call analogy, saying that a tulip growing is a flower being carried up like a candle by an unseen hand. As if, as if — and in those two small words lies the seed of poetry.

Robert Frost's poem "To Earthward" is one of many examples of the sense of touch. First he felt the sand beneath his hand, but as he did so he knew in his mind that it had a significance. It was one of those meaningful things we do, among many that are meaningless. He wrote:

> When stiff and sore and scarred†
> I take away my hand
> From leaning on it hard
> In grass and sand,
>
> The hurt is not enough:
> I long for weight and strength
> To feel the earth as rough
> To all my length.

*Quoted with permission of James Welles Shearer, son of Winifred Welles.

†Quoted from *Complete Poems of Robert Frost*, copyright, 1930, 1949, by Henry Holt and Company, Inc., with permission of the publishers.

It was a handy and a natural likeness for him to make, and that making of likenesses is called imagery, when the thing is more or less pictorial. When we say that Robert Frost writes about New England, what we really mean is that all his images have been taken from what he knows best, the grass and sand, the stone walls, the lanterns at night across the snow, the grindstones, and the farms of that part of the country. He brings to bear on them his special sense of significance, in addition to other special poetic senses.

Sound is a manifestation of life to which poets are extremely sensitive. Volume and pitch in all its million gradations are separated in the poet's ear, and noted. More often in usual people sound is noise. But the poet listens as eagerly as he looks, and then he attaches significance, finds words, and quickens the sound into useful matter for poetry. Since he is strung high by nature, it is as if he can hear the very grass grow sometimes, or the plodding footsteps of an ant, or the passing of time. Sound becomes almost visible to him, especially the arranged and developing sounds we call music; music makes images all its own, and the images in turn have their significance, and their usefulness for poetry.

Taste and smell are perhaps less often noted specifically in poetry, but with his instant choice of the right word, the poet can describe more vividly than usual the sensations of palate and nose. Both these physical senses are somehow either very luxuriantly sensuous, or very gross and even comic. The sense of smell is the only humorous physical sense, though why it is so is difficult to say.

Poets, and especially the more greatly imaginative poets, have a strong sense of space. This sense makes them aware of the universe itself, at its farthest reach, and of the four walls of a room at the other. Archibald MacLeish, in his poem "You, Andrew Marvell," displays this cosmic sense when he tells of the dark coming round the earth, pouring like a tall wave toward him, though it is noontime where he is. This sense makes a man feel that he is riding the earth, which lunges over and over slowly on its axis in the middle of a vast sea of air. Far away and above him glisten the stars and planets, like the one on which he stands in immensity. He feels earth curve away from under his feet; on the beach he feels the broad continent at his back, solid and deep behind him. He has a compass swinging in his breast. Or else he feels the strangeness of being in a room, a block of space, set on top of another block of space, with lights in it and the huge night everywhere outside his thin walls.

The sense of time is an equally powerful sense, and urges many of the poets. It tells the poet that at every latest breath he draws, time is at the same point for every one all over the world. Every one is as much farther from their day of birth as he is; time is running through millions of people. In a strange and exciting poem by Eli Siegel, called " Hot Afternoons Have Been in Montana," we feel this sense reaching backward and forward, when he says that in the field he sits in there were once Indians fighting on a hot afternoon — " we live now and it is hundreds of years after." While the Indians fought and yelled, monks in cool black monasteries thought of God and studied Vergil. It was at the same time. The sense of time and the sense of space give the poet enormous imaginative power over life and the world, drawing to him all he cannot immediately see or touch. With a more obvious magnitude than some of the other senses, these make him feel alive and complete in the life of man. That is part of the reason why there is such a vibration of life in poetry; it is like taking hold of a wire to read good and great poetry. It stings and flashes and quickens all the perceptions.

Although it is a sane and balancing sort of thing to have, among these mind-stretching-senses, the sense of humor, or the feeling for nonsense, is not always present in ˝the combination. The sense of absurdity, in Americans, is usually acute appreciation of incongruity, or of futility. Sheer nonsense is somewhat more of an English habit of pleasure, less cruel, and more enduring in books and magazines. Nevertheless the sense of humor is a distinct additional sense, and while it appears mostly in good light verse, it may color and vary the serious poetry of any writer.

We have already mentioned the sense of curiosity, which is one thing, while the sense of wonder is somewhat different. There is something about the actual make-up of poets, Chard

252

Powers Smith decides, in his *Annals of the Poets,* that gives them wide-open, staring eyes as a usual thing. And they do stare at life in all their waking moments. Conrad Aiken, a poet who glorifies one aspect of life continually, has said that the time may come when all philosophies will give way before man's fundamental sense, that of curiosity. His own has created poetry that seeks always to say what man knows, all that he knows, dark and bright, and that as an end in itself. But the sense of wonder is more innocent. The Englishman, W. H. Davies, has it, of course, and so do all lyric poets. To these, the world and all things in it seem fresh and amazing; it is astounding and wonderful that man should breathe and be able to see a green tree. At its very best, for this reason, lyric poetry recreates the astonished happiness of the Adam in us, a reaction now too often dulled and tired.

It will be noticed that, although most of the senses enumerated could be related and cross-related, so as to make still further new senses, all have in common the quality of intense life. That is the kernel of the secret and the answer to the question. Life does not vibrate with a leaden twang as of a loose string on a split violin idly plucked. The poet is taut with life, shivering almost with the impact of the world upon him, though shivering is a poor word here. He receives the world through his own heightened senses, and because one of them is a sense for words and their most exciting and most beautiful order, he transmits the world to all who will read poetry. He transmits the world alive, even more alive than in reality sometimes. The poetry of the world is a great reserve of life on which we may draw when our own supply of it is low. It comes to us beating with the intensity of the man who felt it and wrote it down; that very beating and rushing is still another of his special senses, the sense of rhythm.

The last and in most ways the greatest of the poet's special senses is the sense of truth, or the sense of salvation, as it may be called. Sometime every poet writes the one poem that sets forth what for him is the highest truth, the truth by which he lives and wishes to live. All his thinking and feeling goes to produce it; on it he is willing to stake his chances of salvation — his chances of poetic, moral, and intellectual integrity being

253

attained in full, and his consequent place in literature. The poet's sense of truth has a more immediate side as well. It describes his sense of pattern or structure in making the poem itself — his own degree of artistry. This sense of truth all artists have, each in their own way. The artist knows when he has created a final perfect thing; it is that instinct that tells him either that it falls short of finality or that it achieves it, to which we have given here the name of the sense of truth.

This is how poetry is written: the life of the world goes on about a man who perceives it through a varied and extremely subtle sensual equipment. This equipment consists of the senses of sight, touch, sound, smell, taste, words, analogy, curiosity, significance, space, time, humor, wonder, rhythm, and truth. Probably this list can be extended. The intensity of them in him impels him to write; he cannot help that. He is an instrument which he must forever perfect, and its purpose is to announce life.

From *The Horn Book* for January, 1937

THE SPRING-GREEN LADY, ELEANOR FARJEON

By Helen Dean Fish

Lady, lady, my Spring-green lady,
May I come into your orchard, lady?
For the leaf is now on the apple bough,
And the sun is bright and the lawn is shady,
Lady, lady, my fair lady,
O my Spring-green lady!*

To read *Martin Pippin in the Apple Orchard* or *Italian Peepshow* or *Kaleidoscope* leaves one sure that back of them is a writer who is lovely and alive and happy and possessed of a rare sense of humor, for everything she writes somehow communicates something of those qualities to the reader.

Eight years ago *Martin Pippin in the Apple Orchard* made this reader so grateful to the author for having written it that I wished to see her and thank her. But even after five years of a growing friendship through correspondence it was with some hesitancy at invading Miss Farjeon's privacy that I wrote to ask if I might call on her when I came to England. I rather hoped to find her in her cottage on the Sussex Downs near Arundel, where she wrote *Martin Pippin* in the heart of Martin's own country, but her reply came from London, bidding me and my friend to tea with her on a June afternoon in her attic room near Hampstead. We were to find her door behind the open one of a garage in a courtyard whose cobbles Keats once trod. But if we couldn't find the door, she bade us lift our voices in " The Star-Spangled Banner " which

*From *Martin Pippin in the Apple Orchard* (Stokes, 1935, o.p.)

would bring her speedily to our rescue. Fortunately this was unnecessary, but she ran down the steps from her attic to welcome us at the door and drew us up to an old, wide, comfortable, low-ceilinged room overflowing with books and music and pictures. There was a kettle on the hob of an ancient, diminutive grate and a table spread with English bread-and-butter, glowing strawberries and two kinds of cakes — the sign, as Miss Farjeon said, of a *real* party. We were at home at once and things crowded to be talked about. The tea came out of a fascinating double caddy made by a sea-faring ancestor, with one side for India and the other for China and an ingenious device to prevent getting them mixed. The tea-cups were every one different and were collected by Miss Farjeon's mother on her wedding journey around the world. When our visit was first planned we hoped that Rachel Field could be one of the callers, and though she could not be, there was a cup set out for her and a chair by the fire and we toasted her in fragrant amber liquid. (Several years later Miss Field very happily drew the gay pictures and cover design for Miss Farjeon's *Come Christmas*.)

The time flew. Miss Farjeon was zestfully interested in every subject — in the skylarks we had heard on the Downs and the nightingales we had *not* heard in the Pope's garden at Avignon; she told us about her winter in Fiesole which gave her *Italian Peepshow* and the days she loves to spend in Brittany in a little farmhouse with rushes on the floor and a candle to light her to bed; about her walks on the Downs to find dew-ponds and talk with shepherds — such walks as gave us her lovely poem, " From Chichester to Alfriston "— and of her plans for a book of tales for children about London names and places — the book which now, just finished, is *The Tale of Tom Tiddler.*

Miss Farjeon, with a sort of fine shyness, has never wished to have her photograph taken for publication, but I think she will not mind if I give her to you in words as well as I can. She is rosy, dark-haired, bright-eyed, and that day wore a crisp print frock with a white ruffled petticoat — as crisp and dainty as if she were the Spring-green lady herself. Indeed, she seems to belong to Sussex and the Downs and Gilman's

256

apple orchard. She is " hearty " in the most delightful sense of the word and in her company you share her genuine, child-like zest for all things — from the book she found on a book-stall that day to the taste of the strawberries and the memory of picking them, warm with sun, under the leaves. She is a person whose eyes and mind and heart are always wide open, though one cannot read her poems without knowing that she has mightily won her joy. But she *has* won it, and has it to give away. Joy is, I think, the keynote of all her stories, her poems, her people, her music.

Eleanor Farjeon is a granddaughter of the actor Joseph Jefferson and the daughter of B. L. Farjeon, the novelist. She was born in England and has lived there all her life. When still in her teens she wrote poetry and light-opera librettos for which she was complimented highly by W. S. Gilbert, librettist of the famous Gilbert and Sullivan operas. Her early writings were chiefly verse and music for children, and her first published books were two volumes of serious verse in 1908 and 1911. Then came *Nursery Rhymes of London Town* in 1916 and 1917, more grown-up poetry in 1918 and several books of singing games and rounds. " Gypsy and Ginger," her first story, was published in 1920, and *Martin Pippin* in 1922 established her literary and artistic reputation more firmly than any of her previous work. *The Soul of Kol Nikon,* a fantasy, followed in 1923, and in 1927 *Joan's Door,* a volume of child poems, and *Italian Peepshow,* a book of delightful, original folk-tales, among which is the inimitably lovely " The King of Tripoli Brings the Pasta." *Come Christmas,* a gay little book of new Christmas poems, bursting full of all the joys of Christmas for young and old, came in 1928, and in 1929, *Kaleidoscope,* a charming story for older boys and girls and adults. It is made of the dreams of youth and tells of a penniless but happy young man about London who needs no more than his penny newspaper to send him adventuring in a world of romance.

And now we have *The Tale of Tom Tiddler,* again a treat for younger readers. Here Miss Farjeon gives us fanciful tales of how the familiar and often amusing names of London streets and byways came to be —Shepherd's Bush and Whitechapel, Lavender Hill and Petticoat Lane, Earl's Court and Jack Straw's Castle and a score more. The American edition includes, in addition to the tales, a number of the delightful " Rhymes of London Town." Who can resist:

> I went up to the Hay-market upon a summer's day,
> I went up to the Hay-market to sell a load of hay,
> To sell a load of hay and a little bit over,
> And I sold it all to a pretty girl for a nosegay of red clover.
> A nosegay of red clover and a hollow golden straw,
> Now wasn't that a bargain, the best you ever saw?
> I whistled on my straw in the market-place all day,
> And the London folk came flocking for to foot it in the hay.

Once you have met Eleanor Farjeon in one of her magical books and lived in her English countryside, you want to read everything she has written and you live in pleasant anticipation of her next book, for you know it will be written out of a rich life.

Poetry quoted in this article with the kind permission of Eleanor Farjeon.

From *The Horn Book* for February, 1930

THE CHILDREN'S BELLS

By Eleanor Farjeon

When the half-muffled City Bells of London rang in commemoration of the Bell Ringers who fell in the war, the bells of St. Clement Danes could not take part owing to a defect in the framework on account of enemy action. (Ed. note: *On October 19, 1958, the bells of St. Clement Danes Church pealed out the old nursery rhyme again, breaking a 19-year silence, when it was re-consecrated as the official church of the Royal Air Force.*)

Where are your Oranges?
Where are your Lemons?
What, are you silent now,
Bells of St. Clement's?
You of all bells that rang
Once in old London,
You, of all bells that sang,
Utterly undone?
You whom all children know
Ere they know letters,
Making Big Ben himself
Call you his betters?
Where are your lovely tones,
Fruitful and mellow,
Full-flavored orange-gold,
Clear lemon-yellow?
Ring again, sing again,
Bells of St. Clement's!
Call as you swing again,
" Oranges! Lemons! "
Fatherless children
Are listening near you —
Sing for the children,
The fathers will hear you.

Reprinted with Eleanor Farjeon's permission from the book of poems published by Oxford University Press, England, entitled *The Children's Bells*.

From *The Horn Book* for July, 1947

A VALENTINE FOR OLD DOLLS

By Rachel Field

Let others sing of cooing doves,
Of beating hearts and new-found loves,
These my poor rhymes shall tell the graces
Of china, wax, or wooden faces;
The charm of curls and painted braids.
Oh sweet, perennially cheerful maids,
Your smiles shall last, though nations fall,
And the young hands that dressed you all
In flowered flounce and ribbons gay
Long since to dust be laid away.
Your years you wear like faint perfume
Of rose-leaves in a quiet room
When winter at the threshold knocks;
Like some old tune a music box
Tinkles as soft as phantom rain
Falling beyond a window pane.
And so, where'er you be today —
On parlor shelf; packed snug away
In attic camphor — still I'll praise
Your stiff set limbs, your timeless gaze,
Knowing full well when I am gone
Thus you will sit, and thus smile on.

Reprinted with the permission of The Macmillan Company.

From *The Horn Book* for July, 1942

CHILD'S PLAY

By Ella Young

Last night we took peeled hazel wands
For rods of magic in our hands,
And when the folk were all abed
Up the steep hillside we sped,
The wind went running with us too:
Everything was strange and new,
The grass was starred with lilies small,
The trees were black and hugely tall,
The tarn so still by day
Had golden fish at play:
And where the holly boughs are red
A phoenix-bird, all silver, shed
So bright a light it seemed to be
The moon that slipped from tree to tree.
Following upon the ground
Silent there ran a scarlet hound,
And with the hound went by us there
Three queens with loosened hair
Of wind-blown gold,
We thought them Guinevere,
Etawin, and Isolde.

From *The Horn Book* for September, 1938

Date Due

Mai 27 2003			
APR 0 1 2003			